THE METHODIST BOOK OF DAILY PRAYER

The Methodist Book of Daily Prayer

Matt Miofsky, General Editor and Contributing Writer

Laceye Warner, Contributing Editor

Abingdon Press
Nashville, TN

THE METHODIST BOOK OF DAILY PRAYER

ISBN: 978-1-7910-2955-5
Library of Congress Control Number: 2023945058

Contents

Introduction

The Methodist Book of Daily Prayer is for pastors, other ministry leaders, and Methodist people of all kinds who seek to strengthen and sustain their spiritual lives with a daily practice of prayer. It offers prayers for morning and evening, plus brief passages of scripture and reflective readings for each day. Wesleyan theology undergirds each selection. Psalms are emphasized. Hymns appear regularly. Classic and familiar writings are included along with original new writing. The practice is structured around the liturgical seasons, following the ancient rhythms which have ordered the practice of our faith since before John and Charles Wesley.

This book was born out of hundreds of conversations with Christians, church leaders, and pastors who are tired. It isn't the kind of fatigue that can be fixed with a personal day, a long weekend, a vacation, or even a sabbatical. This collective exhaustion is much deeper, conceived from habits that are out of rhythm with the God who created us. The solution can't be found in time off, or even in better self-care. This weariness can only be addressed by creating lives from which we do not want to escape. Essential to a whole and fulfilling life is reconnecting with the One who gives us that life. Critical to leading others to Christ is being connected to Christ oneself.

Christians are notorious for talking about things that we do not do. It is easy to say that people need to pray more, connect with God, or spend time each day in devotion. But it is difficult to persist in new habits. There are several reasons we find it hard to keep a daily discipline of prayer and reading. We are busy, our schedules are erratic, our spaces are often cramped, and many of us lack a resource to help us. We don't know where to start with reading the Bible, we aren't always sure what to pray, and many of us want a devotional resource that is thoughtfully curated, historically rooted, theologically nuanced, and enriched by diverse contemporary voices that are engaged in day-to-day ministry. John Wesley used the *Book of Common Prayer*, which those in Anglican traditions still use today. A similar resource—one less cumbersome and more Wesleyan—might assist Methodists everywhere in the very Wesleyan habit of regular prayer and reflection. *The Methodist Book of Daily Prayer* seeks to be that resource.

The Structure

This book is **simple to use**, accessible no matter your experience with scripture. It requires a **small commitment of time**. It is organized by the **Christian year,** with **weekly themes**. It provides text and prompts for **morning and evening prayer practices**. The prayers are provided at the beginning of each week and are to be repeated each day. A new set of prayers is included each week. Each **morning and evening** includes **scripture,** a brief **theological reflection**, and **prayers**. The book is designed for individual use but can easily be used by a group.

The Theological Reflections

The reflections are theologically rich. They vary daily, providing a wide range of forms to engage the heart and mind, including prose, poetry, academic writing, and—of course—hymns. Sources include contemporary writers, all of whom are Methodist pastors, as well as historical Christian works. For a new Christian or someone just beginning a devotional habit, the reflections are accessible, thought-provoking, and relevant to everyday life. For church leaders, the writings offer variety and depth we often find lacking in similar resources. In addition to a manageable and meaningful daily spiritual practice, pastors will find much to provoke a sermon idea or illustration along the way, as the book follows the seasons of the church year.

The Prayers

The prayer texts and prompts are at once universal and specific. They draw from our common human state *and* help us to name our particular, individual circumstances. The morning prayers focus on petitions and Christ-focused living for the day ahead. The evening prayers focus on gratitude and reflection on the day just spent. The prayers can be done in a few minutes or can extend as long as you like. Using the same set of prayers each day, your prayers will develop and change over the course of the week. You might sometimes find this leads to surprising insight. It certainly leads to a profound connection with God.

How to Adopt the Practice

Here are a few suggestions for beginning (or returning to) the habit of daily prayer and reflection: Decide on **a consistent time each day** when you will read and pray. Stick to that specific time as best you can. Choose **a dedicated place** for your daily prayer. It can be a certain chair, a particular room, or a spot in your office. Be sure to **keep this book out in the open** so you see it every day. The daily prayer exercises are interactive, asking you to reflect on and voice your own petitions with the given prompts. Choose a method to **write down your thoughts, your petitions, and points of gratitude**. This is an excellent way to make the habit stick and to track your prayer life over time. The scripture passages are brief and printed in the book. If a passage sparks your interest, **get a Bible and read more**. You might **invite another person to use the resource along with you**. Perhaps check in with a text each week to **encourage each other** to stay consistent. **Consider stacking this new habit with something you already do each day**. Maybe use it as you have your morning coffee, pick it up immediately after dinner, or read it as soon as you finish working out. Find something you do each day and then include this practice before or after it. And **don't be hard on yourself**. If you miss one day, just let it go and jump back in the next.

One logistical note: The book is undated so you may begin or return to it at any time. For assistance in understanding the liturgical seasons, or **to determine which week you are in**, we recommend this site administered by Vanderbilt University: https://lectionary.library.vanderbilt.edu.

Building the Practice Over Time

The importance of this book is in the daily habit that it seeks to form, not the amount of time you spend doing it each day. If at first the practice feels forced, **persist**. Habits are powerful once they are formed, but the formation takes time. As you build this habit, prayer will become easier, richer, and more natural.

This book is meant to be used daily, but devotional habits fluctuate with the seasons of life as our needs and circumstances change. So, this resource is flexible. At certain times, you may read only the scriptures and daily reflections. In another season you may simply use the prayer practices each day, leaving aside the scripture and reflective readings. You may choose to do only the morning *or* evening practices for a time.

The book is also meant to be used year after year. These prayers and reflections will take on new meaning and depth as the seasons of your life and ministry develop and change. If you must, set this book aside for a time, but keep it close at hand, for the opportunity and need for it will return. You can pick up the practice again at any time. Release any guilt over inconsistent efforts. God welcomes us back repeatedly, no matter how far we've strayed or how distant we may feel.

The Power of the Practice

The power of this practice may not be obvious at first, but the *regular* connection to God becomes powerful over time. It **creates space for a healthy ritual of repetition**, which leads to ever-deepening insight and can soothe our disjointed souls. It **connects us across time** with the saints, those faithful ones who've gone before us, who created this path for us. It also **connects us with our contemporaries**—pastors, theologians, and writers living in the recent past and today whose work and devotion we share. It **connects us across dividing lines** of all kinds, presenting voices and perspectives we have not heard or considered. It **undergirds our Wesleyan way of thinking**, reminding us daily what we believe and why. It is an **offering to God**, returning to God one of the most valuable gifts we receive: time.

Most of all, this practice supports our important work, responsibilities, and schedules, while providing a deeply significant rhythm for life, giving shape to our days, weeks, seasons, and years. This rhythm causes us to pause, to be quiet, even to rest. God offers us rest as a gift, and asks us to practice, not for God's sake, but for our own. This rhythm of work and rest, of going out and coming back, living life, and returning to the source of that life is crucial to addressing the deep-seated fatigue we all experience. May God bless you in this new discipline and may you hear God's voice more clearly as you open your heart, mind, and life to God. May this resource help you create a life from which you find no need to escape.

Advent

Hope

Morning Prayer of Petition

God, as I start a new day I renew my hope in you and belief that you are at work in my life. There is a gap between the way the world is and the way you want it to be. That same gap exists in me. May I look beyond, hoping and working alongside you for what will be. Today I name:

- my hopes for what you might do in my life,
- my hopes for what you might do in my relationships and friendships,
- my hopes for what you might do in my church,
- my hopes for what you might do in my neighborhood and community,
- my hopes for what you might do in our country and world.

As I name my hopes to you, enlist me to play a role in the work you are already doing. Amen.

Evening Prayer of Gratitude

God, as the day draws to a close, I confess that I did not always live out of a sense of hope. Forgive me for the way that today I:

- chose cynicism over promise,
- assumed the worst instead of the best in others,
- gave up or gave in instead of standing up or stepping out,
- acted as if your power is not real instead of believing you are able.

As this day draws to a close and as I sleep, renew in me a sense of hope and possibility. Amen.

Day 1

Morning

Therefore, once you have your minds ready for action and you are thinking clearly, place your hope completely on the grace that will be brought to you when Jesus Christ is revealed. (1 Peter 1:13)

1

Reflection

The source of our hope is a consequential matter. We sometimes find ourselves believing in God but not acting like it. This is called functional atheism, which Parker Palmer defines as "the belief that ultimately responsibility for everything rests with me." We might pray, go to church, read scripture, and sing songs about the power of God. But then we stress, over-function, and burn out, all under the misguided notion that our lives are shaped by our own efforts. We place our hope in God, but only in part. Peter reminds us to rely on Jesus—on grace—as our source of complete hope, trusting that God is worthy, not only of our partial faith but all of it.

~Prayer of Petition~

Evening

But I will hope continually and will praise you yet more and more. (Psalm 71:14)

Reflection

What does it mean to "hope continually"?

Perhaps the way to embody hope is to disconnect it from an expected outcome and, instead, to take on a posture that declares a movement toward some alternate reality. Hope can be so fleeting, present one moment and then gone the next, leading to disappointment and discouragement.

But when hope is a posture, hope is rooted in the onward movement toward that alternate reality. It accepts that life will have its ups and downs. This posture allows for one to hope continually because the end of the journey is belovedness, when all would know God's hope, joy, peace, and love.

What is interesting is the way that the psalmist ties these two actions in the future tense. Despite the experiences that have brought the psalmist to write these words, and despite the circumstances that bring the psalmist to cry out for rescue and relief, there is a commitment to hope and praise. It isn't conditional; it is simply a declaration of what is to come.

May our hope be continual, firmly grounded in God's promise of God's preferred future.

~Prayer of Gratitude~

Day 2

Morning

The expectations of the righteous result in joy,
but the hopes of the wicked will perish. (Proverbs 10:28)

Reflection

Hope and hopefulness are not intrinsically good. Money can be both the object and source of hope for a greedy heart. Physical security could be the source of hope for a fearful heart, achievement for a selfish heart, or acclaim for an insecure heart. Each one is fading and temporal, bringing at best only fleeting happiness. And there are many others, of course, but none are worthy objects of our deepest hope, none are truly a source of enduring hope. The proverb challenges us to consider the nature of our own hearts. It calls us to question where our hope comes from and what we hope for. It prompts us to recognize God—God's wisdom and God's presence—as our true sources of hope. This hope leads to deep and lasting joy.

~Prayer of Petition~

Evening

And all who have this hope in him purify themselves even as he is pure. (1 John 3:3)

Reflection

For were you to be disappointed of your Hope, still you lose nothing. But you shall not be disappointed of your Hope: it will come, and will not tarry. Look for it then every Day, every Hour, every Moment. Why not this Hour, this Moment? Certainly you may look for it now. If you believe it is by Faith.
   —John Wesley, *Scripture Way of Salvation*

~Prayer of Gratitude~

Day 3

Morning

Return to the stronghold, prisoners of hope.
   Moreover, declare today that I will return double to you. (Zechariah 9:12)

Reflection

Perhaps you've heard a version of the idea that Christians are never allowed to give up hope. Believers in Jesus are hopelessly hopeful! We cannot stop trusting that God is at work in our lives and in the world. We cannot stop believing that the same spirit that raised Jesus from the dead is at work in our lives as well. We cannot stop putting our confidence in a God who is making all things well. If Christ is risen, if the Holy Spirit is present, if death has been defeated, and if God is reconciling all things to Godself, then pain, suffering, and evil are on a timer. Real though they are, they will not last. To believe in Jesus is to be, as the prophet says, a "prisoner of hope."

~Prayer of Petition~

Evening

I meet the predawn light and cry for help.
I wait for your promise. (Psalm 119:147)

Reflection

Whatever may be the tensions and the stresses of a particular day, there is always lurking close at hand the trailing beauty of forgotten joy or unremembered peace.
—Howard Thurman, *Meditations of the Heart*

~Prayer of Gratitude~

Day 4

Morning

Lord, *show us favor; we hope in you. Be our strength every morning, our salvation in times of distress.* (Isaiah 33:2)

Reflection

What does it mean to place our hope in God? Why would such a hope give us strength and salvation during times of distress? Part of the answer lies in the difference between something that is temporary and something that is eternal. Many people struggle with seasonal affective disorder. When the air is cold and the sky is gray, a depression sets in. If you experience this condition, you learn something over time. The winter season may seem to drag on, but we know it is temporary. It will change, and it will break forth into spring. You can place your hope not in the day-to-day weather, but in the confidence that spring is coming. In life, our hope comes not from our day-to-day circumstances, which can vary, but from a strong confidence that even today, God is working for our good and that something better is coming.

~Prayer of Petition~

Evening

This hope, which is a safe and secure anchor for our whole being, enters the sanctuary behind the curtain. (Hebrews 6:19)

Reflection

Do you ever wonder if Jesus had hope?

Into a world of oppression, a world defined by the rules of empire, Mary births the one called Emmanuel, God with us, and with him would arrive the hopes of all the nations. He would go on to shoulder the burdens of imagining a new and better way, one that is different than the kingdoms of earth, one centered on belovedness, togetherness, and oneness with God and with community . . .

Through it all, did Jesus himself have hope? Did he experience this human emotion of expectancy for a world that could be?

Too often, it is the human condition to connect hope to an uncertain outcome, to assume that hope requires a component of unknowing. And, therefore, one's Christology might then disqualify Jesus from having hope.

But I need Jesus to have had hope so that he might fully be the embodiment of humanity's hope. I need a hope-filled Jesus who lived his life and died his death with the expectancy of a world not yet, so that the ways we model our lives—anchored in his ways—might move us from a world not yet, into a world that could be.

~Prayer of Gratitude~

Day 5

Morning

We even take pride in our problems, because we know that trouble produces endurance, endurance produces character, and character produces hope. This hope doesn't put us to shame. (Romans 5:3-5)

Reflection

Hope is forged in the midst of hardship and struggle. If life were always to unfold the way you expect, then there would be no need for hope. You don't need to long for something that you already have. But life is full of surprises, changed plans, disappointments, and problems. These challenges can either be the occasion for despair or the beginning of a pathway that leads to hope. These troubles can produce perseverance and strength. This kind of strength can shape and mold our hearts and lives. And in the midst of this persistent determination to keep moving forward, we can craft a hope that comes not from a trouble-free life, but from knowing that God is more powerful than our current trials.

~Prayer of Petition~

Evening

I hope, Lord.
My whole being hopes,
*   and I wait for God's promise.* (Psalm 130:5)

Reflection

Come thou long-expected Jesus,
Born to set thy people free,
From our fears and sins relieve us,
Let us find our rest in thee:
Israel's strength and consolation,
Hope of all the earth thou art,
Dear desire of every nation,
Joy of every longing heart.

Born thy people to deliver,
Born a child and yet a king,
Born to reign in us forever,
Now thy gracious kingdom bring;
By thine own eternal Spirit
Rule in all our hearts alone,
By thine all-sufficient merit
Raise us to thy glorious throne.
    —Charles Wesley, "Come, Thou Long-Expected Jesus"

~Prayer of Gratitude~

Peace

Morning Prayer of Petition

Holy God, your son is called Wonderful Counselor, Mighty God, Everlasting Father, and Prince of Peace. Today I pray for peace, plead for peace, and ask you to fill the places in my life and in our world that need your peace:

- I pray for peace in my inner spirit where I am distracted and anxious.
- I pray for peace in my relationships with family, friends, coworkers, neighbors.
- I pray for peace in my community, city, and country where divisiveness seems to reign.
- I pray for peace among people globally, especially where conflict and war are an expected way of life.

As we prepare to celebrate the coming of your son into the world, may the peace He embodies and offers be made real on earth as it is in heaven. Amen.

Evening Prayer of Gratitude

Gracious God, as I look back on this day, it is too easy to focus on places of discord and division. Instead, I give you thanks for the ways you are working in my life for peace and wholeness. Today God, I thank you for:

- the ways you are working to bring peace to my emotional and mental being,
- the way you are working my relationships, especially those that are strained or fractured,
- the ways you are offering a picture of peace in my church or community.

As I rest and look forward to a new day tomorrow, may I have the eyes to see where you are at work for peace in the world, and may I have the courage to join you in that work. Amen.

Day 1

Morning

A child is born to us, a son is given to us,
and authority will be on his shoulders.
He will be named

Advent

> *Wonderful Counselor, Mighty God,*
> *Eternal Father, Prince of Peace.* (Isaiah 9:6)

Reflection

One of the words most often associated with the coming Messiah is *peace*. In a world of division, anger, strife, and conflict, the coming of the Messiah means a coming of peace. Of course, peace is not merely the absence of conflict. But the peace of Jesus is deeper and more challenging. The peace of Christ is a reconciliation, a putting back together of relationships and realities that have been torn apart by sin and suffering. This kind of peace, or wholeness, is radical because it signifies that even the lion will lie down with the lamb, and that even enemies will eat at a common table. The ones far off will be brought near, and the disparities in our world will be made level. The coming of Jesus is the beginning of this kind of peace, and while not yet complete, it only grows as we welcome Christ more into our lives and world.

~Prayer of Petition~

Evening

> *To give light to those who are sitting in darkness*
> *and in the shadow of death,*
> > *to guide us on the path of peace.* (Luke 1:79)

Reflection

"Oh!" I said, "I see it." And somehow I seemed to sink down out of sight of myself, and then rise; it was all in a moment. I seemed to go two ways at once, down and up. Just then such a wave came over me, and such a welling up in my heart, and these words rang through me like a bell: "God in you, God in you," and I thought doing what? Ruling every ambition and desire, and bringing every thought unto captivity and obedience to His will. How I have lived through it I cannot tell, but the blessedness of the love and the peace and power I can never describe. O, what glory filled my soul! The great vacuum in my soul began to fill up; it was like a pleasant draught of cool water, and I felt it.

—Amanda Berry Smith, from *In Her Words* (edited by Amy Oden)

~Prayer of Gratitude~

Day 2

Morning

> *Let the LORD give strength to his people!*
> > *Let the LORD bless his people with peace!* (Psalm 29:11)

Reflection

While peace is an external reality among peoples, countries, and tribes, it is also an internal reality. Conflict resides not only in the world but also in our own hearts. The peace that the Lord offers is at once at work in the world and in our own spirits. As much as it may seem like peace is making slow progress in our world, scripture indicates that it can happen quickly in our lives. The Lord blesses us with a kind of peace rooted in God's presence, which we can experience right here, right now, even in the midst of a conflicted and troubled world. This kind of peace is a gift, one that we can ask for, one that we are told to pray for, and one that can be received even now.

~Prayer of Petition~

Evening

Peace I leave with you. My peace I give you. I give to you not as the world gives. Don't be troubled or afraid. (John 14:27)

Reflection

In 1955 a songwriter, Jill Jackson, penned these words: "Let there be peace on earth and let it begin with me." Her words invite us to take a moment of sacred pause. In that pause, we are called to ask ourselves, "Are we creating an atmosphere where we are cultivating peace or are we cultivating chaos? Are we leading with peace or are we leading with anxiety?" Jesus tells us in John 14:27, "Peace I leave with you. My peace I give to you. I give to you not as the world gives. Don't be troubled or afraid." Jesus understood that we would experience seasons of restlessness and dis-ease. He understood that there will be moments when our peace will be shaken because of death, divorce, injustice, war, oppression, depression, or simply life. Yet, he propels us to have faith in a God who does not leave us comfortless, but gives us the ability to tap into a relationship with a God whose very presence ushers in peace.

~Prayer of Gratitude~

Day 3

Morning

Faithful love and truth have met;
righteousness and peace have kissed. (Psalm 85:10)

Reflection

Another word for *righteousness* is *justice*, and here the psalmist reminds us of the inextricable relationship between justice and peace. There is an unbreakable connection between love and truth. One cannot be present without the other. A peace that covers over hurt, ignores the realities of sin, or fails to name sources of brokenness is not peace at all. Love that does not want to name the truth is not authentic love. Christ's peace is not a superficial focus on everyone getting along and being polite. Christ's peace brings with it righteousness and justice, a naming of what is broken, and making right what is wrong. In Jesus, righteousness and peace are wed together, and wholeness only comes when both are present.

~Prayer of Petition~

Evening

There will be vast authority and endless peace
  for David's throne and for his kingdom,
  establishing and sustaining it
  with justice and righteousness
  now and forever.
The zeal of the LORD of heavenly forces will do this. (Isaiah 9:7)

Reflection

Though opposed, I went forth laboring for God, and he owned and blessed my labors, and has done so wherever I have been until this day. And while I walk obediently, I know he will, though hell may rage and vent its spite.
  —Julia A. J. Foote, "A Brand Plucked from the Fire"

~Prayer of Gratitude~

Day 4

Morning

Glory to God in heaven, and on earth peace among those whom he favors. (Luke 2:14)

Reflection

The angelic announcement of Jesus's birth was a proclamation of peace. This is not the promise of peace but the declaration that what had been waited for was finally here. The birth of Jesus is also the arrival of peace. The natural question is, then: Why is so much conflict still present? The answer is that the work of peace is present but not yet complete; it has been born, but it is not yet fully grown. But the mere arrival offers those who have been waiting for it a reason to celebrate, to be joyful, and to sing. For the peace that comes with Jesus, as the story will eventually show, is one that cannot be stifled, stunted, or stopped.

~Prayer of Petition~

Evening

Pray that Jerusalem has peace:
"Let those who love you have rest.
Let there be peace on your walls;
let there be rest on your fortifications." (Psalm 122:6-7)

Reflection

Psalm 122 is one of the songs of ascent. This means that those who were traveling to Jerusalem to celebrate one of the Jewish festivals would sing them as they were traversing uphill to get to the house of the Lord. In this psalm, the singers are petitioning God for peace because they carry with them intergenerational trauma. Their collective memory has been shaped by slavery, exile, and persecution. Yet, they sing this song of praise. The singers are literally inviting peace to rest on the holy city. They are praying for the walls to be fortified and for God's peace to reign.

During the Advent season, we are invited to pray the words of Psalm 122 for our own cities, communities, and churches. We struggle with our own collective memory of trauma and we all need God's peace to rest on us so that we can overcome it.

~Prayer of Gratitude~

Day 5

Morning

Peace I leave with you. My peace I give you. I give to you not as the world gives. Don't be troubled or afraid. (John 14:27)

Reflection

When kids are little, they are often afraid of the dark. Sometimes, when we were young, we might have even been afraid to enter a dark basement or to be left alone in a dark bedroom, afraid that there were monsters there. But if someone, usually a parent, would go with you to that dark basement, or sit beside you as you fell asleep, well, that made everything better. Their presence didn't make the dark go away, and presumably it didn't mean the monsters weren't still there, but not being alone was powerful enough to give you a peace that allowed you to move forward. The same is true of Jesus. He is Emmanuel, God's very presence always with us. That means that we are not alone. We do not walk the path by ourselves, and we do not face the challenges of life with no one by our side. Instead, we have the power and presence of God with us always. Knowing we are not alone is powerful enough to give us a peace that we can move forward, even in the dark.

~Prayer of Petition~

Evening

Yes, you will go out with celebration,
*   and you will be brought back in peace.*
Even the mountains and the hills will burst into song before you;
*   all the trees of the field will clap their hands.* (Isaiah 55:12)

Reflection

Lord, make me an instrument of thy peace;
Where there is hatred, let me sow love;
Where there is injury, pardon;
Where there is doubt, faith;
Where there is despair, hope;
Where there is darkness, light;
And where there is sadness, joy.
    —Francis of Assisi, "Lord, Make Me an Instrument"

~Prayer of Gratitude~

Love

Morning Prayer of Petition

God of love, as I begin a new day, shape me as a person of love. Help me to be attentive to the people you call me to love and the ways that you are challenging me to grow in love. Today I name:

- one way that I can grow in love of self,
- one person you are challenging me to love more fully,
- one person whose love I need to receive more fully,
- one way I can grow in loving my neighbor or community.

As love comes down at Christmas to meet us, help me to live more fully into that love today. Amen.

Evening Prayer of Gratitude

Good and loving God. As I look back on this day, I am reminded of the ways that you are showing up as love in my life. I am grateful for:

- the family that have and continue to nurture and love me,
- the friends who show up for me when I need them most,
- surprising people that you bring into my life for a season,
- those who have helped me to grow in my ability to love myself and others,
- pastors, spiritual friends, and mentors who have taught me how to love you more fully.

As you came to us in Christ, you continue to come to me through the power of your Spirit and through your people. As I rest tonight, work on my heart that I may receive the lessons of love around me. Amen.

Day 1

Morning

Your faithful love is priceless, God!
Humanity finds refuge in the shadow of your wings. (Psalm 36:7)

Reflection

Have you ever gotten together with old friends that you haven't seen in a while and picked up right where you left off? You find that the relationship you share doesn't seem to diminish over time or space. It is surprisingly resilient through the years and unaffected by all that might have occurred in your life and theirs. There is a Hebrew word, *hesed*, which occurs over 250 times in the Old Testament. It doesn't have an easy, one-word translation in English, but it is usually rendered as *steadfast* or *faithful love*. It isn't a kind of love that is conditional or subject to change. It isn't a love that is stronger when you are good, but weaker when you are bad. Instead, it is a love that is firm, that is solid, that is unchanging and unchangeable. It is a love that doesn't diminish over time and isn't eroded by sins and mistakes. It is solid and dependable; it will be there no matter how long it's been, or what has happened in between.

~Prayer of Petition~

Evening

Love the LORD your God with all your heart, all your being, and all your strength. (Deuteronomy 6:5)

Reflection

When preparing for Christmas, the common texts that are read or recited are:

- Isaiah 9:6
- Luke 1:46-48
- Matthew 1:23

The book of Deuteronomy tends not to be on the radar. And yet, it is the book that establishes the identity of the God of Israel and what that God requires of us to be in relationship with God. Moses, the writer of Deuteronomy and instrument of God's commands, declares: "Hear, O Israel: The LORD is our God, the LORD alone" (Deuteronomy 6:4 NIV). These words are called the *shema*, which is the Jewish affirmation that there is only one God in a world in which there are multiple gods to worship and idolize. Therefore, out of our acknowledgement of the sovereignty of God in our lives, Moses compels us to love God fully and completely.

There are so many things competing for our love and attention. And, yet, we are called to remember and live out the words of Moses, echoed by Jesus: "You shall love the Lord your God with all your heart and with all your soul and with all your mind" (Matthew 22:37 NRSVUE). If our identity is connected to the God we serve, then, prayerfully, our identity is love.

~Prayer of Gratitude~

Day 2

Morning

Knowledge makes people arrogant, but love builds people up. (1 Corinthians 8:1b)

Reflection

Love is a strange word in the English language. We use it to describe our feelings for a good cheeseburger as well as our feelings for our spouse, our favorite sports team or our own children. It is no wonder that we walk around with a lot of definitions of what it means to love, and with quite a bit of confusion about what love really looks like. Paul reminds us that whatever love is, it always builds up, period. Love builds people up, it doesn't harm them or tear them down. Love builds relationships up, it doesn't undermine or betray them. Love builds communities up, it doesn't disparage or weaken them. It is so basic, and yet so clarifying. If you want to know what love looks like, it looks like this: love doesn't harm, it doesn't hurt, it doesn't diminish, it doesn't tear down. Love builds up. Period.

~Prayer of Petition~

Evening

He responded, "You must love the Lord your God with all your heart, with all your being, with all your strength, and with all your mind, and love your neighbor as yourself." (Luke 10:27)

Reflection

Love divine, all loves excelling, joy of heaven, to earth come down;
Fix in us thy humble dwelling; all thy faithful mercies crown!
Jesus, though art all compassion, pure, unbounded love thou art;
Visit us with thy salvation; enter every trembling heart.
    —Charles Wesley, "Love Divine, All Loves Excelling"

~Prayer of Gratitude~

Day 3

Morning

The person who doesn't love does not know God, because God is love. (1 John 4:8)

Reflection

There are people who claim the name of Christ but then act in ways that seem so anti-thetical to what Christ would have done. There are people who know the Bible inside and out, can talk eloquently about God, or are respected leaders in their church. But John reminds us that none of this actually means a person knows God. Why? Because God is love. Therefore the chief characteristic of one who knows God is that they are loving—not smart, active, respected, or eloquent—but loving. If you are a person who has spent a lot of time in prayer, knows what is wrong and right, is committed to church, and guards yourself from sin, but you do not love, then you don't yet know God. This reminder is both a personal challenge for us, and a helpful hint about who around us truly knows God.

~Prayer of Petition~

Evening

I'm convinced that nothing can separate us from God's love in Christ Jesus our Lord: not death or life, not angels or rulers, not present things or future things, not powers or height or depth, or any other thing that is created. (Romans 8:38-39)

Reflection

The end of the year is a time of reflection and examination. We take a moment to acknowledge the triumphs and successes. We lament the challenges and failures. Some may even be experiencing the holiday blues. The National Alliance on Mental Health says that "the holiday blues are temporary feelings of anxiety or depression during the holidays that can be associated with extra stress, unrealistic expectations, or even memories that accompany season." The holiday blues can cause feelings of loneliness and isolation. In those moments, we can convince ourselves that nobody loves us or cares about us. We can find ourselves wrestling with the enemy which can be the inner me. Yet, God calls us to remember the words of the Apostle Paul, "[nothing in all creation] can separate us from the love of God in Christ Jesus our Lord."

This is a challenging season, but hold onto the promise that God never leaves you alone and that no matter what you do say, or experience, God's love for you is never ending and never changing.

~Prayer of Gratitude~

Day 4

Morning

But I say to you, love your enemies and pray for those who harass you. (Matthew 5:44)

Reflection

For Jesus, love is a way of being. Love is not something we can put on or take off; rather, it is the way we understand the world, approach others, and choose to relate. Love is a choice we make about how to live, not something that depends on the behavior of another. That is why Jesus can say something as outrageous as "love your enemies" (Matthew 5:44). If love is something that you extend only some of the time, and only to the people who already love you, then it isn't really a way of life.

It is merely an emotion reserved for special people. Instead, Jesus challenges us to make love a way we live everyday, in every situation, and with each person we meet.

~Prayer of Petition~

Evening

All you who are faithful, love the LORD!
*   The LORD protects those who are loyal,*
*   but he pays the proud back to the fullest degree.* (Psalm 31:23)

Reflection

Love shall be our token;
Love be yours and love be mine;
Love to God and all,
Love for plea and gift and sign.
—Christina Rosetti v. 3 UMH 242

~Prayer of Gratitude~

Day 5

Morning

Who will separate us from Christ's love? (Romans 8:35a)

Reflection

As a child, maybe you had a parent or loved one tell you that nothing you could do would change their love for you. This is often a word of assurance parents give to their kids after the child has screwed up, made a mistake, or done something wrong. It is natural for us to see affection as something we either deserve or don't, as something we earn through good behavior or lose through bad action. It is a hard idea for us to wrap our minds around a love that we cannot break. In Romans, when Paul asks this question, it is rhetorical. It makes a point in a dramatic way. Paul even lists all the potential answers, only to arrive at the right answer, and one that is the simplest of all: nothing. Nothing can separate us from the love of God.

~Prayer of Petition~

Evening

I give you a new commandment: Love each other. Just as I have loved you, so you also must love each other. (John 13:34)

17

Reflection

We become what we love and who we love shapes what we become. If we love things, we become a thing. If we love nothing, we become nothing. Imitation is not a literal mimicking of Christ, rather it means becoming the image of the beloved, an image disclosed through transformation. This means we are to become vessels of God's compassionate love for others.

—Clare of Assisi

~Prayer of Gratitude~

Joy

Morning Prayer of Petition

Steadfast God, you call your people to joy and thanksgiving, but too often I am tempted towards cynicism and a mindset of scarcity. As I wake, forgive me for the ways that I fail to see you at work and rejoice at your presence. Forgive me for:

- people I overlook or take for granted,
- blessings that I do not recognize,
- simple moments that I do not stop and soak up,
- reasons for joy that I do not see or notice.

Today, help me to focus on the reasons I have to be joyful and help me resist a hard heart that no longer sees reasons to rejoice in you. Amen.

Evening Prayer of Gratitude

God of joy and singing, as I reflect on today, may I notice the ways you continue to show up in my life. As the angels rejoice at the birth of Christ, may I learn to rejoice at your presence in my life. I rejoice for:

- one way you cared for me today,
- one way you opened my eyes today,
- one person that was a source of encouragement or comfort today,
- one opportunity you presented to me today,
- one blessing that I overlooked today.

May I have the eyes to see your work, and a heart that finds joy in your daily presence. Amen.

Day 1

Morning

As soon as I heard your greeting, the baby in my womb jumped for joy. (Luke 1:44)

Reflection

Do you know someone who just seems to exude joy? Just being in their presence is enough to raise your spirits, make you laugh, or turn your day around. When Elizabeth greeted Mary, her baby (John the Baptist) jumped for joy in the mere presence of Jesus. Even while in utero, Jesus seemed to have a joyful aura all around him. During his life this would continue. The closer people got to him, the more they could feel it. One touch of his robe would heal. One word from his mouth would calm a storm or cure the sick. One encounter would leave people rushing back home full of joy. Sometimes, we can get stuck in the mess of our own lives and joy can seem impossible to find. But the closer we grow to Jesus, the more we will find the joy that is so elusive.

~Prayer of Petition~

Evening

They offered great sacrifices on that day and rejoiced, for God had made them rejoice with great joy. The women and children also rejoiced, and the sound of the joy in Jerusalem could be heard from far away. (Nehemiah 12:43)

Reflection

During the holiday season, cable networks air movies in which the main character is doing everything possible to make it home for Christmas. Yet, any obstacle one could think of gets in their way—getting caught in a snowstorm, their car breaking down, missing their ride, or getting into a fight with a significant other or a friend. Their only wish is to go home and participate in their family traditions.

The exiled Israelites living in Babylon (post-Babylonian captivity) desired to return home to Jerusalem. But when they reached Jerusalem, they found that its gates had been destroyed and that its temple was no more. Under the leadership of Nehemiah, however, they were able to rebuild and re-establish their identity, their worship practices, and their holy city. Therefore, after all the turmoil of being disconnected, they rejoiced in being together. They rejoiced because not only were these edifices being rebuilt, but so were relationships. Let us, too, rejoice in the opportunity to rebuild relationships and heal old wounds. Let us enjoy being home.

~Prayer of Gratitude~

Day 2

Morning

When they saw the star, they were filled with joy. (Matthew 2:10)

Reflection

If you have ever gotten lost running or hiking, you know the panic that can lodge in your gut when you fear that you have lost your bearings. Similarly, there is an incredible, indescribable sense of joy and relief when you finally see a familiar landmark or recognizable path. You aren't home yet, but there is joy in merely knowing that you aren't lost. For the wise men, each time they hit an obstacle, encountered a detour, or got sidetracked with a distraction, the star would appear and, with it, great joy. You may not always know where you are going or how long it will take you to get there, but Christ is like the North Star. You are never lost and there is immense relief and joy when you keep him in sight.

~Prayer of Petition~

Evening

The angel said, "Don't be afraid! Look! I bring good news to you—wonderful, joyous news for all people. Your savior is born today in David's city. He is Christ the Lord." (Luke 2:10-11)

Reflection

In the Christmas carol *God Rest Ye Merry Gentlemen*, the writer encourages the singers and the hearers of the song to not allow the troubles of the world to alarm them, for Jesus was born "to save us from Satan's [power] when we have gone astray." The song tells the story of the revelation of Jesus to the shepherds and how they were entrusted with the "tidings of comfort and joy."

The angels' appearance to the shepherds demonstrates that God does not care about our socio-economic status. God will send the good news to anyone who is open and willing to receive it. God calls us to share the joy of how an encounter with God can change our lives forever. Will you share that joy today?

~Prayer of Gratitude~

Day 3

Morning

I have said these things to you so that my joy will be in you and your joy will be complete. (John 15:11)

Reflection

There are a lot of things we look to in this world to bring us happiness. Many turn to fulfilling friendships and the love of a family. Some search for happiness and security in money, a 401(k), or material possessions. Others think the key to joy is experiences and adventure, while others think it is achievement and accomplishments. The truth is, a certain amount of joy can be found in many of these things. They bring a partial fulfillment to our lives, and one need not abandon them in order to find Jesus. But what Christ offers is something that none of these can. Christ can complete the joy that we so desperately search for in our life pursuits.

~Prayer of Petition~

Evening

Then the young women will dance for joy;
*   the young and old men will join in.*
I will turn their mourning into laughter
*   and their sadness into joy;*
*   I will comfort them. (*Jeremiah 31:13)

Reflection

And while we were being carried along by those four angels we saw a large open space like a splendid garden landscaped with rose trees and every variety of flower. The trees were as tall as cypresses whose leaves rustled gently and incessantly. And there in that garden-sanctuary were four other angels, more dazzling than the rest. And when they saw us they showed us honor, saying to the other angels in admiration, "Here they are! They have arrived. . . ."

We went up to a place where they walls seemed constructed of light. At the entrance of the place stood four angels who put white robes on those who entered. We went in and heard a unified voice chanting endlessly, "Holy, holy, holy. . . ."

We were all sustained by an indescribable fragrance which completely satisfied us. Then in my joy, I awoke.

—"The Martyrdom of Perpetua" from *In Her Words* (edited by Amy Oden)

~Prayer of Gratitude~

Day 4

Morning

So they left the tomb quickly with fear and great joy and ran to tell his disciples. (Matthew 28:8 NRSVUE)

Reflection

We often associate fear with weakness, cowardice, or a lack of faith. But we know that courage is acting in the face of fear, not without it. Similarly, we often think that in order to be happy we can't also be sad. To be joyful means to be overwhelmingly optimistic about life and confident about the road ahead. But this is a lie. Joy and fear are not mutually exclusive, as we see from the women at the tomb. To be joyful doesn't mean to be happy all the time, or always confident. Joy is a daily choice, an anchor that holds us steady no matter what emotions we are going through or feel.

~Prayer of Petition~

Evening

Let those who plant with tears
reap the harvest with joyful shouts. (Psalm 126:5)

Reflection

There are Christians whose lives seem like Lent without Easter. I realize of course that joy is not expressed the same way at all times in life, especially at moments of great difficulty. Joy adapts and changes, but it always endures, even as a flicker of light born of our personal certainty that, when everything is said and done, we are infinitely loved.
    —Pope Francis, *Evangelii Gaudium*

~Prayer of Gratitude~

Day 5

Morning

The angel said, "Don't be afraid! Look! I bring good news to you—wonderful, joyous news for all people. (Luke 2:10)

Reflection

What is the best news you have ever received? Maybe it was word that a relative was coming home, or the phone call telling you the test was negative (or positive!). Maybe it was when someone said, "I forgive you," or when the doctor assured you everything was going to be okay. There is something about great news that immediately takes over our spirits, drowns out the smaller details, and puts everything into perspective. There is something about Christmas that can make small problems recede and help us refocus on what is most important. As the day draws near, petty differences seem less significant and everyday problems don't seem as burdensome. The birth of Jesus was this kind of news. It is so big, so transformative, that it can make our everyday struggles pale in comparison to the great joy he brings.

~Prayer of Petition~

Evening

The people walking in darkness have seen a great light.
    On those living in a pitch-dark land, light has dawned.
You have made the nation great;
    you have increased its joy.
They rejoiced before you as with joy at the harvest,
    as those who divide plunder rejoice. (Isaiah 9:2-3)

Advent

Reflection

Jesus, joy of our desiring, holy wisdom, love most bright;
Drawn by thee, our souls aspiring sour to uncreated light.
Word of God, our flesh that fashioned, with the fire of life impassioned,
Striving still to truth unknown, souring, dying round thy throne.
    —Martin Janus, "Jesus, Joy of Our Desiring"

~Prayer of Gratitude~

Christmas

WEEK 5

Light

Morning Prayer of Petition

Holy God, in Christ you came to be the light in the darkness. You came to be the light in my darkness. This Christmas, I pray that you would shine light into my life:

- Be a light in my family, where there is discord or hurt.
- Be a light in my work or school, where I am tired or weary.
- Be a light in my spirit, where I am struggling or searching.
- Be a light in my faith, where I am wavering or doubting.

As you shine your light into the world, may I live in that light and reflect it more fully to others. Amen.

Evening Prayer of Gratitude

God of light, every good and perfect gift comes from you, and without you we would not have anything. This evening I stop, pause, and give thanks for the ways that you have been light to me this Christmas. Thank you for:

- the ways you showed up for me through others today,
- how you helped me to see in new ways today,
- revealing what I need to confront today,
- illuminating a new direction or opportunity or understanding for me today.

Continue to be the light of my life and the light that emanates out from me to others. Amen.

Day 1

Morning

Because of our God's deep compassion,
the dawn from heaven will break upon us,
to give light to those who are sitting in darkness (Luke 1:78-79a)

Reflection

Sitting in darkness is a powerful metaphor for those seasons of suffering in our life. Isolation, pain, grief, or tragedy can all feel like sitting alone in the dark. Such seasons in life were often seen as punishment from God for mistakes or sins. We often feel that way. We desperately search for understanding why something is happening to us, many times believing it to be from God. But as Zechariah's song reminds us, it is not God's anger that subjects us to a solitary confinement of darkness. Rather, it is God's deep compassion that meets us in the darkness, breaking upon us as light that illuminates a way forward.

~Prayer of Petition~

Evening

The light shines in the darkness, and the darkness doesn't extinguish the light. (John 1:5)

Reflection

There is something about Christmas that is known to us in the contrasts. A decorated Christmas tree looks nice in the daytime, but at night its lights sparkle, and we are mesmerized by the glow. In the same way, we can recognize light because we have experienced darkness. The wonder of Christmas is that the true light—the light that illumines everyone—has come into the world. Later, in John's Gospel, Jesus will tell us: "I am the light of the world" (John 8:12). Candles melt, lightbulbs burn out, and Christmas lights get put away. But Jesus—the true light—never dims or fades. And not only is he the light, but he also gives his light to those who follow him and commands us to be the light of the world. We cannot generate this kind of light. We must first receive the light and then be willing to share it with the world.

~Prayer of Gratitude~

Day 2

Morning

The people walking in darkness have seen a great light.
On those living in a pitch-dark land, light has dawned. (Isaiah 9:2)

Reflection

Have you ever woken up early just to watch the sunrise? To really take in the beauty of the morning, you have to get up well before dawn, when it is still pitch-dark. The reason is because the sun doesn't rise all at once. It isn't like a light switch. Instead, the hue of the sky slowly begins to change, as if illuminated from some unknown source. Streaks of light begin breaking through as the sun emerges on the horizon. The dawning of the light takes time, but eventually the darkness is dissipated by the light. The arrival of Jesus at Christmas doesn't change our lives all at once. But like the dawning of the sun—slowly, steadily—the light of Christ begins to shine in our lives, eventually transforming even the darkest parts and places.

~Prayer of Petition~

Evening

It's a light for revelation to the Gentiles
and a glory for your people Israel. (Luke 2:32)

Reflection

Silent night, holy night,
Son of God, loves' pure light;
Radiant beams from thy holy face
with the dawn of redeeming grace,
Jesus, Lord, at thy birth,
Jesus, Lord, at thy birth.
 —Joseph Mohr, "Silent Night"

~Prayer of Gratitude~

Day 3

Morning

Jesus spoke to the people again, saying, "I am the light of the world. Whoever follows me won't walk in darkness but will have the light of life." (John 8:12)

Reflection

In many older homes and buildings, there are rooms, or basements, that we would rather not see. Whether it is a cracking foundation, leaky wall, or an aging furnace, there are certain parts of a home that we prefer to keep in the dark. We keep them out of sight and out of mind, at least until somethingt breaks. Our lives can also be like this. There are certain realities that we prefer not to think about, face, or deal with. Whether it is a sin that we harbor, a trauma that we stuff away, or a growing conflict that we prefer to ignore, there is much about our lives that we are content to keep in the dark. But the light of Christ does more than just warm or illuminate; it also reveals. In this revelation, we are forced to look at the whole of our lives, recognizing that the pathway to healing begins by first being willing to see something that, until now, we had kept in the dark.

~Prayer of Petition~

Evening

The sun will no longer be your light by day,
nor will the moon shine for illumination by night.
The LORD will be your everlasting light;
your God will be your glory. (Isaiah 60:19)

Reflection

For most of human history, people lived without the convenience of artificial light. They lived based on the sun's light, and when day was done, so was their work. The sun still orders our days in many ways, but we have become accustomed to being able to work, play, eat, and live on the time frame we choose because we can make light available to us anytime we want. This gives us the illusion that we control our days, and—to some degree—our lives. The challenge inherent in Isaiah's words is that it is the Lord who is in control and who gives us light. It is not through our own power, might, or clever intellect that we can see the path in front of us; rather, it is because the Lord is the light of our lives. Coming to rely fully on the light that comes only from God is the journey of discipleship.

~Prayer of Gratitude~

Day 4

Morning

In the same way, let your light shine before people, so they can see the good things you do and praise your Father who is in heaven. (Matthew 5:16)

Reflection

So much of the light we see isn't directly from the source, but is instead reflected off of something else. Perhaps the best example is the moon, which on a clear night, lights up the dark. It has no light of its own, but rather reflects the light it receives from the sun. Objects can either absorb the light they receive or reflect it so that others can benefit from it. Jesus tells his followers that they are meant to live reflectively in the world. Jesus's followers do not simply absorb the blessings and benefits that come from a life with God, but are meant to reflect those gifts so that others may experience them.

~Prayer of Petition~

Evening

Do not rejoice over me, my enemy,
  because when I fall, I will rise;
    if I sit in darkness, the Lord is my light. (Micah 7:8)

Reflection

When I look back 79 years ago, I see myself coming from the home life of slaves. My mother and father were slaves in America. We were hungry and thirsting for help, for light, for that thing that would help us to grow and become what we believed our God and your God wanted us to be. We wanted light, intelligence; we wanted that spiritual guidance that would guide us into that full manhood and womanhood that could help bless the world.

—Mary McLeod Bethune, "Address to a World Assembly for Moral Re-Armament"

~Prayer of Gratitude~

Day 5

Morning

The city doesn't need the sun or the moon to shine on it, because God's glory is its light, and its lamp is the Lamb. The nations will walk by its light, and the kings of the earth will bring their glory into it. (Revelation 21:23-24)

Reflection

All light in our world is temporary. We have a cycle of night and day because of the way the earth spins on its axis. We have seasons of relative dark and cold because of the way the earth rotates around the sun. Similarly, in our lives, we have seasons that are full of light and others that are characterized by darkness. These seasons aren't always predictable, and when we are in a season of darkness, it can feel permanent. But the book of Revelation reminds us that a day is coming when there will no longer be periods of light and dark, day and night. Instead, the glory of God will permanently be present and, in the presence of that light, our lives will no longer vacillate between joy and pain, hope and despair, death and life. In God's presence, the light is eternal.

~Prayer of Petition~

Evening

Come, house of Jacob,
  let's walk by the Lord's light. (Isaiah 2:5)

Christmas

Reflection

Long my imprisoned spirit lay, fast bound in sin and nature's night thine eye diffused a quickening ray: I woke, the dungeon flamed with light; my chains fell off, my heart was free, I rose, went forth, and followed thee.
   —Charles Wesley, "And Can It Be that I Should Gain"

~Prayer of Gratitude~

New

Morning Prayer of Petition

God of new birth and new life, second chances and new beginnings, on the cusp of the ending of one year and the beginning of another, I invite you to continue your work of making me new. As I enter a new year I pray:

- for that which I need to leave behind in order to embrace something new,
- for big decisions that I need to make,
- for areas of my life where I hope for new opportunities,
- for habits that I hope to prioritize,
- for areas of my faith that I want to grow in.

As you make all things new, I pray that your Holy Spirit would work in me to reshape me, that I may live in a new way for you this year.

Evening Prayer of Gratitude

God of endings and beginnings, you have been at work in my life, and there is new work yet ahead that you intend to do in me. As I reflect on the ending of one year, and ready myself for that which is new, I see the ways that you have been at work in my life. I name and thank you for the ways that you used this past year to:

- teach me,
- challenge me,
- care for me,
- bless me,
- strengthen me.

As I move forward in faith to a new leg of my journey, I take with me all that you have and are doing in my life. I pray that you would give me the eyes to see and the heart to receive the ways that you are daily at work for me and for my good. Amen.

Day 1

Morning

So then, if anyone is in Christ, that person is part of the new creation. The old things have gone away, and look, new things have arrived! (2 Corinthians 5:17)

Reflection

Sometimes, in an effort to save money and be responsible, people will try to fix things that are broken. But, eventually, certain items just can't be patched up, rewired, or salvaged. Instead, it is time to replace them. Paul reminds us that Jesus doesn't just come to improve our lives by rounding them out or fixing them up. He ushers in a new creation! Old things aren't fixed; they go away. Old habits aren't salvaged; they are thrown out. Old ways of seeing things aren't improved; they are left behind. New life in Christ is both hopeful and challenging. In Christ, you don't get an improved life. You get a new one.

~Prayer of Petition~

Evening

*He put a new song in my mouth,
     a song of praise for our God.
Many people will learn of this and be amazed;
     they will trust the LORD.* (Psalm 40:3)

Reflection

Go, tell it on the mountain, over the hills and everywhere;
Go, tell it on the mountain, that Jesus Christ is born. . . .
Down in a lowly manger the humble Christ was born,
And God sent us salvation that blessed Christmas morn.
     —"Go, Tell It on the Mountain"

~Prayer of Gratitude~

Day 2

Morning

Take off the old human nature with its practices and put on the new nature, which is renewed in knowledge by conforming to the image of the one who created it. (Colossians 3:9b-10)

Reflection

Some of us have clothes, like a sweatshirt or slippers, that are old, worn out, and have long since lost their color. But we love them because they are comfortable. Much of our lives can be this way, too. We have habits, narratives, and ways of seeing the world that may no longer work for us. They may even hold us back. But we hold on to them because they are familiar and comfortable. When Christ is born into our lives, he asks us to take off ways of life that are familiar and comfortable and put on a new way of life, one that is stitched and sewn by him.

~Prayer of Petition~

Evening

My comfort during my suffering is this:
your word gives me new life. (Psalm 119:50)

Reflection

Hark! The herald angels sing, "Glory to the newborn King;
Peace on earth, and mercy mild, God and sinners reconciled!"
Joyful, all ye nations rise, join the triumph of the skies;
With the angelic host proclaim, "Christ is born in Bethlehem!"
—Charles Wesley, "Hark! the Herald Angels Sing"

~Prayer of Gratitude~

Day 3

Morning

No one pours new wine into old wineskins. If they did, the wineskins would burst, the wine would spill, and the wineskins would be ruined. Instead, people pour new wine into new wineskins so that both are kept safe. (Matthew 9:17)

Reflection

Some people in twelve-step recovery programs will talk about the decision to get sober as impacting not just one part of their life, but every part. For example, a person in recovery can't just stop drinking and then not change anything else. If they keep the same habits, go to the same bars, hang out with the same crowd, and manage stress the same way, the change won't last. Instead, the decision to stop drinking is often accompanied by holistic life changes. They build new social habits, make different friends, and develop new ways of dealing with stress and anxiety. The change they want to make requires a more holistic change to their life. You might be struggling with work, a relationship, parenting, stress, or health and want Jesus to help. But, often, Jesus doesn't just change one isolated part of our lives without also asking us to consider the whole. Changing one part often requires addressing the whole; otherwise, we risk losing the new thing that God is doing in us.

~Prayer of Petition~

Evening

Look! I'm doing a new thing;
*   now it sprouts up; don't you recognize it?*
I'm making a way in the desert,
*   paths in the wilderness.* (Isaiah 43:19)

Reflection

We love this image from Isaiah about rivers in the desert, and we have become so accustomed to hearing the scripture that we do not often stop to think about the logistics of such a vision. The desert is inhospitable to new things. While there are certainly species that make their home in the desert, they have had to develop over a long period of time to be able to survive there. A new species would not have the same adaptability and therefore, could not thrive. But, in Isaiah, there is a promise that God is going to do a new thing by bringing forth a river in the desert. The geography of our own lives has deserts as well. There are places in our hearts that are hostile to new things, where the conditions make life hard. Even in these places, God is promising to break forth and bring something new. Do you not perceive it?

~Prayer of Gratitude~

Day 4

Morning

I give you a new commandment: Love each other. Just as I have loved you, so you also must love each other. (John 13:34)

Reflection

When kids are young, parents often have rules about what they aren't allowed to do. As kids get older, this list of what they cannot do only grows in length and complexity. Eventually, as kids grow up, you can no longer parent them with a list of rules. Instead, you need a new way of doing things. Many people see Jesus and faith as a force that restricts their lives, giving them an ever-increasing and burdensome set of rules to follow. But Jesus gives his followers a new commandment, a new way of seeing life with God. Faith isn't about all the things we are not supposed to do, nor is it about a list of behaviors that are wrong. Jesus changes all that by, instead, giving us one thing to do, and one thing to be known by. Love each other.

~Prayer of Petition~

Evening

Sing to the LORD a new song!
*   Sing to the LORD, all the earth!* (Psalm 96:1)

Reflection

The saying goes "everything old is new again," insinuating that, somehow, nothing is actually new. In Ecclesiastes, the wisdom writer tells us there is nothing new under the sun. Even so, our United Methodist order for morning prayer says, "New every morning is your love, great God of light." We have a complicated relationship with newness: we honor tradition and sing old hymns and songs, yet there is a command in this psalm to sing a new song. The work is ours, then, to look for God in the ways that God has always promised to be made known to us: in fellowship and community, in worship and the sacraments, in prayer and scripture reading. We can be confident that no matter how old we get, there are still new ways for us to encounter the grace and love of God, and new ways we will experience God. At Christmas, especially, we give thanks to God for Jesus, who is always being given to us, and because of whom, we can sing a new song.

~Prayer of Gratitude~

Day 5

Morning

Jesus said to them, "I assure you who have followed me that, when everything is made new, when the Human One sits on his magnificent throne, you also will sit on twelve thrones overseeing the twelve tribes of Israel." (Matthew 19:28)

Reflection

It is easy to read the verse above and miss just how radical it really is. Jesus tells the people that everything will be made new. Not a few things, not just the messy things, not the broken things, but everything. It is a reminder that sin has a way of working and weaving its way into all aspects of our lives and world. It isn't just people that are sinful, but systems are as well—systems of government and policing, churches and institutions, colleges and schools, neighborhoods and communities. Christ doesn't just save hearts and convert individuals; Jesus confronts sin wherever it is found. When Jesus takes his throne, it will only be after he has made everything new.

~Prayer of Petition~

Evening

When you let loose your breath, they are created,
and you make the surface of the ground brand-new again. (Psalm 104:30)

Christmas

Reflection

Finish, then, thy new creation; pure and spotless let us be.
Let us see thy great salvation perfectly restored in thee;
Changed from glory into glory, till in heaven we take our place,
Till we cast our crowns before thee, lost in wonder, love, and praise.
    —Charles Wesley, "Love Divine, All Loves Excelling"

~Prayer of Gratitude~

Epiphany

Believe

Morning Prayer of Petition

Holy God, I believe but help my unbelief. As I seek to know you more fully and follow you more faithfully, I confess that I struggle with doubt. Help me today to:

- confess areas of doubt in my faith,
- name the places where I chose my own way rather than trusting in you,
- believe that you can work in areas of my life where I lack hope,
- grow strong in an area of my faith.

God, even in my searching and wondering, strengthen in me a faith to trust you more fully and to believe in your power to work in my life. Amen.

Evening Prayer of Gratitude

Tonight God, I come to you with thanksgiving for the ways that you have shown yourself to me. Thank you for showing up to me today:

- through other people,
- through small moments of wonder or joy,
- through moments of difficulty or distress,
- through signs that reveal your presence.

May I sleep knowing that you are at work in my life and wake up believing that you hold something new in store for me each day. Amen.

Day 1

Morning

Do not let your hearts be troubled. Believe in God; believe also in me. (John 14:1 NRSVUE)

Reflection

We often think of the word *believe* as an intellectual ascent to certain doctrines and dogmas. But, when Jesus uses the word, that is almost never what he means. Instead, *believe*

Epiphany

is a relational word, often better translated as *trust*. A child learns early on to trust a parent. Good friends learn that they can rely on or trust each other during times of struggle. Similarly, Jesus reminds the disciples to believe or trust in him during times of anxiety, fear, or uncertainty. This isn't to believe something merely in our heads, it is to believe in someone with our hearts, and to learn to trust that, during times of trouble, we do not walk alone.

~Prayer of Petition~

Evening

Jesus replied, "This is what God requires, that you believe in him whom God sent." (John 6:29)

Reflection

Let earth and heaven combine,
Angels and men agree
To praise in songs divine
Th' incarnate deity,
Our God contracted to a span,
Incomprehensibly made man.
He deigns in flesh t' appear,
Widest extremes to join,
To bring our vileness near,
And make us all divine;
And we the life of God shall know,
For God is manifest below.
Made perfect first in love,
And sanctified by grace,
We shall from earth remove,
And see his glorious face;
His love shall then be fully showed,
And man shall all be lost in God.
  —Charles Wesley, "Let Earth and Heaven Combine"

~Prayer of Gratitude~

Day 2

Morning

Therefore I say to you, whatever you pray and ask for, believe that you will receive it, and it will be so for you. (Mark 11:24)

Reflection

Do you believe that God can do surprising and miraculous things in your life? Psychologists have long noted that our expectations shape what we experience. Known as the Pygmalion Effect, our expectations change our reality. If we only expect small possibilities and progress for our lives, we often experience just that. But if we expect and believe that God can do far more than we can imagine, then we have taken the first step toward greater possibilities for our lives. It isn't magic, and God is no genie in a bottle, but earnestly praying for something, and asking God for it, raises our awareness, focuses our energy, and opens our hearts in a way that greatly increases our ability to receive what God wants to give us.

~Prayer of Petition~

Evening

Jesus replied, "Do you believe because you see me? Happy are those who don't see and yet believe." (John 20:29)

Reflection

It is by grace that we believe in God (Ephesians 2:8-9; John 6:44). What is important about this notion of faith as a gift from God is the understanding that faith brings out certain dimensions in life. Faith as gift from God provides us with an orientation that is a product of our faith in Jesus Christ. It evokes certain feelings in us; it represents a new form of spirituality (1 Corinthians 1:23, 2:10-16; Ephesians 1:15-19).

—Bonganjalo Goba, "What Is Faith? A Black South African Perspective," from *Lift Every Voice: Constructing Christian Theologies from the Underside*

~Prayer of Gratitude~

Day 3

Morning

The seed on the rock are those who receive the word joyfully when they hear it, but they have no root. They believe for a while but fall away when they are tempted. (Luke 8:13)

Reflection

Believing in Jesus is often imagined as a one-time decision. Many Christians recount the moment they were saved and came to faith in Christ. But Jesus reminds his followers that believing is not a single decision. Rather, belief is a continual and daily choice that we make to trust God with our lives, obey God within our work, honor God in our behavior, and center God in our hearts. Believing is an ongoing activity that we participate in every day, not a passive decision that we make once. It is possible to believe strongly but, then through neglect, allow that belief to dissipate and slip away. Most of us drift in our beliefs at times. But just as belief can be neglected, we can return to it at any time. Today can be a day to refocus your attention toward God, trust God, and put faith back into a place of priority in your life.

~Prayer of Petition~

Evening

In the same way, faith is dead when it doesn't result in faithful activity. (James 2:17)

Reflection

A couple and their young daughter were getting off the elevator as I stood waiting on the ground level. "Your flowers are beautiful," I said, before adding how much I love the magnificent proteas grown in South Africa. The man didn't skip a beat before saying, "Please take them," as he placed them in my hands. I responded with a hint of confusion before he added, "We are leaving and were not sure what to do with them." Observing my reaction as I admired the flowers up close, the woman then said, "Look at God," before describing the joy of being able to bless someone. Her words of praise were pure in response to God seemingly orchestrating an opportunity to share something beautiful with another person.

What might you offer another person to bring them delight? What gift might you place in the hands of someone who might need or enjoy it more than you? What talent, resource, or treasure could produce a ripple of goodness? What if such moments are, in fact, epiphanies—moments to say, "Look at God," and believe?

~Prayer of Gratitude~

Day 4

Morning

Then he said to Thomas, "Put your finger here. Look at my hands. Put your hand into my side. No more disbelief. Believe." (John 20:27)

Reflection

Many of us struggle to believe in something until we have concrete evidence that it is real. We can approach God in an overly rational way, needing logical arguments or seeking proof of God's existence. This is understandable. It isn't bad to question God and to seek greater understanding. Thomas wanted evidence of Jesus's resurrection and proof of what the other disciples had told him. But believing in Jesus is rarely arrived at through philosophical arguments or irrefutable evidence. After all of our inquiries, questions, and doubts, sometimes we have to trust in a God whom we cannot completely prove exists. Jesus at once honored Thomas's questions and doubts, and also challenged him to move beyond his need for all of the answers and believe!

~Prayer of Petition~

Evening

Immediately the father of the child cried out, "I believe; help my unbelief!" (Mark 9:24 NRSVUE)

Reflection

It can be easy to stand in worship and profess the faith found in the ancient creeds, "I believe in God the Father Almighty and in Jesus Christ . . ." Our recitation continues as we affirm our belief in the miracles of the virgin birth and the resurrection of the dead. Yes! We believe all we profess to be true. But then someone invites us to believe there is a miracle with their name on it—a resounding "Yes" after a season of "No's." We have been trying to have a child for years only to miscarry six times. Will you pray we can conceive a child? I have been diagnosed with stage-four inflammatory breast cancer. Will you pray for me to be healed? "Of course," we respond, before speaking a prayer punctuated by unspoken doubt, a silent honesty that often struggles to believe miracles still happen. What would it take for us to be as honest with God as with the father of a son suffering from seizures? What if belief starts with bringing our needs before Jesus and allowing his belief in what is possible to be stronger than our doubt? I believe; please help my unbelief, Jesus.

~Prayer of Gratitude~

Day 5

Morning

It's impossible to please God without faith because the one who draws near to God must believe that he exists and that he rewards people who try to find him. (Hebrews 11:6)

Reflection

In church, we often sing songs, recite prayers, and participate in rituals without really thinking about what we are proclaiming. We sing about giving our whole life to God, but then walk out of church struggling to give even a few moments a day to God. We pray about forgiveness but then refuse to offer forgiveness to others. We speak of love but then snap at our kids or spouse. To truly experience God in your life, you cannot simply go through the motions of church, worship, or prayer. You must believe that which you are proclaiming, and seek to live it out. When you do, it not only pleases God, but it also allows you to experience the power of God in your life.

Epiphany

Evening

He also saw the face cloth that had been on Jesus' head. It wasn't with the other clothes but was folded up in its own place. (John 20:7)

Reflection

Sustain me God, as I confront
the tempest that has stilled.
Help me endure the task ahead
reclaim and then rebuild.
I know that out of death comes life,
with time will come relief.
For even now, Lord, I believe.
Lord, help my unbelief.
    — Jacque B. Jones, "You Formed Creation by Your Word"

~Prayer of Gratitude~

Anointing

Morning Prayer of Petition

Holy God, you send your Spirit to rest and anoint your people, to set us apart for your work in the world. Now I set apart a few minutes today to remember the circumstances in which you've placed me. As I go about my day, help me to see the way you've set me apart to:

- speak words of encouragement to someone around me,
- offer forgiveness to someone who needs it,
- notice those in my life who are hurting or suffering,
- pray for the specific needs of my community and city.

Help me to remember that I am anointed, set apart, and help me to see the opportunities I have today to serve you in the world. Amen.

Evening Prayer of Gratitude

God of anointing and blessing, you are always working for the good of those who love and serve you. Thank you for the ways that you have showed up for me today, set apart time and space for me to see you. Thank you for:

- moments of truth and discovery,
- opportunities you are opening for me,
- ways that you are teaching me,
- people that you put around me.

Continue to work in my heart to trust you, to see you at work in my life, and to believe that you can set apart and use me in extraordinary ways. Amen.

Day 1

Morning

When Jesus was baptized, he immediately came up out of the water. Heaven was opened to him, and he saw the Spirit of God coming down like a dove and resting on him. (Matthew 3:16)

Reflection

Methodists believe in grace that is independent of our activity. God's grace is with us before we come to faith; it leads us to faith in Jesus and continues to sanctify us as we follow Jesus. This grace is a gift of the Holy Spirit, which comes before anything we do to deserve it. This idea of a grace that we do not earn or deserve is so hard for most of us to accept. In practice, we constantly think that our behavior must impact how much or little God loves us or does for us. But in our baptism, God claims us and anoints us with the Spirit before we do anything at all to deserve it. Nothing that we do afterward can either add to or take away from that gift. It's good to remember this.

~Prayer of Petition~

Evening

So Samuel took the horn of oil and anointed him right there in front of his brothers. The LORD's *spirit came over David from that point forward.* (1 Samuel 16:13)

Reflection

There's something uniquely beautiful about this moment in 1 Samuel. Israel has asked for a king to govern them—a rejection of God and God's rule over their lives—so Samuel goes and first anoints Saul. Saul rules until he turns from God, and Samuel is tasked to anoint another. And it is here that we find Samuel, anointing David, the new king, filled mightily with the spirit of the Lord.

Too often, we place so much emphasis on David, on the one who is anointed, that I wonder if we sometimes forget about Samuel?

Society encourages us, even requires us at times, to operate from the box of individualism, making ourselves the protagonists of every story. Surely, we are the anointed ones, the ones filled with the Spirit to take on the issues of society, to bring about peace and justice in the world. And yet, for every David (and for every Saul, for that matter), Samuel was present, listening intently to the wisdom and direction of God. Samuel was present to participate in God's unfolding story, to do the anointing of another. Who has God placed in your life for you to bless and anoint?

~Prayer of Gratitude~

Day 2

Morning

The Spirit of the Lord is upon me,
because the Lord has anointed me.
He has sent me to preach good news to the poor,
to proclaim release to the prisoners
and recovery of sight to the blind,
to liberate the oppressed,
and to proclaim the year of the Lord's favor. (Luke 4:18-19)

Reflection

In Hebrew the word *Messiah* means the anointed one. In ancient Israel, the act of anointing with oil was used to confer special status on a person, like a king. It also signified that such a person was set apart for a special purpose. Jesus's anointing was quite different from that of the typical king, as was the way he lived out that special role. Jesus was not anointed with oil by people but with the Holy Spirit by God. Jesus was not set apart to rule with earthly might, but to preach good news to the poor and release to the captives. Those of us who follow Jesus are also set apart for a special purpose. But that purpose isn't found in arrogance of believing we have all the answers. Rather, our anointing, our purpose, should be good news to the poor and oppressed.

~Prayer of Petition~

Evening

Now I know that the LORD saves his anointed one;
*   God answers his anointed one*
*   from his heavenly sanctuary,*
*   answering with mighty acts of salvation*
*   achieved by his strong hand.* (Psalm 20:6)

Reflection

My heart beat, my limbs trembled, and my voice was faint. . . . After I took my text [from the Bible], it appeared to me as if I had nothing to do but open my mouth, and the Lord filled it. . . .

I preached and felt joy in my soul. . . . My mind was cleared and the Scriptures opened themselves to my mind and I felt strengthened; some shouted, others wept. . . . The fire kindled. . . . The prayers of God's people helped me, and the power of God, like the dew of heaven, was let down upon us.

I endeavored to speak as God gave ability. . . . I felt free, the tongue was loosed, the lip was touched, and the heart was warm. . . . The Lord owned the word, and the hearty Amens that went up caused the woods to echo.

O how careful ought we to be, lest through our by-laws of church government and discipline, we bring into disrepute even the word of life. For as unseemly as it may appear now-a-days for a woman to preach, it should be remembered that nothing is impossible with God. And why should it be thought impossible, heterodox, or improper, for a woman to preach? Seeing the Savior died for the woman as well as the man.

—Jarena Lee, *The Religious Experience and Journal of Jarena Lee*

~Prayer of Gratitude~

45

Day 3

Morning

You didn't anoint my head with oil, but she has poured perfumed oil on my feet. (Luke 7:46)

Reflection

There is an irony in seeing Jesus as the Messiah and savior. The more holy a person is, the closer they believe themselves to be to God, the harder it is to see Jesus as a savior. Why? Because holy people don't need saving. Conversely the greater the sinner, the easier it is to confess Jesus as a savior. Why? Because sinners know their deep need for saving. In the story above, the woman who was a well-known sinner in town understands Jesus's identity much better than the religious leaders at the same dinner. Her anointing of Jesus's feet is an act of recognition and of worship. Our closeness to Jesus is not connected to how holy we are, but rather to how much we see our own need for a savior.

~Prayer of Petition~

Evening

But you have an anointing from the holy one, and all of you know the truth. (1 John 2:20)

Reflection

It is fascinating that John connects the idea of being anointed by the Holy One with the idea that all have knowledge. When I think of anointing, I often think about the intangibles. I think of things like a divine call on one's life, or God-given wisdom, or supernatural strength, or unshakeable perseverance. But John connects being anointed with knowledge—with facts, with information, with an understanding acquired through experience or education.

But perhaps being anointed is simply that—pausing to reflect on the journey of our lives thus far and experiencing God's faithfulness through it all. By naming and accepting God's work in our lives, we can name God's presence, articulate God's call, and accept that the knowledge we acquire throughout our lives informs us to live more fully into God's preferred future.

~Prayer of Gratitude~

Day 4

Morning

On the day when Moses finished setting up the dwelling, he anointed and made it holy. All its equipment, as well as the altar and all its equipment, he also anointed and made holy. (Numbers 7:1)

Reflection

The Hebrew scriptures remind us that we not only anoint or set apart people for a special purpose, but we also set apart space and time for holy purposes. The Sabbath was a time set apart for rest, renewal, and reconnecting with God. The tabernacle, and later the temple, were set apart as special places to encounter and worship God. While God is present always and in everything, it is useful to set aside a special place and time to connect, worship, and spend time with God. What time do you set aside for God? Is there a special place that is reserved for this time of connection? Anointing a time and space for God can remind you of the priority and importance of this relationship in your life.

~Prayer of Petition~

Evening

The LORD *is his people's strength;*
  he is a fortress of protection for his anointed one. (Psalm 28:8)

Reflection

So let the tears come
as anointing,
as consecration,
and then
let them go.

Let this blessing
gather itself around you.

Let it give you
what you will need
for this journey.

You will not remember
the words—
they do not matter.

All you need to remember
is how it sounded
when you stood
in the place of death
and heard the living
call your name.
     —Jan Richardson, "The Magdalene's Blessing"

~Prayer of Gratitude~

Day 5

Morning

When the Sabbath was over, Mary Magdalene, Mary the mother of James, and Salome bought spices so that they could go and anoint Jesus' dead body. (Mark 16:1)

Reflection

The scriptures go overboard to remind us that Jesus is not just any ordinary person, and that he shouldn't be treated as such. Jesus was given the name anointed one at his birth—anointed by the Spirit in his baptism, anointed by a sinful person during his life, and by the women followers after his death. If anointing is to set apart as holy, it raises the question of how we will recognize and set Jesus apart in our own lives. It could be through acts of extravagant generosity, acts of prayer, worship, or service to those whom Jesus came to save. We have the invitation and the opportunity to set apart our relationship with Jesus as something special; something different; something worthy of attention, sacrifice, and devotion.

~Prayer of Petition~

Evening

God is the one who establishes us with you in Christ and who anointed us. (2 Corinthians 1:21)

Reflection

The testimony of the Spirit is an inward impression on the soul, whereby the Spirit of God directly "witnesses to my spirit that I am a child of God"; that Jesus Christ hath loved me, and given himself for me; that all my sins are blotted out, and I, even I, am reconciled to God. . . .

The Spirit of God does give a believer such a testimony of his adoption that while it is present to the soul he can no more doubt the reality of his sonship than he can doubt of the shining of the sun while he stands in the full blaze of his beams.

—John Wesley, "The Witness of the Spirit"

~Prayer of Gratitude~

Temptation

Morning Prayer of Petition

God of protection and strength, each day there are forces that pull me away from you. As I begin a new day, call my attention to the temptations that lurk in my own life. Protect me from the temptation:

- to see other people as enemies or competition,
- to grow cynical about what is possible in my life,
- to hoard resources and think that material wealth is the path to happiness,
- to live for myself and close my eyes to the need around me.

Guard my heart today, God, as I seek to follow you. Amen.

Evening Prayer of Gratitude

Holy one, every day your Spirit is protecting me. Even today I see that you are active in leading me towards the good and forgiving me for sins. With a heart of gratitude, I:

- name the ways you guided me today,
- name the ways you protected me today,
- name the ways you provided for me today,
- name the ways you forgave me today.

Continue to lead me not into temptation but deliver me from evil. Amen.

Day 1

Morning

Then the Spirit led Jesus up into the wilderness so that the devil might tempt him. (Matthew 4:1)

Reflection

The church proclaims that Jesus is fully human. Jesus had to manage a human body, experience the range of human emotions, deal with the complexities of family relationships, and even experience what it was like to be tempted. Temptation itself is not sin, but neither is it something to treat casually. Temptation is a liminal experience. It sits just beyond what is healthy and right, but just shy of sin. Like the wilderness in which Jesus experienced it, temptation is a dangerous space. You cannot avoid it, but neither should you seek it out or entertain it for long. Temptation itself is not a sin.

Jesus experienced it. But, like Jesus, we must be swift to confront, name, and separate ourselves from that temptation, lest we give it a foothold in our lives.

~Prayer of Petition~

Evening

When wrongdoings become too much for me,
*   you forgive our sins.* (Psalm 65:3)

Reflection

It is tempting to forget the signs of the times, to individualize evil on a personal scale, as a sign of moral deficit. In this week of Epiphany we remember how wisdom-seekers from afar brought insight into the imperial structures at work in Jesus's geopolitical context. When we pray, "the kingdom and power and glory are yours, forever," to God, we make a political statement regarding the power arrangements of our current day. How am I implicated? How am I tempted to take my social privileges, of race, class, gender, or citizenship, for granted? How does the ordering of society make harm inevitable for the most precarious, globally? How does the Spirit re-orient me to resist the familiar flow of how the world works?
    —Hyemin Na

~Prayer of Gratitude~

Day 2

Morning

Those who stand firm during testing are blessed. They are tried and true. They will receive the life God has promised to those who love him as their reward. (James 1:12)

Reflection

Temptation works incrementally. Its goal is not always to get you to fall all at once, but rather to inch you closer to a danger zone. After a long and stressful day, temptation convinces you that one or two cocktails won't hurt. When you are struggling in your marriage, temptation urges you to just confide in someone. When finances are tight, temptation assures you that a little more on the credit card won't hurt. Temptation starts with small steps, encouraging you to blur your previously clear boundaries, compromise your otherwise solid principles, or nuance a previously straightforward value. Therefore standing firm and not allowing temptation to move us is the best way to keep temptation from leading us down a dangerous pathway.

~Prayer of Petition~

Evening

And don't lead us into temptation,
but rescue us from the evil one. (Matthew 6:13)

Reflection

How are we to understand Jesus's instruction in Matthew 6:13 to pray: "Don't lead us into temptation"?

Greek mythology describes sirens as beautiful creatures whose enchanting songs tempt sailors to their deaths. In Homer's *Odyssey*, we learn of Odysseus's encounter with sirens when he stopped up the ears of his crew with wax to prevent them from hearing their songs.

On the other hand, when Jason and the Argonauts encounter sirens, they instruct the great musician Orpheus to play the lyre. His music overpowers the song of the sirens and they are saved.

In the Christian life, pride often causes us to think old temptations can no longer cause us to stumble. We assume Christ's work in our lives will subdue the temptations to sin just as Orpheus's song drowned out the sirens.

While sanctifying grace leads the desires of a Christian to become increasingly aligned with God's desires, Jesus's instruction that we pray not to be lead into temptation provides a necessary check on our pride. In this life, there will always be temptations to sin we cannot resist. And it is these temptations that we should pray and work to avoid.

~Prayer of Gratitude~

Day 3

Morning

Brothers and sisters, if a person is caught doing something wrong, you who are spiritual should restore someone like this with a spirit of gentleness. Watch out for yourselves so you won't be tempted too. (Galatians 6:1)

Reflection

When someone else has a cough or cold, we take greater care when we are around them. Why? Because we know that colds can be contagious. But emotions, dispositions, and even behavior can be contagious as well. If we spend a lot of time with negative people, it isn't surprising when we start to get negative ourselves. Being around gossip makes it easier to gossip. Watching friends constantly make irresponsible financial choices normalizes the practice for us. Compassion for others, even those who are caught up in unhealthy and unhelpful behavior, is part of our call as followers of Jesus. But we also must remember that to be in the consistent proximity of a behavior increases our own exposure to the temptation that behavior might present in our own lives.

~Prayer of Petition~

Evening

Look at my suffering and trouble—
forgive all my sins! (Psalm 25:18)

Reflection

Forgiveness is costly. It cost Jesus his life and it costs us control of our lives.

How terrifyingly difficult it is to join with Psalm 25:18 in praying "Look at my suffering and trouble—forgive all my sins!" What an easy prayer Psalm 25 would be to pray if the psalmist had just omitted the word *all*!

We have little trouble asking God to relieve our suffering and to forgive those sins that do nothing but make our lives miserable. But what about the hidden temptations we profess to hate, yet secretly love? The unhealthy coping mechanisms we are not yet ready to unlearn? The darkness in our hearts we have not yet allowed the light of Christ to expose?

To pray for God to forgive all our sins is to give up control and to submit ourselves to whatever manner it pleases God to employ to remove all our sins from us.

The Bible is clear. Jesus died for all, and Jesus died to forgive all our sins. God, grant us the courage to allow the purpose of our prayers to match the purpose of Christ's sacrifice. Take note of our struggles and forgive all our sins!

~Prayer of Gratitude~

Day 4

Morning

No one who is tested should say, "God is tempting me!" This is because God is not tempted by any form of evil, nor does he tempt anyone. (James 1:13)

Reflection

Temptation is not a divine test. It is easy and convenient to sometimes see it that way. God must be dangling this thing in front of me to determine the strength of my resolve or the firmness of my faith. But God is not the source of temptation. God is for us, not against us. When we face temptation, it can be dangerous to imagine God on the other side of that enticement because that means that we are alone on this side of it. But instead, scripture reminds us that God is with us. God is alongside us. We don't face temptation alone or only with our own strength. Instead, God offers us a power and strength to face temptation, and promises to be with us in that struggle.

~Prayer of Petition~

Evening

Forgive us our sins,
> *for we also forgive everyone who has wronged us.*
And don't lead us into temptation. (Luke 11:4)

Reflection

The greatest test of character is the ability to stand prosperity. In moments of success which come to earnest devoted souls, comes [sic] also the temptation to use power and influence for selfish ambition or turning aside from the paths of virtue.

—Ida B. Wells-Barnett, "The Requisites of True Leadership," in *Can I Get a Witness? Prophetic Religious Voices of African American Women, An Anthology*

~Prayer of Gratitude~

Day 5

Morning

Everyone is tempted by their own cravings; they are lured away and enticed by them. Once those cravings conceive, they give birth to sin; and when sin grows up, it gives birth to death. (James 1:14-15)

Reflection

There is an old adage that says sheep nibble their way lost. They don't intend to separate themselves from the flock or the shepherd. Instead, they begin eating and just keep nibbling and nibbling and nibbling until suddenly they pop their heads up and discover that they are far away from where they are supposed to be. James talks about a progression that begins with human desire and ends with death. It is a dramatic move from something so ordinary to something so serious and final. But it reminds us that very few of us wake up one day and decide to do something that has severe consequences for our lives. Usually, people don't wake up and decide to become a thief, cheat on their spouse, form an addiction, or embezzle from their employer. Instead, if we aren't attentive and careful, we begin with a behavior that seems okay, move to habits that are increasingly harder to justify, and end up down a path that is far away from where we intended our lives to go.

~Prayer of Petition~

Evening

God of our salvation, help us
> *for the glory of your name!*
Deliver us and cover our sins
> *for the sake of your name!* (Psalm 79:9)

Epiphany

Reflection

Empty, waiting to be fed;
first the water, then the bread
and the wine, God's offering:
Jesus Christ, the living spring.
As the ages come and go,
lives to you, like rivers, flow:
those who doubt and those who know,
nonetheless will find it so.
    —Daniel Charles Damon, "Broken, Bitter, Bruised We Come"

~Prayer of Gratitude~

Bless

Morning Prayer of Petition

Good and gracious God, you bless my life so that I can be a blessing in the lives of other people. As I approach today, show me how to be a blessing:

- to my family members and those whom I see every day,
- to colleagues, classmates, or those with whom I work,
- to my neighbors and those who live around me,
- to those that are hurting or suffering in my community and world.

Lead me to live beyond myself today, so that I may be salt and light in the world. Amen.

Evening Prayer of Gratitude

Mighty God, all day long you are working for my good. I too often get caught up in what is happening for others and struggle to focus on the ways you are blessing me. Open my eyes to see the ways that even today you blessed me:

- in surprising moments,
- through other people,
- by opening doors and providing opportunities,
- in using my mistakes or shortcomings to teach me,
- by offering me opportunities to impact other people.

Keep me focused on the work that you are doing in and through me, and may I not neglect to see you blessing my life or ignore your call to bless others. Amen.

Day 1

Morning

I will make of you a great nation and will bless you. I will make your name respected, and you will be a blessing. (Genesis 12:2)

Reflection

It is easy to talk about blessings when we are on the receiving end of them. We pray for God to bless us, and we regularly respond to positive outcomes in our lives as evidence of that blessing. Everything from a good parking spot to a healthy family is often interpreted as a blessing from God. But rarely do we consider our obligation in blessing. We are happy to receive God's favor, but we often don't ask the next question: What am I called to do with this blessing? God doesn't intend for us to be containers ready to receive good things but to be conduits that are ready to pass the blessings we receive on to others. We are blessed for a reason, to be a blessing in the lives of others.

~Prayer of Petition~

Evening

The LORD bless you and protect you.
The LORD make his face shine on you and be gracious to you.
The LORD lift up his face to you and grant you peace. (Numbers 6:24-26)

Reflection

Strong, gentle children, God made you beautiful,
gave you the wisdom and power you need;
speak in the stillness all you are looking for;
live out your calling to love and to lead.
Strong, knowing children, utter your cry aloud,
honor the wisdom God gave you at birth;
speak to your elders till they have heard your voice;
sing out your vision of healing on earth.
　　—Daniel Charles Damon, "Strong, Gentle Children"

~Prayer of Gratitude~

Day 2

Morning

Bless the God and Father of our Lord Jesus Christ! He has blessed us in Christ with every spiritual blessing that comes from heaven. (Ephesians 1:3)

Reflection

It is tempting to see blessings and material provisions in our lives. We look at other people and often proclaim them blessed simply by observing outward appearances. Nice houses, fancy cars, good looking families, and luxury vacation photos plastered on social media all seem to point to someone who has it made. When we notice these things, it follows that many of us become jealous, and begin to compare our lives to theirs. Be careful about this. God blesses each of you in different ways. God's blessings aren't material; they are spiritual. God blesses us with a peace that surpasses understanding, or resilience to get through seasons of struggle. God's blessings come in the form of forgiveness, freedom, calm, hope, friendship, and purpose. If you want to see

God's unique blessing in your life, focus less on the outward appearance of others, and instead on the contours of your own spirit.

~Prayer of Petition~

Evening

Of David, when he pretended to be crazy before Abimelech, who banished him so that he left.
I will bless the LORD at all times;
> *his praise will always be in my mouth.* (Psalm 34:1)

Reflection

Wanted: More Praise. I cannot help believing that the world will be a better and a happier place when people are praised more and blamed less; when we utter in their hearing the good we think and also gently intimate the criticisms we hope may be of service. For the world grows smaller every day. It will be but a family circle after a while.

—Frances Willard

~Prayer of Gratitude~

Day 3

Morning

Bless people who harass you—bless and don't curse them. (Romans 12:14)

Reflection

We think of blessing as tied to circumstances. When things go well, we are blessed by God. When they do not, we are cursed or forgotten. Similarly, we offer our blessing to those that we love and support. Often, at a wedding there is an opportunity for family and friends to offer such a blessing. But if we do not support the person, or worse, if we have been harmed by them, we withhold our blessing. But the gospel does not follow such a logic. The gospel asks us to bless other people regardless of their actions or behaviors. That is because blessing is an act tied not to circumstances or other people's behavior, but to our own disposition toward the world. We can either choose to be light, salt, and blessing whatever circumstances we find ourselves in, or we can choose a path of anger, resentment, or "curse." To bless is not to give permission to bad behavior, nor does it mean we can't draw boundaries. Instead, to bless is simply to always ask, "What is the most loving thing I can do right now?" no matter the situation.

~Prayer of Petition~

Evening

Sing to the LORD! Bless his name!
  Share the news of his saving work every single day! (Psalm 96:2)

Reflection

Often, we forget how much our words and actions truly do matter and that they have considerable effect on all of creation. God created something good out of nothing, simply by choosing to speak up, call forth, and say what would become a new world of holy imagination. Every word released from our lips has a substance or consequential quality to them, for good or ill.

Each one of us has the capacity for blessing others on a daily basis. We bless God by speaking light and life into the realities of others, working against all that threatens to bind and strangle the beauty of creation without and within. When one is diminishing oneself, find ways to expand their self-concept to remember their belovedness. When someone feels alone, help them to claim again their rightful place in God's family. When questions arise and someone feels ashamed, remind them that their curiosity is a sign of their engagement with faith rather than of being distanced from their faith.

This is the work of modern-day creatives, mystics, and prophets—to redeem that which is broken for being blessed. It is its own rich form of active resistance.

~Prayer of Gratitude~

Day 4

Morning

He said: "Naked I came from my mother's womb; naked I will return there. The LORD has given; the LORD has taken; bless the LORD's name." (Job 1:21)

Reflection

To bless is to consecrate or make holy. When we bless God's name, we rightly recognize God as holy and mighty, gracious and steadfast in God's love for us. When we bless God with words and prayers, songs and worship, we are expressing our fundamental belief about who God is and what God is capable of doing. It is easy and natural to bless God in good times. After all, when life is going our way, God is doing what we expect and want God to do. But what's our response during seasons of hardship, suffering, or disappointment? The temptation can be to question God, doubt God, or even curse God. While all of these reactions to suffering are fair, and even biblical, Job reminds us of another way. We can choose to trust that, even in seasons of struggle, God is present, sustains us, and is for us in every way. It is for this reason that we can bless God, even in hardship, even in disappointment, and even when life isn't going our way. God may give, and God may take, but in all of it, we bless God because we believe that throughout history and throughout our lives, God is at work in all things for our good.

~Prayer of Petition~

Evening

Let my whole being bless the LORD!
Let everything inside me bless his holy name! (Psalm 103:1)

Reflection

Lord, I hear of showers of blessing
Thou art scattering, full and free—
Showers, the thirsty land refreshing;
Let some dropping fall on me. Even me.

Pass me not, O God, our Father,
Sinful though my heart may be!
Thou might'st leave me, but the rather
Let thy mercy light on me. Even me.

Pass me not, O tender Saviour,
Let me love thee cling to thee!
I am longing for thy favour;
When thou comest, call for me! Even me.

Pass me not, O mighty Spirit!
Thou canst make the blind to see:
Witnesser of Jesus' merit!
Speak some word of power to me. Even me.

Pass me not, but pardon bringing
Bind my heart, O Lord, to Thee
All my heart to Thee is springing;
Blessing others, oh! Bless me,
Even me.
　　　—Charles Wesley, "Lord, I Hear of Showers of Blessing"

~Prayer of Gratitude~

Day 5

Morning

Because you, LORD, bless the righteous.
You cover them with favor like a shield. (Psalm 5:12)

Reflection

Growing up, young people take in millions of messages about who they are. Most of us form a sense of identity from the words, behaviors, and narratives that we receive from those around us. Many of us have so internalized these narratives that we begin to believe that we are who others say we are. But God reminds us that we are blessed. You are created by God, redeemed and forgiven, and ultimately blessed and favored. No matter what others say about you, or what narratives they write concerning you, God's favor constitutes our identities. Like a shield, God's blessing holds and protects us from anyone or anything that seeks to tell us that we are anything less than God's very own.

~Prayer of Petition~

Evening

Bless the Lord God of Israel
because he has come to help and has delivered his people. (Luke 1:68)

Reflection

I have not knowledge, wisdom, insight, thought,
Nor understanding, fit to justify
Thee in Thy work, O Perfect! thou has brought
Me up to this; and lo! what Thou has wrought,
I cannot comprehend. But I can cry,
"O enemy, the Maker hath not done;
One day thou shalt behold, and from the sight shalt run."

Thou workest perfectly. And if it seem
Some things are not so well, 'tis but because
They are too loving deep, too lofty wise,
For me, poor child, to understand their laws.
My highest wisdom, half is but a dream;
My love runs helpless like a falling stream;
Thy good embraces ill, and lo! its illness dies.
    —George MacDonald, *A Guide to Prayer for All God's People*

~Prayer of Gratitude~

Reveal

Morning Prayer of Petition

Unknown God, you are constantly teaching me and showing me who you are and who you call me to be. Today, wake me up to the ways that you are revealing yourself to me:

- through challenges and struggles,
- through difficult decisions or choices in front of me,
- through other people that I interact with,
- through the needs and hurts of the world.

May I be alive to your movement and work today God, and please make yourself known to me. Amen.

Evening Prayer of Gratitude

Holy one, you make yourself known each day through holy scripture, the creation around me, and your Spirit, which fills all things. I give thanks for the ways you revealed yourself to me today:

- in small moments of insight or revelation,
- in relationships that change my perspective,
- in hardship that strengthens my resolve,
- in moments of grace.

Continue to reveal yourself to me that I may grow in love of you and service to your people in the world. Amen.

Day 1

Morning

Whenever the evil spirits saw him, they fell down at his feet and shouted, "You are God's Son!" But he strictly ordered them not to reveal who he was. (Mark 3:11-12)

Reflection

There is a pattern often noticed in churches. New people visit only to sneak out the door quickly right before the benediction. They elude the pastor and greeters, and make it clear they are not yet ready to be known. Then, finally, often after several visits, they decide to stop and introduce themselves. To allow someone to know you is a great act of vulnerability. To know someone, even just their name, is sacred. It is arrogant to think that we can ever fully know another person, much less God. There-fore we approach others and God with humility, curiosity, and great respect. Since we never fully know another, each new day brings the possibility of new revelation.

~Prayer of Petition~

Evening

I appeared to Abraham, Isaac, and Jacob as God Almighty, but I didn't reveal myself to them by my name "The LORD." (Exodus 6:3)

Reflection

God is knowable yet never fully known.

Imagine for a moment that you have a glass jar. You walk down to the ocean and you fill your jar with water. Now imagine your friend comes down with their glass jar, although shaped differently. They, too, fill it with ocean water. Each of you simultane-ously has a full cup of water.

Now imagine that everyone in the world fills their jars with ocean water. Each one is holding a portion of ocean water, but never the whole of the ocean.

Depending on where one is standing, the water is likely to look and feel differ-ently. It might be clear or murky. It might be colder or warmer. But, nevertheless, it is the ocean's water.

This is what it is like to know God. We can know pieces of God, but never the entirety of God. And what we know of God depends on our own experiences.

God reveals Godself in different ways and places and people. God is constantly revealing Godself to us. Let us pay attention. Let us tune our hearts and minds to hear God's whisper. Let us open ourselves to the gentle nudge of God saying, "I'm right here."

~Prayer of Gratitude~

Day 2

Morning

My Father has handed all things over to me. No one knows the Son except the Father. And nobody knows the Father except the Son and anyone to whom the Son wants to reveal him. (Matthew 11:27)

Reflection

Christian theology teaches that there are two ways to know God. One is through the world and our observations of it. This general or natural revelation is accessible to all people anywhere. But theology also teaches us that there are certain characteristics and aspects of God we can never know unless God chooses to reveal them to us in a unique or supernatural way. This special revelation is what God reveals to us through scripture, miracles, and, most of all, in the person of Jesus. It is true that God is mystery, and on our own we can never hope to know God. But Jesus came that we might know who God is, what God cares about, and what God's purposes are for us and our world. Jesus is the exact imprint of God and the revelation of God's very being. The God who is mystery can finally be known through Jesus. The closer we get to Jesus, the more we will know about God.

~Prayer of Petition~

Evening

You should respond when I correct you.
   Look, I'll pour out my spirit on you.
   I'll reveal my words to you. (Proverbs 1:23)

Reflection

The incarnation is a revealing of God in the world. We humans tend to be tangible beings. We like to see, know, taste, hear, and feel. In God's compassion for us, Jesus is born.

It is in Jesus that we get to see how God responds to the world. Through Jesus's life, we witness how God moves in and out of love, anger, gratitude, fear, compassion, courage, and abandonment.

Jesus provides examples of how to treat the outcast, powerful, marginalized, religious, sick, apathetic, and criminal (spoiler alert: he treats them with love).

God's revelation doesn't just happen in a church building. It often happens when and where we least expect it.

However, we can cultivate practices that intentionally invite this revelation.

The more we read scripture, sit in silence, walk in nature, or talk with a friend, the more God will reveal to us. And the better we understand God's true nature, the more we are able to reflect it back to a world that is desperately in need of God's love, harmony, and grace.

~Prayer of Gratitude~

Day 3

Morning

God sent me to reveal the secret plan that had been hidden since the beginning of time by God, who created everything. (Ephesians 3:9)

Reflection

Many of us think of God as having a specific plan for our lives. We can spend a lot of our time and energy trying to figure out that plan. Others eschew this notion altogether, and do not look to God for specific direction or guidance. After all, does God really care which job we take or where we live? Both kinds of people are right. God may not have a specific point-by-point plan for each decision of your life, but God does have a purpose and plan for creation, and your role in it. Like any good parent, God does have hopes and dreams for you, and a desire for how you choose to live your life. As we grow in our relationship with God, God reveals those purposes and plans to us. God may not dictate what decision you make, but God cares about how we make decisions. God may not care what you spend your money on, but God cares about how you approach your resources. God may not have a specific career in mind for you, but God cares about how you use the gifts given to you.

~Prayer of Petition~

Evening

Call to me and I will answer and reveal to you wondrous secrets that you haven't known. (Jeremiah 33:3)

Reflection

How do we know what we know about God? Or, how is God made known to us? John Wesley's answer is, "Through God's revelation." God has been revealed in Christ. What has been revealed in Christ is God's love. There is no better interpretation of this revelation of God in Christ than Scripture. Scripture teaches that Christ in our hearts is a "divine evidence or conviction" of God's free, unmerited love to us as sinners (Sermon 17: "Circumcision of the Heart"). Wesley cautions against over-valuing or undervaluing the role that reason plays in revelation. Reason may help in our understanding, but it cannot produce faith, hope, or love. It is the work of the Holy Spirit who reveals Jesus Christ to us and makes Scripture real to us. Revelation is ultimately the Holy Spirit making Christ known to us.
   —*The Wesley Study Bible*

~Prayer of Gratitude~

Day 4

Morning

Whoever has my commandments and keeps them loves me. Whoever loves me will be loved by my Father, and I will love them and reveal myself to them. (John 14:21)

Reflection

Love is not primarily a feeling, but an action. To say that we love a friend but then ignore the habits and practices of friendship is not love. We can't claim to love a spouse while regularly neglecting the behaviors that demonstrate that love. In scripture, we aren't asked to feel love but rather to practice it toward God and others. Love is showing patience and kindness. Love doesn't manipulate or seek its own advantage. It is one thing to say that we love Jesus, but loving Jesus means being obedient to the commandments of Jesus and the way of life that he teaches. Loving Jesus is a choice we make each day with our behavior, not a sentiment that we claim to have. It is in our loving Jesus through obedience that he reveals more of himself to us. It is by following Jesus's commandments that we grow closer to Christ.

~Prayer of Petition~

Evening

The king declared to Daniel, "No doubt about it: your God is God of gods, Lord of kings, and a revealer of mysteries because you were able to reveal this mystery!" (Daniel 2:47)

Reflection

Love all God's creation, both the whole and every grain of sand. Love every leaf, every ray of light. Love the animals, love the plants, love each separate thing. If thou love each thing thou wilt perceive the mystery of God in all; and when once thou perceive this, thou wilt thenceforward grow every day to a fuller understanding of it: until thou come at last to love the whole world with a love that will then be all-embracing and universal.
—Fyodor Dostoevsky, *The Brothers Karamazov*

~Prayer of Gratitude~

Day 5

Morning

So all of us who are spiritually mature should think this way, and if anyone thinks differently, God will reveal it to him or her. (Philippians 3:15)

Reflection

In some churches, much is made of doubting God or not fully believing everything that is taught. Some churches fear people who don't fully comply with the faith that is taught. But faith and understanding are progressive in the scripture. We come to know and understand God more fully as we journey on a relationship with God. Jesus even told his disciples that if they knew everything there was to know about God right now, they couldn't handle it! Instead, as we stay connected to God in our doubts, struggles, and questioning, God rewards us by revealing more and more of Godself. Maturity is not eliminating doubt and questions. Maturity is understanding that staying connected to God through these doubts and questions leads to an even deeper and richer faith.

Epiphany

~Prayer of Petition~

Evening

The LORD has made his salvation widely known;
    he has revealed his righteousness
    in the eyes of all the nations. (Psalm 98:2)

Reflection

A man can no more diminish God's glory by refusing to worship Him than a lunatic can put out the sun by scribbling the word "darkness" on the walls of his cell.
    —C. S. Lewis, *The Problem of Pain*

~Prayer of Gratitude~

Covenant

Morning Prayer of Petition

Steadfast God, you are faithful to the covenant you make with your people, extending across time and space. May I be made faithful in my relationships, with you, and with others in my life. Today I pray for my relationship:

- with family,
- with friends and neighbors,
- with those I find difficult to bear,
- with those I too easily neglect or take for granted,
- with you.

Help me to be faithful as you are faithful. Amen.

Evening Prayer of Gratitude

Faithful God, just as you made covenant with the patriarchs and matriarchs of faith, so you continue to be steadfast in your relationship with us today. With gratitude I thank you for the ways that you are faithful to me:

- for opportunities that you give me,
- for resources that you surround me with,
- for help and ways that you surround me with care,
- for meaningful work, relationships, and projects.

Stir up in me a heart of gratitude that I may reflect your faithfulness to me in those that I seek to love. Amen.

Day 1

Morning

I will make a covenant between us and I will give you many, many descendants. (Genesis 17:2)

Reflection

A covenant is a relationship between two people who make promises to each other. The most well-known example in modern culture is marriage. Two people form a relationship based on promises they make to love each other for richer and poorer, in sickness and in health, until death parts them. Covenants bind two parties together, and they aren't easily undone, even if one side violates the terms. Foundational to the scriptures is the idea that God has chosen to make a covenant with us. For better or worse, in good times and in bad, God has sworn to be our God, just as the Israelites swore to be God's people. While we as humans regularly violate the promises made, the relationship is never broken. Why? Because even in the midst of human neglect, unfaithfulness, and rebellion, God never stops upholding God's end of the bargain. Our covenant with God may be strained, stretched, and neglected by us, but it is never broken because God is ever faithful. What this means is that, at any time, we can re-engage the relationship that God is waiting to have with us.

~Prayer of Petition~

Evening

You are the heirs of the prophets and the covenant that God made with your ancestors when he told Abraham, Through your descendants, all the families on earth will be blessed. (Acts 3:25)

Reflection

Can you feel the season turning
as an age of listening starts,
tuned to cries of deepest yearning,
changing minds and lives and hearts?
Sisters, brothers, bound together,
joining hands through time and space,
can you feel the season turning
toward the tender green of grace?
　　—Mary Louise Bringle, "Can You Feel the Season Turning"

~Prayer of Gratitude~

Day 2

Morning

You said, "I made a covenant with my chosen one;
　　I promised my servant David:
　　　'I will establish your offspring forever;
　　I will build up your throne from one generation to the next.'" (Psalm 89:3-4)

Reflection

God's promises are generational. We mistakenly believe that God only made promises and covenants with people in biblical times. We wish that we could benefit from that kind of relationship with God, that kind of assurance that God is with us and active in our lives. God makes promises not just to individuals, but also to families, tribes, nations, and people. God's promises were not confined to one time period, but have extended from generation to generation. This means that what we read about in scripture is also about us. God's promises are for you and your family. These promises are not historical; rather, we live in the power of these promises today.

~Prayer of Petition~

Evening

He has shown the mercy promised to our ancestors,
and remembered his holy covenant. (Luke 1:72)

Reflection

Will you hold me in the light with prayer and song? Hold me in the light of God. Will you weep and cry with me? Will you ache and sigh with me? Hold me in the light of God.

Hmmm

We will hold you in the light and walk with you. Come into the light of God. We will share your tears with you; we will face your fears with you. Come into the light of God.

—Adam M L Tice

~Prayer of Gratitude~

Day 3

Morning

All the LORD's paths are loving and faithful
for those who keep his covenant and laws. (Psalm 25:10)

Reflection

Have you ever tried to use a new device or appliance without reading the instruction manual? In our eagerness or stubbornness, we often just start using something without ever fully understanding how it works. Often we can go days, months, or years using something incorrectly, in a way that never quite maximizes its capabilities. Sometimes, in a moment of humility, we read the instructions and realize, "Oh, that is how this works . . ." Devices work better when you use them as they were designed to be used. The same is true for us. God designed and created us, and God gave us instructions on how to live. But in our eagerness or stubbornness, we often forge our own paths and want to live our own way. When we do, we live in ways that never maximize our possibilities and potential. Returning to God's instruction can unlock a life that is far greater than the one we imagine. We work better when we live as we were designed to live!

~Prayer of Petition~

Evening

He has qualified us as ministers of a new covenant, not based on what is written but on the Spirit, because what is written kills, but the Spirit gives life. (2 Corinthians 3:6)

Reflection

The problem with rules is not that we have them, but that they must be interpreted by both context and relationship. No matter how well-intentioned or well-written, when rules and policies are disconnected from the particularities of life with real people, it can lead to legalism, foster injustice, and stifle authentic community. It is no wonder, then, that God insists on a new, covenantal community "not of the letter but of the Spirit" (2 Corinthians 3:6 NIV)—a covenant that is wholly defined by grace, not by enforcement. Too often, we set up systems of fences designed to delineate who's in or out, right or wrong, worthy or unworthy. Not only this, but we also judge each other on our fidelity to the systems, conveniently forgetting that our fundamental posture as Christians is grace and never judgment. If we allow the entirety of our collective life together to be wholly defined by this new covenant of grace, it will transform us. I wonder what would happen if we were brave enough to not just move the fence boundaries but to tear them down altogether?

~Prayer of Gratitude~

Day 4

Morning

This is my blood of the covenant, which is poured out for many so that their sins may be forgiven. (Matthew 26:28)

Reflection

Covenants often require sacrifice. When two people or parties agree to be in a relationship, certain things are often given up or left behind. We see this most clearly in Jesus's death. It sounds harsh, even violent, to link Jesus's blood to the new covenant he makes with us. But Jesus's death shows us the depth of his willingness to sacrifice anything and everything to have a relationship with us. Our response to this sacrifice is a willingness to give up some of our pride, aspirations, or desired outcomes in order to trust and follow him. Ultimately, Jesus came that we might have a more abundant life than the one we create on our own. But to experience that life requires a relationship that often starts by a willingness to give something up.

~Prayer of Petition~

Evening

I won't break my covenant.
> *I won't renege on what crossed my lips.* (Psalm 89:34)

Reflection

Covenant is about relationship, and one cannot overstate the contrast between the covenantal faithfulness of God and the human impulse to divide and conquer. This impulse gives an effective strategy for accomplishing certain goals yet devalues relationships, turning the connective tissue of lives shared together into a mere commodity to be exploited. And though we might readily assign negative intentions to those who do so, we engage this impulse unwittingly each time we use personal preferences, convenience, and even self-actualization as reasons for pulling away from others. Sometimes, we might even use religious language to cast a veneer of sacred purpose to our unwillingness to continue in relationship—because relationships are hard and demand a self-giving faithfulness that we all at once crave yet resist. Thus is the wonder of God's covenantal faithfulness toward us—that even when we pull away, God leans toward us, insisting on the priority of relationship and unconditionally refusing to break covenant with us. Can we rest in God's covenantal embrace, knowing that God is for us even when we are not? Can we, in turn, embrace each other?

~Prayer of Gratitude~

Day 5

Morning

This is the covenant that I will make with the house of Israel
> *after those days, says the Lord.*
I will place my laws in their minds,
> *and write them on their hearts.*
I will be their God,
> *and they will be my people.* (Hebrews 8:10)

Reflection

We often think of God as someone that we have to pursue and find. But God does not have to be found. Our relationship with God is not like our relationship with other people. It is qualitatively different. After all, when we enter into a relationship with others, it is finite, temporal, and limited. We remain who we are, and they remain who they are. We cannot fundamentally change them, just as they cannot fundamentally change us. But God is different. God created us and knows us. God knit us together and we are God's handiwork. God writes on our very hearts and lives. God is within us. We don't have to journey somewhere to find God. God has already found us.

~Prayer of Petition~

Evening

God remembers his covenant forever,
the word he commanded to a thousand generations. (Psalm 105:8)

Reflection

How long hath he borne with us? How perverse hath our manners in the various stages of life been before him? And yet you and I are not in hell: O let us lift up our voices with the prophet Jeremiah, and cry, Tis of the Lord's mercies we are not consumed. The whole scripture holds him out in that character. St. Paul calls him a gracious and merciful high priest, and God himself in the same epistle, says, I will be merciful to their unrighteousness, and their sins will I remember no more; and again, Return for I am merciful saith the Lord. Now as the darling attribute of God is mercy, so it is one pointed out for our imitation above any other; and many precious promises are annexed to the observance thereof.

—Mary Bosanquet Fletcher, "Merciful"

~Prayer of Gratitude~

Week 13

Healing

Morning Prayer of Petition

God of our salvation, in Christ you showed yourself to be the Great Physician, healing us in body, mind, and spirit. There is much in my world that needs your healing power today:

- for those that suffer from illness and disease,
- for those that struggle with mental health,
- for those who live in the midst of violence and trauma,
- for conflict in our world,
- for relationships that are fractured and broken.

Pour out your healing power on us that we may experience your shalom. Amen.

Evening Prayer of Gratitude

Gracious God, even now you are at work in my life and in the world, redeeming, blessing, rescuing, and healing. May you open my heart to see the ways that you are at work in:

- my relationships that are strained,
- my inner being when I struggle or despair,
- my family when circumstances are difficult or uncertain,
- my community when it seems divided and fractured,
- my world, which seems chaotic and broken.

Continue to show me the ways that you are working beneath the surface, bringing all things under your power and salvation. Amen.

Day 1

Morning

Heal me, Lord, and I'll be healed.
Save me and I'll be saved,
for you are my heart's desire. (Jeremiah 17:14)

Reflection

There is a difference between curing and healing. Curing relates to the relief of a physical disease or illness. Healing is more holistic, addressing the mind, spirit, and body. A cure is also temporary. We can stave off disease or illness but ultimately our bodies

73

are mortal. There is no cure for death. But the healing God offers is eternal; it is something we can receive and experience in this life as well as extending to the next. A cure is sometimes possible; healing is always possible. While Jesus often cures people of disease in scripture as evidence of his power, the more consequential and eternal gift he offers is that of healing—something that Jesus extends to all people.

~Prayer of Petition~

Evening

Have mercy on me, LORD,
*   because I'm frail.*
Heal me, LORD,
*   because my bones are shaking in terror!* (Psalm 6:2)

Reflection

When we think about healing, we often think about physical healing. When we pray for healing, it is often for someone who is sick, chronically ill, or hospitalized. The psalm that we read today reminds us that healing takes many forms, and that God has the power to heal all of our broken facets. The psalmist writes that not only are their bones shaking in terror, but that they are also "frail," feeling that listlessness that so often comes when our bodies and spirits fail us. The poet appears to be fearful and growing weak. The good news today is that God has the power to heal: to heal broken bones and shaken spirits. Today, take a moment to invite God into your fears. Ask God to think through your questions and concerns for the day ahead. Ask God to restore the deep hope that casts out all fears.

~Prayer of Gratitude~

Day 2

Morning

That evening people brought to Jesus many who were demon-possessed. He threw the spirits out with just a word. He healed everyone who was sick. (Matthew 8:16)

Reflection

Jesus first made a name for himself not as a teacher or preacher, but as a healer. People who were sick would come to him, and he would cure them of every kind of disease. Ancients had a different understanding of what it meant to be sick. While we usually limit sickness to medical ailments, we too are afflicted by more than physical disease. Marriages can be on life support, relationships can go toxic, or our ability to experience joy can be severely impaired. Our spiritual vision can be obscured, our hearts can be hardened (and not from cholesterol), and our emotional energy can be zapped. We are invited to turn to Jesus, not merely during times of physical illness, but much more in all the ailments and struggles that we experience, and the healing he offers extends to all areas of our lives.

~Prayer of Petition~

Evening

Right then, Jesus healed many of their diseases, illnesses, and evil spirits, and he gave sight to a number of blind people. Then he replied to John's disciples, "Go, report to John what you have seen and heard. Those who were blind are able to see. Those who were crippled now walk. People with skin diseases are cleansed. Those who were deaf now hear. Those who were dead are raised up. And good news is preached to the poor." (Luke 7:21-22)

Reflection

There is a balm in Gilead to make the wounded whole; there is a balm in Gilead
To heal the sin sick soul.
Sometimes I feel discouraged and think my works in vain.
But then the Holy Spirit revives my soul again.
  —African American Spiritual, "There Is a Balm in Gilead"

~Prayer of Gratitude~

Day 3

Morning

Lord, my God, I cried out to you for help,
    and you healed me.
Lord, you brought me up from the grave,
    brought me back to life from among those going down to the pit. (Psalm 30:2-3)

Reflection

Many of us know what it is like to hit rock bottom. It is the moment your own power and capabilities run out, when your life seems to have no way forward, and your hope is all but extinguished. Rock bottom is hitting the lowest point in your life. The scriptures, and especially the psalms of lament, give us a guide as to how to proceed through these moments. First, laments require honesty about everything that we feel, even toward God. Anger, rage, sadness, and regret are all expressed honestly to God. Second, lament holds on to hope, questioning, but never giving up on God's power to make a way when there is no way. There is honesty and hope, transparency and trust. Lament will eventually break through to something new and teach us that our low point is never our last point.

~Prayer of Petition~

Epiphany

Evening

Come, let's return to the LORD;
*   for it is he who has injured us and will heal us;*
*   he has struck us down, but he will bind us up.* (Hosea 6:1)

Reflection

What comfort can our worship bring
on bleak and empty days
to those who cannot bear to sing
when pain is missed in praise?
What sorrow can we dare to own?
What anger, loss and fears?
Not just in joy is God made known,
but also in our tears.
    —Adam M L Tice, "What Comfort Can Our Worship Bring"

~Prayer of Gratitude~

Day 4

Morning

One day when Jesus was teaching, Pharisees and legal experts were sitting nearby. They had come from every village in Galilee and Judea, and from Jerusalem. Now the power of the Lord was with Jesus to heal. (Luke 5:17)

Reflection

Wherever there is healing and transformation, there will also be skeptics. Whether among your family and friends, coworkers or social circles, there may be people who scoff and question any change in your life. We have to be careful not to allow the onlookers to distract us from the new direction God is leading us through or the change God is making in us. Healing is not a one-time moment of magic. It is a pathway toward renewal, transformation, and restoration. Along the way, healing will require confronting old wounds, naming hard truths, giving up comfortable patterns, and courageously embracing new beginnings. Through it all, set your eyes firmly on where God is leading you, and not on those who seek to keep you where you are.

~Prayer of Petition~

Evening

In fact, I didn't even consider myself worthy to come to you. Just say the word and my servant will be healed. (Luke 7:7)

Reflection

O God, hear every longing sigh
as voices rise and strain
and meet us in that honest cry
where praise is voiced in pain.
    —Adam M L Tice, "O God, Hear Every Longing Sigh"

~Prayer of Gratitude~

Day 5

Morning

I have seen their ways, but I will heal them.
    I will guide them,
        and reward them with comfort. (Isaiah 57:18a)

Reflection

Much is made of sin and guilt in western Christianity. We so often see our mistakes
and misdeeds as incurring guilt and therefore needing forgiveness. But scripture also
talks about the human problem as one of illness. Sin is a condition whereby we do not
do what we should. And what we don't want to do, we do. Many of us can resonate
with the frustration and futility of trying to do what is right, and failing. When we find
ourselves incapable of doing what God requires, scripture reminds us that God's healing is given as a gift to us. With that healing comes a sense of peace, comfort, strength,
and guidance. God has the capacity to restore us to a place of wholeness, guiding us to
a life no longer bogged down by the condition of sin.

~Prayer of Petition~

Evening

*Heal the sick, raise the dead, cleanse those with skin diseases, and throw out demons. You
received without having to pay. Therefore, give without demanding payment.* (Matthew 10:8)

Reflection

In business, the act of "give and take" is a calculated and important component of
success. A business owner must price and sell a product in order to earn income for
themselves and their investors. Hopefully, the life of faith operates on less calculated
equations. The verse we read today inspired the hymn written by Carol Owens in
1972 entitled "Freely, Freely." The hymn sings, "Freely, freely, you have received,
freely, freely give," and with its three-fourths time it moves like waltz. A waltz is a
counted dance, but not a calculated one. There are three steps, but how those are

taken by each participant is different at different times. One steps forward, the other steps back; one twirls, the other assists. The image of a dance is helpful as we ponder what God has done for us and how we respond to God's initiative. The giving and receiving from God and to God, from others and to others, is not a calculated "give and take," but a calling inspired by movements of gift and grace. Let us not focus on how many times we have healed or been healed, on what we have earned or not, but, rather, let us make sure that we all keep dancing this beautiful life God has given us.

~Prayer of Gratitude~

Compassion

Morning Prayer of Petition

God of mercy and compassion, often my heart is hardened towards those situations and people that need love. Today slow my pace so I can notice and respond in compassion to:

- those close to me whom I might overlook or neglect,
- people who are left out or overlooked,
- people who are consistently treated unjustly,
- those who anger or frustrate me.

Shape my heart to mirror for others the compassion you have for me. Amen.

Evening Prayer of Gratitude

Ever present God, even today you surprise me and show up for me. In thanksgiving, I name:

- the ways you cared for me today,
- the people who spoke encouraging words to me today,
- moments when you made yourself known to me today,
- opportunities you offered me to care for others.

Thank you for your love and compassion towards me. Help me to see your mercy anew each day, that I may live out of the abundance you show for me. Amen.

Day 1

Morning

But you, my Lord,
are a God of compassion and mercy;
you are very patient and full of faithful love. (Psalm 86:15)

Reflection

God has a funny sense of time. God has the ability to see the long game, especially when it comes to people. God can see us for who God created us to be and who we are becoming. This allows God to love us even through seasons of rebellion, neglect, ignorance, and sin. Through all of this, God's care for us is never diminished, and God's work in us is never abandoned. Implicit in compassion is a love that is patient and long-lasting. God doesn't condone wrongdoing or overlook inaction on our part. But, in compassion, God's love waits patiently for us to become the people we are called and created to be. Today, perhaps you need to receive this compassion, living out of it and in response to it. Or perhaps you need to mirror this compassion with someone in your life whom you love, but who is not yet the person they are called to be.

~Prayer of Petition~

Evening

Nonetheless, the LORD is waiting to be merciful to you,
and will rise up to show you compassion.
The LORD is a God of justice;
happy are all who wait for him. (Isaiah 30:18)

Reflection

God weeps with us who weep and mourn;
God's tears flow down with ours,
and God's own heart is bruised and worn
from all the heavy hours
of watching while the soul's bright fire
burned lower day by day,
and pulse and breath and love's desire
dimmed down to ash and clay.
    —Thomas H. Troeger, "God Weeps with Us Who Weep and Mourn"

~Prayer of Gratitude~

Day 2

Morning

Now when Jesus saw the crowds, he had compassion for them because they were troubled and helpless, like sheep without a shepherd. (Matthew 9:36)

Reflection

It isn't flattering to be compared to sheep. They are often characterized as dumb, prone to getting lost, and helpless against predators. All this is true, if they are alone. Sheep need two things to thrive: a flock and a shepherd. They aren't meant to navigate the wilderness alone, and they aren't meant to wander without guidance. As people, we are prone to doing life alone, and without any guidance outside of ourselves. But we don't have to do it this way. We have a flock—the church—and a shepherd in Jesus. You do not have to face the wilderness of your own life alone.

~Prayer of Petition~

Evening

He has compassion on the weak and the needy;
  he saves the lives of those who are in need. (Psalm 72:13)

Reflection

Through tears and sorrow, God, we share
a sense of your vast grief:
the weight of bearing every prayer
for healing and relief,
the burden of our questions why,
the doubts that they engage,
and as our friends and loved ones die,
our hopelessness and rage.
  —Thomas H. Troeger, "God Weeps with Us Who Weep and Mourn"

~Prayer of Gratitude~

Day 3

Morning

The LORD said, "I'll make all my goodness pass in front of you, and I'll proclaim before you the name, 'The LORD.' I will be kind to whomever I wish to be kind, and I will have compassion to whomever I wish to be compassionate." (Exodus 33:19)

Reflection

There are many of us who believe we do not deserve compassion. We beat ourselves up for past sins and punish ourselves for mistakes. It is tempting to see compassion as complicity or being comfortable with sin. But that is not how God views us or our sin. Compassion from God does not come after we get our lives all straightened out. It comes first. It passes in front of us before we deserve it. God's compassion isn't the reward for living right; instead it is the proactive work of God that can turn our lives in new directions. God's compassion is in front of you and over you, even now. We no longer have to live out of a self-imposed guilt, but rather, we can live out of a new-found freedom, which God's compassion makes possible.

~Prayer of Petition~

Evening

Therefore, as God's choice, holy and loved, put on compassion, kindness, humility, gentleness, and patience. (Colossians 3:12)

Epiphany

Reflection

What is "compassion"? Com (with), passion (suffers): God is compassionate; God isn't remote, but God suffers with all who suffer. But how? Through us. We embody God's heartfelt compassion here on earth in what we do as the body of Christ. . . . Compassion isn't a mood but a responsibility, a privilege, an action. John Wesley insisted that it is better to carry aid to the poor than to send it. Instead of lobbing charity over a wall, we go. When we "suffer with," we embody God's compassion.

 —*The Wesley Study Bible*

~Prayer of Gratitude~

Day 4

Morning

So now you, LORD—
> *don't hold back any of your compassion from me.*
Let your loyal love and faithfulness always protect me. (Psalm 40:11)

Reflection

When children get hurt, usually they can depend on a loving parent to be there to help them. Most of us had the care and compassion of a parent. They were a safety net, allowing us to take risks or try new things, knowing that they would be there for us if something went wrong. Their love for us provided protection, even when we ventured out on our own. There is security in knowing that you can depend on the compassion of someone who loves you. God's compassion and faithfulness toward us is rock solid. It is a homebase that we can return to and a foundation that we can depend on. Such compassion and care protect us as we take risks, work for justice, and do God's work in a world that doesn't always welcome it.

~Prayer of Petition~

Evening

So he got up and went to his father.
"While he was still a long way off, his father saw him and was moved with compassion. His father ran to him, hugged him, and kissed him." (Luke 15:20)

Reflection

Softly and tenderly Jesus is calling,
calling for you and for me;
see, on the portals he's waiting and watching,
watching for you and for me.

Why should we tarry when Jesus is pleading,
pleading for you and for me?
Why should we linger and heed not his mercies,
mercies for you and for me?

Come home, come home;
you who are weary come home;
earnestly, tenderly, Jesus is calling,
calling, O sinner, come home!

—Will L. Thompson, "Softly and Tenderly"

~Prayer of Gratitude~

Day 5

Morning

Because of our God's deep compassion,
the dawn from heaven will break upon us. (Luke 1:78)

Reflection

Have you ever done something wrong and had to come clean with someone about it? Even with small infractions, there is a nervousness and anxiety that wells up in us when we know we will disappoint someone. We might be tempted to hide the misstep or not be fully honest about what we have done. But that lack of transparency only further weighs us down. When we finally come clean, we often find that the person is not only less upset than we expected, but also has compassion for what has happened, offering us forgiveness instead of anger. When we experience that compassion, it is like a weight has been lifted, or a shackle loosened. It is like the dawning of a new day for us, and we can live with freedom again. That is what it's like everytime we stop running from God, and turn toward God with full transparency about who we've been and what we've done. It is like the beginning of a brand new day.

~Prayer of Petition~

Evening

The LORD is good to everyone and everything;
God's compassion extends to all his handiwork! (Psalm 145:9)

Reflection

And yet because, like us, you weep,
we trust you will receive
and in your tender heart will keep
the ones for whom we grieve,

Epiphany

while with your tears our hearts will taste
the deep, dear core of things
from which both life and death are graced
by love's renewing springs.
 —Thomas H. Troeger, "God Weeps with Us Who Weep and Mourn"

~Prayer of Gratitude~

Lent

Listening

Morning Prayer of Petition

God of the still small voice, today slow me down and calm my spirit so that I can hear you:

- calling me out of my comfort zone,
- prompting me to reach out to a friend,
- nudging me to speak up and make my voice known,
- convicting me to confront that which is unhealthy in my own life.

May I be more attentive today to the ways your Spirit is speaking to me, and may I have the willingness to listen. Amen.

Evening Prayer of Gratitude

Mighty God, with a word you brought the creation into being and ever since you have been speaking life into existence. Thank you for the ways that you speak to me, for:

- moments of realization and clarity,
- new insights and perspective,
- reminders of encouragement and hope,
- challenges and circumstances that push me to grow or change.

Open my ears, that I may hear your voice more clearly each day. Amen.

Day 1

Morning

While he was still speaking, look, a bright cloud overshadowed them. A voice from the cloud said, "This is my Son whom I dearly love. I am very pleased with him. Listen to him!" Hearing this, the disciples fell on their faces, filled with awe. (Matthew 17:5-6)

Reflection

As kids, we often don't listen to the grownups around us. Perhaps you had a parent at some point say to you, "If you hear me, then why don't you listen?!" We all know there is a difference between hearing and listening. Hearing is taking in the words that someone else is speaking. But listening means something more. Listening implies an obedience, doing something with the words you hear. Many of us read scripture and know the words that Jesus speaks. Some of us might even spend a great amount of time studying those words, their context, their history, and their interpretations. But as leaders, we must be careful not to merely hear Jesus but to also listen to him. Discipleship is not merely understanding his words but is also the obedience to follow them.

~Prayer of Petition~

Evening

Listen, my people, to my teaching;
  tilt your ears toward the words of my mouth. (Psalm 78:1)

Reflection

It is a surprising thing to learn that God, whom we call all-powerful, mighty, and Lord, does not usually speak with force. God, who made the wind and the waves, who gave the lion his roar, and the bear her growl, does not often shout. Instead, God prefers to whisper. God's voice comes to us most frequently in quiet ways, not heard with our ears, but with our heart. Hearing that quiet voice of God requires us to listen with intention and care. It requires stillness. It requires silence. It requires attentiveness.

God will not force communication upon us; we have to choose to listen. This means when we pray, we need to not only talk to God, but also to listen. Prayer needs to contain moments of openness, trusting that God has something to say to us. God's promptings might sound like a voice in our heads, or a knowing in our gut, or an image that appears to us. It takes patience and practice, but if we ask, God will speak. God will give us insight, convict us of our errors, reassure us, or inspire us to act. When we listen, the power and wisdom contained in that quiet and holy voice will be worth the wait.

~Prayer of Gratitude~

Day 2

Morning

Moses told this to the Israelites. But they didn't listen to Moses, because of their complete exhaustion and their hard labor. (Exodus 6:9)

Reflection

Several studies show that when we are tired, not only do our default behaviors change but so do our personalities. We are literally different people when we get fatigued.

Weariness can stunt our curiosity, hamper our creativity, sap our patience, and impair our ability to listen to others who care about us. There is a danger in trying to live in a constant state of fatigue. When you are tired, be careful and be more intentional to seek out and listen to the voices of people who care about you. Ask others if they can see things that you can't see. Be even more deliberate even in listening to words that you don't want to hear. Often when we are tired, others can see things that in our exhaustion we can't see. Listening to them can help point us toward a healthier way of living.

~Prayer of Petition~

Evening

If you listen to these case laws and follow them carefully, the LORD your God will keep the covenant and display the loyalty that he promised your ancestors. (Deuteronomy 7:12)

Reflection

We must learn to differ without denouncing; to listen without distrust; to reserve judgment. "Judge not, that ye be not judged. For with what judgment ye judge, ye shall be judged. And with what measure ye mete, it shall be measured unto you again" (Matthew 7:1-3 KJV). You know the words, my friends.

—Mary McLeod Bethune, "The Lesson of Tolerance"

~Prayer of Gratitude~

Day 3

Morning

Listen, Job; hear me;
be quiet, and I will speak. (Job 33:31)

Reflection

Have you ever gone out into the woods, away from all manufactured noise and artificial light? Without a phone buzzing or music playing, the sheer quiet can be striking and overwhelming. But if you sit in that quiet long enough, the forest begins to come alive around you. You begin to hear things that you never noticed before, like the sound of limbs swaying, the melodic chirping of birds, the howling of the wind, or even the crunching of leaves from nearby animals. These sounds are always available to us. We just don't often stop and quiet ourselves long enough to hear them. We often wish God would speak more clearly to us, but have you ever wondered if the problem isn't with God speaking, but with our ability to listen? As you create margin in your life, care for your bodies, and make space for your spirit, you will also find that your ability to listen heightens and you can begin to see and hear God all around you. God is always present. What fluctuates is your ability to actually listen.

~Prayer of Petition~

Evening

He replied, "My mother and brothers are those who listen to God's word and do it." (Luke 8:21)

Reflection

Jesus says that listening to God is what makes us family. That's a short list of qualifications to call someone a brother or sister. It means that geography doesn't matter. Age doesn't matter. Income doesn't matter. Language, skin color, sexual orientation or gender identity, height, weight, spiritual credentials, life experience, ability, and disability—none of it matters. All that is needed to be a part of the family of God is to hear the word of God, pay attention, and do it.

Jesus also seems to be saying that we are not expected to hear alone, in isolation. Rather, we listen together. He implies that the very act of listening to the word of God is communal, as it makes us siblings. Listening to the word of God draws us closer to other people and unites us in a powerful and deep way. This is part of the way God transforms us. As we seek the will of God, we must do it with others. These relationships with one another shape us and help us grow. And they help us truly hear God's will for the world. Listening to God, as a family, leads us to holiness.

~Prayer of Gratitude~

Day 4

Morning

The religious experts said to Pharaoh, "This is something only God could do!" But Pharaoh was stubborn, and he wouldn't listen to them, just as the LORD had said. (Exodus 8:19)

Reflection

We have all dealt with people (or kids) who dig their heels in and, despite our best efforts, simply won't listen to us. In their stubbornness they have formed an opinion that is not open for negotiation and will not change. In scripture, this is often called hard-heartedness. Despite what we say, many of us are closed to new information. We are unwilling to change, indifferent to new voices, and stubbornly unwilling to listen to God or others. Listening, however, implies a posture of openness, a humility that recognizes that you may not understand something fully, and a teachable spirit that is willing to change in light of new information. The prerequisite for listening is humility, a recognition that there is still a need for growth.

~Prayer of Petition~

Evening

He said, "Whoever has ears to listen should pay attention!" (Mark 4:9)

Reflection

Vocation . . . comes from listening. I must listen to my life and try to understand what it is truly about—quite apart from what I would like it to be about—or my life will never represent anything real in the world, no matter how earnest my intentions.

That insight is hidden in the word *vocation* itself, which is rooted in the Latin for "voice." Vocation does not mean a goal that I pursue. It means a calling that I hear. Before I can tell my life what I want to do with it, I must listen to my life telling me who I am. I must listen for the truths and values at the heart of my own identity, not the standards by which I must live but the standards by which I cannot help but live if I am living my own life.

—Parker Palmer, *Let Your Life Speak*

~Prayer of Gratitude~

Day 5

Morning

Joshua said to the Israelites, "Come close. Listen to the words of the LORD your God." (Joshua 3:9)

Reflection

Have you ever been at a dinner with a large group of people? It is difficult to hear the person at the other end of the table. It is common sense, but the ability to hear someone is proportional to how close you are to them. The same is true, spiritually. It is harder to hear God speaking to us if we have drifted in our faith. When we make little time for prayer, neglect any quiet space, stop worshipping, or no longer read scripture for our own growth, it is no wonder that we struggle to hear God. If you want to be more in tune with the voice of God, begin practicing those disciplines that move you closer to God. The closer you get, the easier it will be to hear.

~Prayer of Petition~

Evening

Listen, my people, I'm warning you!
If only you would listen to me, Israel. (Psalm 81:8)

Reflection

The sorrowing, the sick, the unwanted, the lonely, both young and old, rich and poor, all come to my window. No one listens, they tell me, and so I listen and tell them what they have just told me. And I sit in silence, listening, letting them grieve. "Julian, you are wise," they say, "You have been gifted with understanding." All I did was listen.

For I believe full surely that God's spirit is in us all, giving light, wisdom, understanding, speaking words in us when we cannot speak, showing us gently what we would not see; what we are afraid to see; so that we may show pity, mercy, forgiveness to ourselves.

    —Julian of Norwich, *Revelations of Divine Love*

~Prayer of Gratitude~

Fasting

Morning Prayer of Petition

Holy One, in Christ you gave up everything to enter into solidarity with your people. Today, may I resist the temptation to constantly consume all that is around me. Help me resist:

- the tendency to get lost in social media,
- the hyperfocus on the way I look or appear to others,
- the temptation to compare myself to those around me,
- the urge to lash out or speak harshly to those around me.

As I actively abstain from what is easy in our world, may my focus be on following Jesus more fully. Amen.

Evening Prayer of Gratitude

God of mountains and valleys, deserts and dry places, I am grateful for the ways I have seen you today:

- for the people who remind me of your goodness,
- for the simple beauty of nature that reminds me of your presence,
- for the life-giving moments in my day when I felt close to you,
- for ways life is opening up and developing for me.

As I resist the urge to busy my heart and mind constantly with all that is around me, may my attention be more fixed on the ways you work in my life. Amen.

Day 1

Morning

After Jesus had fasted for forty days and forty nights, he was starving. (Matthew 4:2)

Reflection

Fasting had many functions in scripture but it was almost always accompanied by prayer. Abstaining from food heightened a person's sense of dependence on God and therefore enhanced one's ability to listen for God's direction. This is why we see Jesus begin his public ministry not with a bunch of activity, but with a forty-day fast in the wilderness. Before Jesus began his work, he modeled the kind of deep listening that the work would require. Sometimes, in our zeal to work and produce, we neglect listening to the direction that God wants us to take. When we do this, we can often run far and fast in the wrong direction. Fasting can be a way of intentionally stopping, abstaining long enough to begin to detect the direction God is calling us to move.

~Prayer of Petition~

Evening

I then turned my face to my Lord God, asking for an answer with prayer and pleading, and with fasting, mourning clothes, and ashes. (Daniel 9:3)

Reflection

The monastic way is very different. Obedience, fasting and prayer are laughed at, yet only through them lies the way to real, true freedom. I cut off any superfluous and unnecessary desires, I subdue my proud and wanton will and chastise it with obedience, and with God's help I attain freedom of spirit and with it spiritual joy. Who is more capable of conceiving a great idea and serving it—the rich man in his isolation or the man who has freed himself from the tyranny of material things?

—Fyodor Dostoevsky, *The Brothers Karamazov*

~Prayer of Gratitude~

Day 2

Morning

As they were worshipping the Lord and fasting, the Holy Spirit said, "Appoint Barnabas and Saul to the work I have called them to undertake." (Acts 13:2)

Reflection

How do worship and fasting fit together? Worship is about praising God, and fasting is often seen as a kind of self-imposed punishment. But moving toward God is often a move away from the world, or at least away from the things of the world that distract us. It is easy to get bogged down by what is right in front of us—our phones, our schedules, our to-do list, or our emails. Sometimes the move to set aside or remove some of these day-to-day necessities, at least for a time, can facilitate a movement toward God. Authentic worship often requires us to set aside the things that distract us. Fasting and worship can be two sides of the same coin.

~Prayer of Petition~

Evening

Yet even now, says the LORD,
  return to me with all your hearts,
    with fasting, with weeping, and with sorrow. (Joel 2:12)

Reflection

Lord, who throughout these forty days
for us didst fast and pray,
teach us with thee to mourn our sins
and close by thee to stay.

As thou with Satan didst contend,
and didst the victory win,
O give us strength in thee to fight,
in thee to conquer sin.

As thou didst hunger bear, and thirst,
so teach us, gracious Lord,
to die to self, and chiefly live
by thy most holy word.
      —Claudia F. Hernaman, "Lord, Who Throughout These Forty Days"

~Prayer of Gratitude~

Day 3

Morning

And when you fast, don't put on a sad face like the hypocrites. They distort their faces so people will know they are fasting. I assure you that they have their reward. (Matthew 6:16)

Reflection

Pride gets in the way of so much in our lives. We may give generously, pray often, study scripture faithfully, or live a spiritually disciplined life—but we want people to know about it. Why? Do we want credit for our faithfulness, do we want to be praised, or do we expect a certain amount of heavenly extra credit for the work we are putting in? God desires our faithfulness, and spiritual disciplines are an important avenue for growing closer to God and hearing God's voice more clearly in our lives. But we also should be careful. When God is leading us in growth, the evil one lies close at hand to hijack or distract us from that growth. Even in our acts of faithfulness, we should check our motives, desires, and attitudes to guard against those influences that would seek to turn these virtues into vices.

~Prayer of Petition~

Evening

Isn't this the fast I choose:
> *releasing wicked restraints, untying the ropes of a yoke,*
> *setting free the mistreated,*
> *and breaking every yoke?* (Isaiah 58:6)

Reflection

Fasting is one of those spiritual practices that is often seen as a personal act of piety. It is something that we take on, perhaps during a season of the church year, like Lent, in order to focus our attention away from physical needs and toward the spiritual. When we fast, we may choose to refrain from certain pleasures, or restrict ourselves to eating on particular days of the week, as an exercise in self-restraint and discipline.

This is well and good, but the prophet Isaiah calls us to a different kind of fast: "Is not this the fast that I choose: to loose the bonds of injustice, to undo the straps of the yoke, to let the oppressed go free, and to break every yoke?" (Isaiah 58:6 NRSVUE).

The prophet tells us that God hungers for justice and liberation, and desires that we rein in our other appetites like greed, selfishness, and exploiting creation. This type of fast is communal and public, requiring us to act in visible and sacrificial ways as expressions of our faith.

Both types of fasts are important, faithful, and necessary. We cannot do one and not the other.

~Prayer of Gratitude~

Day 4

Morning

She was now an 84-year-old widow. She never left the temple area but worshipped God with fasting and prayer night and day. (Luke 2:37)

Reflection

We live in a world of same-day deliveries and on-demand access. Even compared to a generation ago, we have lost the habit of waiting. We want what we want, when we want it. But growing close to God and learning to hear God's voice in our lives is a pursuit that takes time. Spiritual disciplines like fasting, praying, and reading scripture don't necessarily pay off in days or even in weeks. But as we dedicate ourselves to these practices over time, we begin to reap the benefits that they promise. While access to God is 24/7, there is no short cut to growing close to God and maturing in our faith. But disciplines like fasting will shape us over time into the people we want to be. Don't give up on these disciplines too early or be discouraged if they do not instantly make a difference in your life. Instead, remember that they take time and, like so many things in our spiritual lives, they require the art of patience.

~Prayer of Petition~

Evening

Jesus responded, "The wedding guests can't mourn while the groom is still with them, can they? But the days will come when the groom will be taken away from them, and then they'll fast." (Matthew 9:15)

Reflection

And through these days of penitence,
and through thy passiontide,
yea, evermore in life and death,
Jesus, with us abide.

Abide with us, that so, this life
of suffering over past,
an Easter of unending joy
we may attain at last.
—Claudia F. Hernaman, "Lord, Who Throughout These Forty Days"

~Prayer of Gratitude~

Day 5

Morning

All who want to save their lives will lose them. But all who lose their lives because of me will find them. (Matthew 16:25)

Reflection

It is natural to think of loss as, well, loss! But Jesus's math is a little different. Jesus tells us that loss can be gain. Before we can gain new things in our lives, we often must leave behind something old. If you want to make time for a new habit, you must scratch something off your daily to-do list. If you want to prioritize time with family, you might need to let go of extra time at work. If you want to cultivate generosity, you sometimes need to abstain from spending on unnecessary wants. If it is important to care for your body physically, and your mind mentally, you sometimes must pass up on food and drink that don't contribute to your overall goals. When it comes to following Jesus, disciples regularly confront a decision: to give up or let go of something that they want to do and trust Jesus's way. Faith is letting go of what we have and what we want, with the trust and confidence that Jesus can lead us to something better.

~Prayer of Petition~

Evening

So we fasted and prayed to our God for this, and he responded to us. (Ezra 8:23)

Reflection

In preparation for an annual physical exam, I was instructed to fast for twelve hours before my appointment so that they could test my blood for things like sugar levels, cholesterol, and iron. Without fasting, the test results would be inaccurate, and the doctor would not be able to fully assess my physical health. These blood tests can't tell you everything that's going on inside your body, of course, but they can provide important data that help indicate abnormalities and disease. They can also evaluate whether a patient needs to be on medication, take vitamins, or change their diet.

Fasting can also help us evaluate our spiritual health. Without the distraction of the physical things we put into our bodies, such as food, alcohol, caffeine, or sugar, we can start to assess what it is that our souls need. Fasting can help us achieve a spiritual diagnosis, allowing us to confess the transgressions that have separated us from God's presence and to return to God. One of the names of God is Great Physician because, in relationship with God, we are offered healing and wholeness for all our spiritual ills. Come, beloved, the doctor is in.

~Prayer of Gratitude~

Prayer

Morning Prayer of Petition

Ever present God, you are always listening to your children, and call me to make my hopes and petitions known to you. Today I name that which weighs heavy on my heart:

- for that which I need today,
- for those in my life hurting or suffering,
- for decisions or choices I am facing,
- for local, national, and global leaders,
- for your people far away who are often overlooked, underserved, or treated unjustly.

Hear my prayers, O God, and help me to listen to the ways you are speaking back into my life. Amen.

Evening Prayer of Gratitude

Sovereign God, you see fit to move, speak, and show your presence in your own way and at your own time. Help me to look back and see that even today you are active in my life. I am grateful for the ways that today you:

- supported me,
- guided me,
- confronted me,
- helped me not feel alone,
- opened my eyes,
- softened my heart.

As I speak to you, may I also more readily listen to the ways you are speaking to me. Amen.

Day 1

Morning

Early in the morning, well before sunrise, Jesus rose and went to a deserted place where he could be alone in prayer. (Mark 1:35)

Reflection

Jesus spent time alone in prayer. With limited time on earth and all that he was called to do, he chose to make time to travel out to a deserted place and pray. Why? Jesus already had all that he needed. Was there really a prayer concern that he couldn't himself address? Prayer is about more than asking God for things you need. Prayer is an investment in a relationship with God. It is hard to be friends with someone you spend little time with and rarely see. For a friendship to start, grow, and remain vital, you have to invest time and energy in the relationship. Jesus knew how important it was to spend time with God to maintain a closeness with God. He models for us the centrality of not neglecting the relationships that are most important in our lives when we are busy, especially the one we have with God.

~Prayer of Petition~

Evening

God will turn to the prayer of the impoverished;
he won't despise their prayers. (Psalm 102:17)

Reflection

[Being] prayerful is more an orientation than a set of words or a right ritual. If prayer is "being ourselves with God," prayerful attention indicates a willingness to be ourselves, unedited and unguarded. "Prayerful" means being real, not a smiley-face version of ourselves. Paying prayerful attention means paying real attention, not just going through the motions.

Moreover, prayerful means nonjudgmental in the sense of being available and openhearted. A prayerful posture does not assume to already know what our paying attention will reveal. That means we cannot pre-judge or frontload what we will discover when we pay prayerful attention. Rather, we are more open to discovery than judgment, more to listening than speaking. Prayerful attention expects to discover something about what God is up to. Thus, prayerful attention is curious and unhurried.

—Amy Oden, *Right Here, Right Now: The Practice of Christian Mindfulness*

~Prayer of Gratitude~

Day 2

Morning

For this reason, confess your sins to each other and pray for each other so that you may be healed. The prayer of the righteous person is powerful in what it can achieve. (James 5:16)

Reflection

Prayer changes things. That is a controversial statement in some circles. But prayer has power that goes beyond internal or psychological. We shouldn't shy away from naming our petitions to God. We shouldn't be scared to pray for healing, to ask for miracles, or to expect the unexpected. Believing in the power of prayer doesn't mean God will always show up exactly the way we expect, but it does mean that God will always show up. Some of us tend to lower our expectations of God so that we are not disappointed. As a result, we stop believing and looking for God to do powerful work in our lives. Instead, pray as if you believe that prayer is powerful, and that God can do what we alone cannot.

~Prayer of Petition~

Evening

During that time, Jesus went out to the mountain to pray, and he prayed to God all night long. (Luke 6:12)

Reflection

Prayer is the fundamental activity of the Christian; to be in the image of God means to communicate with God. Many people are intimidated by prayer, believing that there is a right and wrong way, and thinking that they will somehow offend God or make fools of themselves if they do it wrongly. It is helpful to know that our monastic ancestors were convinced that prayer is natural to us, like breathing, if we only discover it in ourselves. It is something we do, but even more, it is a gift of God to us. We do not even have to enter God's presence in prayer, because we are already in God's presence. It may be helpful to think not of entering God's presence but rather of making ourselves accessible to prayer. Prayer shapes us and transforms us. It centers us in God and at the same time in ourselves. It is always changing, as we are always becoming new in God.

—Roberta Bondi, *To Love as God Loves: Conversations with the Early Church*

~Prayer of Gratitude~

Day 3

Morning

Peter and John were going up to the temple at three o'clock in the afternoon, the established prayer time. (Acts 3:1)

Reflection

Creating and sustaining a prayer life is challenging, especially with the lives we have. Rushing from one place to the next, rarely having a down moment, and always being able to pick up a device when we are bored leaves little time to build prayer into our lives. That is why it is important to not only intend to pray, but also to set up a habit of prayer. Setting up a habit is easier when you have a dedicated time, place, and way to pray. Some people pray first thing in the morning, right before their cup of coffee. Others will pray midday, along with eating their lunch. Many people set up a particular spot for prayer in their home. The particulars vary, but if you want to be better at praying, work to create a habit. Pick a time, create a space, and find a routine way of praying. As you do, you will find it easier to grow the practice into a habit that gets easier over time.

~Prayer of Petition~

Evening

The LORD has listened to my request.
The LORD accepts my prayer. (Psalm 6:9)

Reflection

Sitting still in my pew with eyes closed and hands folded together, listening to words that the pastor says.
Gathered around an abundant table, hand-in-hand with family and friends; heads bowed, stomachs rumbling.
Quietly kneeling beside the bed late at night, whispering my gratitudes and hopes.
Raising my arms in a crowd of other worshippers, singing my heart out.
Walking a labyrinth with slow steps and even breaths, into the center and out again.
Holding prayer beads, and turning each one as I repeat ancient prayers.
Lying on a mat, facing the sky, hands crossed over my chest, and feeling my breath.
Writing reflections in a journal, naming people and situations that fill my heart.
Lighting a candle. Burning incense.
Repeating words I memorized as a child.
Saying nothing, but simply listening through my breath for God's still, small voice.
All of this is prayer, and there are many other ways to pray, too.
Prayer takes many forms, invites all kinds of practices.
There is no one right way to pray—in fact, there are thousands.
And God hears each and every one.
Thanks be to God.

~Prayer of Gratitude~

Day 4

Morning

Be happy in your hope, stand your ground when you're in trouble, and devote yourselves to prayer. (Romans 12:12)

Reflection

Elite athletes will tell you that the most important workouts are the ones they don't feel like doing. Even if they struggle, are slow, or don't perform well, doing the activity even when they don't feel like it pays off. One missed workout can hurt more than three great ones can help. Devotion is doing something, not just when you feel like it, but especially when you don't. Anything of great value in our lives requires devotion. A healthy, long-lasting relationship, making a difference over time in a job, or parenting kids all require devotion and making commitments to certain activities, especially when we aren't feeling it. The same is true about our relationship with God. There will be times when God feels far away, our doubts seem stronger than faith, or life just leaves us feeling unmotivated or worn out. Finding time to pray and connect with God, especially in these seasons, can help your relationship with God more than you think. Sometimes our biggest breakthroughs with God come during seasons of struggle.

~Prayer of Petition~

Evening

Let your ear be attentive and your eyes open to hear the prayer of your servant, which I now pray before you night and day for your servants, the people of Israel. "I confess the sins of the people of Israel, which we have committed against you. Both I and my family have sinned." (Nehemiah 1:6)

Reflection

When you have entered into your closets, and shut the doors, then pray to your father, who seeth in secret, that he would open your eyes to see whether slavery is sinful, and if it is, that he would enable you to bear a faithful, open and unshrinking testimony against it, and to do whatsoever your hands find to do, leaving the consequences entirely to him, who still says to us whenever we try to reason away duty from the fear of consequences, "What is that to thee, follow thou me."

—Angelina E. Grimké, "Appeal to Christian Women of the South"

~Prayer of Gratitude~

Day 5

Morning

But God definitely listened
He heard the sound of my prayer.
Bless God! He didn't reject my prayer;
he didn't withhold his faithful love from me. (Psalm 66:19-20)

Reflection

Some people think that praying is a bother to God. "With all that is going on in the world, does God really care about my relatively small problems and challenges?" The answer is *yes*. God does. The reality of great tragedy in the world and unspeakable evil in the lives of others does not negate God's care and concern for you. God's energy doesn't diminish, and more prayer does not mean less attention. God's love is endless, and God's power is limitless. Therefore, we can open up to God in prayer, no matter how weighty our concerns, knowing that God is eager to hear us.

~Prayer of Petition~

Evening

Don't be anxious about anything; rather, bring up all of your requests to God in your prayers and petitions, along with giving thanks. Then the peace of God that exceeds all understanding will keep your hearts and minds safe in Christ Jesus. (Philippians 4:6-7)

Reflection

It's easy to say, "Don't worry," but it's hard not to. We live in an age of anxiety, where worries are a constant companion—concerns for our family and friends, our children, work, health, finances, politics, and the planet. Our anxious minds turn over all the potentials and possibilities, the worst case scenarios, the what-if's.

Paul's letter to the Philippians tells us not to worry but instead to pray and to give thanks in all circumstances. Although it might feel like simple platitudes, we know that this encouragement is rooted in deep faith. Paul was facing imprisonment and death, and he had endured much suffering and persecution because of his commitment to the gospel. Surely Paul had many worries and yet he knew that prayer helps ease our anxiety. Reflecting on that for which we are grateful, even in the midst of our worries and fears, can help us connect with that deep peace we have in Christ. This is the peace that Jesus promised to his disciples: a peace that passes all understanding and keeps our hearts and minds focused on what we can do and what we can control. It allows us to release the rest to God.

~Prayer of Gratitude~

Judgment

Morning Prayer of Petition

Just God, you rightly judge the world, not to condemn but to redeem. Search my own heart, and open my eyes to:

- my sin, which leads me away from you,
- my resistance to following you,
- my fear, which keeps me from acting,
- my cynicism, which robs me of hope.

As you shine a light into my life today, help me to know that your judgments are aimed at my salvation. Amen.

Evening Prayer of Gratitude

Merciful God, you are slow to anger and quick to show compassion on your people. Thank you for your mercy and forgiveness in my life, revealed through:

- the grace others have shown me,
- the second chances and new opportunities given to me,
- the new doorways being opened for me,
- the burdens and guilt lifted from me.

God, I thank you for your mercies which are new every day. Amen.

Day 1

Morning

I will quickly bring my victory. My salvation is on its way, and my arm will judge the peoples. The coastlands hope for me; they wait for my judgment. (Isaiah 51:5)

Reflection

We tend to see judgment in a negative light. This is particularly true when we sit in a position of relative ease and power. But for the one wronged, or worse, for the one subjugated by another, judgment is good news. Judgment represents accountability and freedom. When you consider systems of the world that are unequal, oppressive, and unjust, then judgment is an essential part of creation's redemption and consummation. It is a key step in God setting all things right. In our lives, judgment can have a similar function. Rather than see judgment as a negative, we can instead see it as a hard but important step toward our own redemption, salvation, and perfection in love.

~Prayer of Petition~

Evening

Now when the Human One comes in his majesty and all his angels are with him, he will sit on his majestic throne. All the nations will be gathered in front of him. He will separate them from each other, just as a shepherd separates the sheep from the goats. He will put the sheep on his right side. But the goats he will put on his left. (Matthew 25:31-33)

Reflection

Unless you are familiar with farm animals, you could be forgiven for thinking there's not much difference between sheep and goats. They are about the same size, and they make similar sounds; they all have four legs and horns, and when they are all mixed in together, there's an indistinguishable and overwhelming scent.

Perhaps that's why it takes a shepherd, someone with a keen knowledge of these creatures, to be able to separate the one from the other, to look at each one individually and know to which herd they belong. When you look closely, you can see the differences, clear as day.

When the Son of Man comes, what will matter about our lives will be how we treat those who are the most vulnerable among us. He will be able to tell the difference in our actions, between those who show mercy and compassion—caring for and loving those who are poor, sick, and imprisoned—and those who don't. He will know the choices we make with our time and our resources, and whether we show kindness to others and tend to their needs, as would Christ himself.

~Prayer of Gratitude~

Day 2

Morning

God will definitely bring every deed to judgment, including every hidden thing, whether good or bad. (Ecclesiastes 12:14)

Reflection

Have you ever kept a secret that started gnawing away at you? Sharing it would bring sudden pain and hurt, so keeping it hidden seemed safer. But in the long run, Jesus cannot heal that which he doesn't first reveal. When a sin or mistake is brought into the light of judgment, it often is accompanied by pain and hurt, for us and for those we have hurt. Judgment is a decisive moment, but it is not God's final say about your life. Judgment is not a permanent reality but a mile-marker on the road to redemption.

~Prayer of Petition~

Evening

I've sinned against you—you alone.
I've committed evil in your sight.
That's why you are justified when you render your verdict,
completely correct when you issue your judgment. (Psalm 51:4)

Reflection

The title *Judgment* evokes images of power and respect. Picture a courtroom, of a person cloaked in a black robe, presiding over a trial where someone is accused of committing a crime. Evidence is presented either to incriminate or exonerate the defendant. And, in the end, the judge weighs the evidence and issues a ruling—either innocent or guilty—and, if guilty, decides what the punishment ought to be.

When we think of God as judge over our lives, it can feel intimidating and uncomfortable. We might feel defensive, explaining our choices in an effort to persuade the judge in our favor. Or we might simply throw ourselves on the mercy of this judge, begging for leniency. We unburden ourselves in confession, hoping that our contrition will result in a less severe punishment.

But here is the good news: our God is "merciful and gracious, slow to anger, and abounding in steadfast love" (Exodus 34:6 NRSVUE). When we stand before God, God already knows everything about us and is prepared to offer us forgiveness and the chance to start over. This grace allows us to come before God with our whole selves, and to receive God's mercy yet again.

~Prayer of Gratitude~

Day 3

Morning

They cried out with a loud voice, "Holy and true Master, how long will you wait before you pass judgment? How long before you require justice for our blood, which was shed by those who live on earth?" (Revelation 6:10)

Reflection

Judgment is closely associated with fairness. We get agitated on a visceral level when another person does something wrong, but is never called out, never held to account for what they have done. Worse yet is when such a person actually gets rewarded instead of punished. Yet the world is full of examples of good things happening to bad people, or bad things happening to good people. There is nothing that can make us doubt God more than this kind of unfairness that seems to be baked in to the universe. In this kind of world, judgment is good news. The book of Revelation promises that a day is coming when God will make this unfair world, fair. Judgment is the promise that there is ultimately no suffering that is not addressed, no perpetration of evil that is not confronted, and *not* injustice that is not set right. Like so many things, this judgment does not happen on our own timing, or in the way that we always expect. But God's judgment is coming, and when it does, every tear will be wiped away, and there will be no more mourning. For the world will be set right.

~Prayer of Petition~

Evening

Please don't bring your servant to judgment,
because no living thing is righteous before you. (Psalm 143:2)

Reflection

Be thou my vision, O Lord of my heart;
Naught be all else to me, save that thou art;
Thou my best thought, by day or by night,
Waking or sleeping, thy presence my light.

Be thou my Wisdom, and thou my true Word;
I ever with thee and thou with me, Lord;
Thou my great Father, and I thy true son,
Thou in me dwelling, and I with thee one.

Riches I heed not, nor man's empty praise;
Thou mine inheritance, now and always;
Thou and thou only, first in my heart,
High King of heaven, my treasure thou art.

High King of heaven, my victory won,
May I reach heaven's joys, O bright heaven's Sun!
Heart of my own heart, whatever befall,
Still be my Vision, O Ruler of all.
       —Ancient Irish; translated by Mary E. Byrne, "Be Thou My Vision"

~Prayer of Gratitude~

Day 4

Morning

This is how love has been perfected in us, so that we can have confidence on the Judgment Day, because we are exactly the same as God is in this world. (1 John 4:17)

Reflection

Have you ever met a new person, started talking, and then suddenly found out you have a friend in common? The new person sees you differently considering who you know. Or perhaps you are interviewing for a job and, in a sea of candidates, your resumé stands out because of a particular person that has recommended you. Or consider an ambassador who is welcomed into an important place, not because of who they are but because of who they represent. Relationships matter and change the way people see us. When we become followers of Jesus, God's spirit dwells in us, inhabits us, and makes a home in our hearts. On our own, none of us would pass the scrutiny of God's judgment. But we need not fear judgment because we are not viewed independently or on our own. We are viewed through the Christ we follow and the Spirit that dwells in us. Relationships matter, and our relationship with Jesus changes the way we approach the idea of judgment.

~Prayer of Petition~

Evening

*God didn't send his Son into the world to judge the world, but that the world might be saved through him. (*John 3:17*)*

Reflection

Those who are fully in the truth cannot possess a prejudiced or sectarian spirit. As they hold fellowship with Christ, they cannot reject those whom he has received, nor receive those whom he rejects, but all are brought into a blessed harmony with God and each other.
 —Julia A. J. Foote, "A Brand Plucked from the Fire"

~Prayer of Gratitude~

Day 5

Morning

*In every way, then, speak and act as people who will be judged by the law of freedom. There will be no mercy in judgment for anyone who hasn't shown mercy. Mercy overrules judgment. (*James 2:12-13*)*

Reflection

Mercy is often defined as not getting what you deserve. We understand this idea from experience. We make a mistake as a child and instead of punishing us, a parent goes easy on us. As adults we often screw up and instead of a boss, spouse, or friend responding with anger, the person responds with more kindness and understanding than we expect. Mercy doesn't negate the wrongdoing or condone a misdeed. We still are judged and we still must own our mistakes. It is just that the verdict is not what we expect. God does not, indeed cannot, merely overlook our sin. Confession, repentance, and authentic desire to change all matter to God. But scripture tells us that mercy overrules judgment, that it supersedes the sentence we might otherwise deserve. Instead, God's response to our sin is not punishment, but rather forgiveness and an opportunity to live in new ways.

~Prayer of Petition~

Evening

Don't judge, so that you won't be judged. You'll receive the same judgment you give. Whatever you deal out will be dealt out to you. (Matthew 7:1-2)

Reflection

No condemnation now I dread,
Jesus, and all in him, is mine;
alive in him, my living Head,
and clothed in righteousness divine,
bold I approach the eternal throne,
and claim the crown, through Christ my own.
 —Charles Wesley, "And Can It Be that I Should Gain"

~Prayer of Gratitude~

Forgiveness

Morning Prayer of Petition

Gracious God, you meet my mistakes and sin with grace and forgiveness. Remind me today to follow your example by:

- assuming the best in those around me,
- speaking honestly to those who disappoint me,
- offering forgiveness to those who hurt me,
- reconciling relationships if and where possible.

Lord, just as you have forgiven me, embolden me to forgive those around me. Amen.

Evening Prayer of Gratitude

Compassionate God, thank you for the ways you offer me grace, forgive my sin, and give me new chances to serve you. I am aware of your forgiveness today:

- through people who love me even when I disappoint,
- in the second chances I received,
- in opportunities to help others even though I am imperfect,
- with clean slates to write new stories.

God, thank you for forgiving my trespasses today and helping me to forgive those who trespass against me. Amen.

Day 1

Morning

Please, for the sake of your good name, LORD, forgive my sins, which are many! (Psalm 25:11)

Reflection

Pride so often gets in the way of forgiveness. When we are first faced with the realization that we have hurt someone, many of us respond immediately with defensiveness. We try to justify our actions, convince ourselves that we didn't do anything wrong, or blame the other for overreacting or misunderstanding. Some of us spend a good deal of our lives dodging and deflecting responsibility for actions that hurt others. From coworkers who grow frustrated with us, to family members who try to point out problematic behavior, to friends who grow tired of dealing with us—there is a temptation to see problems with others but never with ourselves. But forgiveness requires a confession and recognition that sometimes the problem is us. There is freedom in simply naming that we have sinned, admitting that we make mistakes, and recognizing that we have hurt other people. Only when we come clean with God, others, and ourselves is the freedom of forgiveness possible.

~Prayer of Petition~

Evening

Let the wicked abandon their ways
    and the sinful their schemes.
Let them return to the LORD so that he may have mercy on them,
    to our God, because he is generous with forgiveness. (Isaiah 55:7)

Reflection

Blessed assurance, Jesus is mine!
O what a foretaste of glory divine!
Heir of salvation, purchase of God,
born of his Spirit, washed in his blood.
This is my story, this is my song,
praising my Savior all the day long;
this is my story, this is my song,
praising my Savior all the day long.
    —Fanny J. Crosby, "Blessed Assurance, Jesus Is Mine!"

~Prayer of Gratitude~

Day 2

Morning

Peter replied, "Change your hearts and lives. Each of you must be baptized in the name of Jesus Christ for the forgiveness of your sins. Then you will receive the gift of the Holy Spirit." (Acts 2:38)

Reflection

Repentance and forgiveness are inextricably linked. While God offers forgiveness freely, God desires not simply to remove a sense of guilt from our lives, but also to empower us to change. When we seek forgiveness without repentance, we get stuck in a cycle of returning to the same sin we just committed. If forgiveness is sought only to remove a sense of guilt, then we are in danger of getting stuck in a sin spiral. We sin, feel guilty, seek forgiveness, feel ashamed for having sinned, and then in that shame, return to sinning again. Repentance breaks this cycle. Repentance is a commitment to changing actions, routines, and relationships. Repentance is turning in a new direction so that we can embrace a new way of living. This doesn't ensure that we will never sin again, but it does mean that we choose to no longer stay in the situations and habits that we know will lead us right back to sinning.

~Prayer of Petition~

Evening

Above all, show sincere love to each other, because love brings about the forgiveness of many sins. (1 Peter 4:8)

Reflection

I'm not sure when it started, but sometime recently I became aware that the Roman Catholic Church was using a new term for confession: the *Sacrament of Reconciliation*. It seems that the church is trying to reframe this rite to make it more inviting to those who might be put off by the idea of sitting inside a confessional and telling their sins to a priest. Now, they are focusing on the goal of confession, which is to be reconciled to God and to one another. And the reason why we need to be reconciled is because our sin creates a separation between us and God. Because of what we have done or left undone, there is a distance between us and the God who loves us and who desires to be in relationship with us. The only way to repair this relationship is through repentance and accepting God's forgiveness. It's true that confessing our sins can feel uncomfortable. It can be hard to face up to our whole selves when we have caused harm. And, yet, the isolation and alienation that comes with sin is not something we have to bear. We can be forgiven. We can be reconciled. Thanks be to God.

~Prayer of Gratitude~

Day 3

Morning

When wrongdoings become too much for me, you forgive our sins. (Psalm 65:3)

Reflection

We like to be able to do things for ourselves and to control our own destinies. But forgiveness doesn't work this way. Forgiveness requires dependence on God. Forgiveness is a gift whose cost is borne by the one who is wronged. We often talk about the difficulty of forgiving ourselves. That is because we don't grant ourselves forgiveness; instead we ask for it. This puts us in a place of dependency when we recognize that we do not control our own forgiveness but rather we must seek it. It is in God's power to offer it and grant it. We don't need to forgive ourselves and, in fact, we can't. Instead, our work is to humbly ask for it, and then to accept it as a gift from God.

~Prayer of Petition~

Evening

We have been ransomed through his Son's blood, and we have forgiveness for our failures based on his overflowing grace. (Ephesians 1:7)

Reflection

Forgiving and being reconciled to our enemies or our loved ones are not about pretending that things are other than they are. It is not about patting one another on the back and turning a blind eye to the wrong. True reconciliation exposes the awfulness, the abuse, the hurt, the truth. It could even sometimes make things worse. It is a risky undertaking but in the end it is worthwhile, because in the end only an honest confrontation with reality can bring real healing. Superficial reconciliation can bring only superficial healing.
—Desmond Tutu

~Prayer of Gratitude~

Day 4

Morning

I will cleanse them of all the wrongdoing they committed against me, and I will forgive them for all of their guilt and rebellion. (Jeremiah 33:8)

Reflection

Have you ever spilled something on a nice rug or carpet and had to clean it up? There are several different kinds of stain removers, each working in a different way. Cheap cleaners contain bleach and peroxide, essentially changing the color of the stain so that you can no longer see it. More expensive cleaners contain acids and chemicals that actually break down the molecules of the stain, allowing it to be removed all together. In the former case, the stain remains; in the latter, it is gone. When it comes to our sin, many of us try to go the cheap route. We don't really want to remove the sin, we just want to cover it up so that it cannot be seen. But like a stain, often that sin begins to show again because the underlying motives and reasons for having done it have never really been addressed. While harder, and perhaps more costly, God wants to heal what is underneath our sin, cleanse us, and remove that sin altogether.

~Prayer of Petition~

Evening

When Jesus saw their faith, he said, "Friend, your sins are forgiven." (Luke 5:20)

Reflection

Perfect submission, perfect delight,
visions of rapture now burst on my sight;
angels descending bring from above
echoes of mercy, whispers of love.
This is my story, this is my song,
praising my Savior all the day long;
this is my story, this is my song,
praising my Savior all the day long.
 —Fanny J. Crosby, "Blessed Assurance, Jesus Is Mine!"

~Prayer of Gratitude~

Day 5

Morning

Therefore, brothers and sisters, know this: Through Jesus we proclaim forgiveness of sins to you. From all those sins from which you couldn't be put in right relationship with God through Moses' Law, through Jesus everyone who believes is put in right relationship with God. (Acts 13:38-39)

Reflection

There is a difference between forgiveness and reconciliation. Forgiveness is the act of releasing anger or vengeance against another. Reconciliation is the restoration of a relationship that has been broken by wrongdoing. In our human relationships, forgiveness is a choice that we make to no longer allow another person dominion over our emotional well-being. We release those feelings of anger and the need for revenge. However, forgiveness does not mean reconciliation. Sometimes you can repair a relationship with another person who has hurt you. Sometimes that reconciliation is impossible this side of heaven. But God is different. Not only does God forgive us, releasing any judgment that we might deserve, but God also restores a relationship with us. This is the good news! God does not choose to hold our sin against us. Instead, through Jesus, God restores us to a place of love and honor in God's family.

~Prayer of Petition~

Evening

If you forgive others their sins, your heavenly Father will also forgive you. But if you don't forgive others, neither will your Father forgive your sins. (Matthew 6:14-15)

Reflection

The writer Anne Lamott once said, "Not forgiving is like drinking rat poison and then waiting for the rat to die" (*Traveling Mercies: Some Thoughts on Faith*). We often struggle with forgiving others because we think that, when we forgive, we are doing something for them, for the person who committed the offense against us. But what if forgiveness were really about ourselves, our own spiritual liberation, and setting ourselves free from the burden of carrying resentment and anger toward another?

One definition of forgiveness is a conscious, deliberate decision to release feelings of resentment or vengeance toward a person who has harmed you, regardless of whether they actually deserve your forgiveness. When we forgive, we release the hold that another person has over us, the hurt that they have caused us, and the ways in which we have been bound up together because we could not forgive. Forgiveness doesn't mean that we have to reconcile, to forget, and to move on. We can still maintain boundaries with a person who has hurt us, especially if we think they could do it again. And it doesn't happen overnight. But by the grace of God, we can stop poisoning ourselves.

~Prayer of Gratitude~

Sacrifice

Morning Prayer of Petition

Holy Lord, this week I remember the great sacrifice you made for me on the cross. Show me where you call me to follow in your footsteps:

- giving up my pride and ego,
- letting go of material goods to live more simply,
- sacrificing personal ambition to listen to your call,
- eschewing immediate gratification for the sake of long-term gain.

As I receive the great gift you offer me on the cross, give me the courage and will to take up my own cross to follow you. Amen.

Evening Prayer of Gratitude

Redeeming God, your sacrifice on the cross brings about life for your creation. Help me to gratefully breathe in:

- hope in place of fear,
- grace in place of resentment,
- joy in place of despair,
- courage in place of fear,
- calm in place of anxiety.

Open my heart to receive the gift of new life that you are preparing for me in Christ. Amen.

Day 1

Morning

This is love: it is not that we loved God but that he loved us and sent his Son as the sacrifice that deals with our sins. (1 John 4:10)

Reflection

Often, when we talk about or hear the word *sacrifice*, we think of pain, hurt, loss, and perhaps even violence. But John says that sacrifice, God's sacrifice, is an act of love. More specifically, God's sacrifice on behalf of our sin is a demonstration and a result of God's love for us. But how? It is one of the trickiest questions in Christian theology. Think about forgiveness in our personal relationships. Forgiving someone who hurt you costs you something—it can cost you hurt and pain, nights of tears, stress, and anguish, retributive justice, or a desire for revenge. Whatever it is, any of you who have had to forgive someone knows that there is a cost associated with it. To forgive means that you must give up something in exchange for an inner peace. Our sin requires the same of God. Forgiving us and letting go of the consequences of our sin costs God something. The cross is ultimately a demonstration of that cost, and God's willingness to absorb it so that we might have a new relationship with God.

~Prayer of Petition~

Evening

I will sacrifice to you freely;
I will give thanks to your name, LORD,
because it's so good. (Psalm 54:6)

Reflection

He left his Father's throne above
(so free, so infinite his grace!),
emptied himself of all but love,
and bled for Adam's helpless race.
—Charles Wesley, "And Can It Be That I Should Gain"

~Prayer of Gratitude~

Day 2

Morning

Some time later, Cain presented an offering to the LORD from the land's crops while Abel presented his flock's oldest offspring with their fat. The LORD looked favorably on Abel and his sacrifice but didn't look favorably on Cain and his sacrifice. (Genesis 4:3-5a)

Reflection

One of the earliest expressions of worship came in the form of offering, particularly the offering of a sacrifice. A proper sacrifice showed a person's commitment to God, expressed a heart of gratitude, and acknowledged God as the source of blessing. When someone gave up an item of great value for God, it demonstrated an internal commitment to put God first and a heart of gratitude. The outward sacrifice was meant to convey an inward disposition, desire, or attitude. But it is possible for people to practice the external acts of faith, without the commensurate internal disposition of the heart. We can fulfill outward obligations without the corresponding attitude or desire to honor God. While sacrifices are important, the condition of the heart is more important, for it is one's heart that makes a sacrifice pleasing. Sometimes we can fall into the trap of going through the motions, fulfilling bare minimum expectations, or checking religious boxes. But we must take care that our sacrifice is pleasing to God, that our hearts are aligned with our outward actions, for this is what makes a sacrifice pleasing and acceptable.

~Prayer of Petition~

Evening

Go and learn what this means: I want mercy and not sacrifice. I didn't come to call righteous people, but sinners. (Matthew 9:13)

Reflection

What does a Christian look like? My memories go back to the very respectable clothes that people wore to church when I was a kid: men in suits and ties, women in dresses with big shoulder pads.

The truth is, if we are to be faithful to the gospel, we should worry less about what a Christian looks like and worry more about what a Christian does. In the Gospel of Matthew, Jesus says, "I want mercy and not sacrifice. I didn't come to call righteous people, but sinners." Jesus does not mean sacrifice is out of the question. After all, sacrifice involves tending to the needs of others. What Jesus means is that if you are making a sacrifice just for the look of it, you've missed the point entirely. There are no suits and ties required. Being a Christian looks like loving God and loving one's neighbor, work that is less about being respectable and more about the adventure of faith.

In her great little book, *Teaching a Stone to Talk*, the writer Annie Dillard says this: "It is madness to wear ladies' straw hats and velvet hats to church; we should all be wearing crash helmets."

~Prayer of Gratitude~

Day 3

Morning

Don't sacrifice to the LORD your God any oxen or sheep that have defects of any kind, because that is detestable to the LORD your God. (Deuteronomy 17:1)

Reflection

Have you ever regifted something you didn't want? Or, even worse, have you ever found out that something you received was not thoughtfully purchased for you, but rather a recycled gift that held little value to the one giving it? The value the item has to the giver impacts the impression it makes on the receiver. Without thinking, it is easy for us to give God our leftovers.

After we pay our bills and buy all the things we want, if there is some money left over, then maybe we will give it to God. Once we work, run around to events, attend every sporting activity, or stream a new show, if we have any time left over, then we will offer some to God. After filling up our days with everything that we need and want to do, if we have any energy left, we might offer some up to God. But God doesn't want our leftovers. Instead, scripture encourages us to offer God the first part of our time, energy, and money. It encourages us to give God our best, not our leftovers. The more it means to us, the more it will mean when we offer it to God.

~Prayer of Petition~

Evening

Offer God a sacrifice of thanksgiving!
Fulfill the promises you made to the Most High! (Psalm 50:14)

Reflection

What wondrous love is this, O my soul, O my soul,
what wondrous love is this, O my soul!
What wondrous love is this that caused the Lord of bliss
to bear the dreadful curse for my soul, for my soul,
to bear the dreadful curse for my soul.

What wondrous love is this, O my soul, O my soul,
what wondrous love is this, O my soul!
What wondrous love is this, that caused the Lord of life
to lay aside his crown for my soul, for my soul,
to lay aside his crown for my soul.
    —"What Wondrous Love Is This"

~Prayer of Gratitude~

Day 4

Morning

I desire faithful love and not sacrifice, the knowledge of God instead of entirely burned offerings. (Hosea 6:6)

Reflection

While sacrifice is often imagined as material and literal, scripture indicates that what God most wants runs deeper. Love can be, and often is, sacrificial. To love a friend faithfully sometimes requires giving up some of what you want for the sake of what the other might need at a particular time. In any healthy marriage, loving a spouse often means enduring hardship, offering forgiveness, or serving selflessly. To put it more bluntly, when you are in a relationship with someone else, it is no longer all about you. Sometimes the "you" sacrifices for the "us." The same is true for God. While many treat God as a personal genie who is supposed to be there when we need God and otherwise stay in the bottle, this is not what an authentic relationship with God looks like. Sometimes to love and trust God, we have to set aside our own desires, sacrifice our own immediate impulses, or give up our own self-devised plans. God ultimately wants nothing more than a relationship with us. And, as in all relationships, this includes a love that considers a higher value than just the self.

~Prayer of Petition~

Evening

Acting with righteousness and justice
*   is more valued by the LORD than sacrifice.* (Proverbs 21:3)

Reflection

To God and to the Lamb I will sing, I will sing,
to God and to the Lamb, I will sing;
to God and to the Lamb who is the great I AM,
while millions join the theme I will sing, I will sing;
while millions join the theme I will sing.

And when from death I'm free, I'll sing on, I'll sing on,
and when from death I'm free, I'll sing on;
and when from death I'm free, I'll sing and joyful be,
and through eternity I'll sing on, I'll sing on,
and through eternity I'll sing on.
    —"What Wondrous Love Is This"

~Prayer of Gratitude~

Day 5

Morning

So let's continually offer up a sacrifice of praise through him, which is the fruit from our lips that confess his name. (Hebrews 13:15)

Reflection

Sacrifice is not primarily about something lost; it is about something given. It isn't to be thought of only as a deficit incurred but a credit that is granted. Sacrifice isn't forced or coerced, but can only be a proper sacrifice if it is freely given. Sacrifice is a choice, and not one that we have to make, but that we get to make. In this sense, it is a sacrifice each time we offer love, gratitude, forgiveness, patience, prayer, or praise. It may cost us something, but it also provides something for another. It may require denying ourselves certain desires, but for the purpose of providing a need for another. Sacrifice may mean dying to self, but it also means offering life. In this way, sacrifice is woven into what it means to have a relationship with God. From God we are continually receiving, so we can continually give. From God we are continually collecting, so we can continually offer. From God we are continually gaining, so we can always give up. In this way, God enables us to choose a life of sacrifice continually.

~Prayer of Petition~

Evening

So, brothers and sisters, because of God's mercies, I encourage you to present your bodies as a living sacrifice that is holy and pleasing to God. This is your appropriate priestly service. (Romans 12:1)

Reflection

The word *sacrifice* conjures up a number of images, none of them particularly enjoyable. As children, we are taught that sacrifice involves giving something up: a toy, our time, the chance to have a fun experience. And, as children, we struggle to sacrifice gracefully. Our stuff, our time, our energy is all we have! Adults don't do much better, though we may be able to keep the tantrums to a minimum. The truth is, while Christians are called to sacrifice, we are called to consider sacrifice as a way of life and not something that leaves us deficient. This is what it means to be a holy and living sacrifice: that we do give thanksgiving to God, but we also recognize that offering to God this thanksgiving does not leave us with less than we had before. Offering thanksgiving to God makes us whole! There are of course times when we must give of ourselves in difficult ways; this is the nature of love, after all. And yet the sacrifice God calls us to is not about having less. It is about being more.

~Prayer of Gratitude~

Easter

Resurrection

Morning Prayer of Petition

God of despair and hope, endings and new beginnings, death and life, I thank you today for the good news of the resurrection of your son Jesus. Through him, you give life to the world and all that is in it. I lift up to you that in my life and in the world that needs your resurrection power:

- for my family and those I love who need you,
- for the problems and injustices that plague my community,
- for my church and its future,
- for the world and the chaos that swirls in it,
- for those anywhere who are rejected, alone, or feel far away from you.

May the first fruits of Christ's resurrection from the dead give me hope for the promise of new life in my world today. Amen.

Evening Prayer of Gratitude

God of new life, help me to know that you are already at work in my life bringing hope from despair:

- in my grief, sadness, or disappointment,
- in my loneliness, isolation, or fear,
- in my eagerness, impatience, and anxiety,
- in my confusion, discernment, and decisions.

May your gift of new life feel tangible to me tonight and give me the peace that comes from knowing that in you, there is always a future with hope. Amen.

Day 1

Morning

From that time Jesus began to show his disciples that he had to go to Jerusalem and suffer many things from the elders, chief priests, and legal experts, and that he had to be killed and raised on the third day. (Matthew 16:21)

Easter

Reflection

Early Jewish thought did not include a belief in life after death. But, later, Jewish apocalyptic literature developed the conviction that there would be a resurrection from the dead. Unlike other religions, the Jewish community never believed in the immortality of the soul or the discardable nature of the body. Instead, they believed that a person was created as a psychosomatic whole. They saw value in the created order. They also believed that death was real and inescapable. It is this last point that we continue to struggle with. Jesus's disciples didn't understand why he had to die. We struggle with this idea as well. We want new life, but we want it without death. We want new direction, new possibility, and new birth, but we so often want it without giving up, losing, or having to let go of something old. Jesus reminds us that new life is possible, hope is real, and life is our ultimate destiny. But he also reminds us that all of it comes through resurrection, that is, it only comes on the other side of death, not without it.

~Prayer of Petition~

Evening

Martha replied, "I know that he will rise in the resurrection on the last day." Jesus said to her, "I am the resurrection and the life. Whoever believes in me will live, even though they die." (John 11:24-25)

Reflection

In the resurrection we see life, which cannot be separated from God by sin, nor destroyed by death.

Jesus was the resurrection before he ever died and rose again. In John 11:25, when he tells Martha he is already the resurrection and life, he is testifying to the truth that the Son of God already holds power over life, death, and life beyond death. Jesus did not gain power over death through his death and resurrection. He demonstrated his power over death through his death and resurrection.

The cross and empty tomb bring to fulfillment the mission begun in the annunciation and virgin birth. The God who bound the world by the laws of physics and circumscribed life to the principles of biology broke into a world turned against its creator to show the full power of life, a power biology cannot contain nor physics explain.

For those who seek this resurrection life, Christ offers not merely religious requirements, but himself. Only the One who is the resurrection can offer resurrection life to those who seek it.

~Prayer of Gratitude~

Day 2

Morning

May the God and Father of our Lord Jesus Christ be blessed! On account of his vast mercy, he has given us new birth. You have been born anew into a living hope through the resurrection of Jesus Christ from the dead. (1 Peter 1:3)

Reflection

Hope comes from the firm conviction that the present is not permanent and that your temporary situation is not your eternal destination. Hope exists in the gap between the now and the not-yet. Resurrection gives birth to hope because it is a promise that what is right now, is not what will be. The resurrection of Jesus is not only his victory over death, but it is also an anticipation of our own future. The result is an ability to live in a sinful, broken, and unjust world without giving up or giving in. We seek to love now because eventually love will win. We work for justice now because eventually justice will reign. We seek to restore and rebuild now because eventually God will restore all things. And we live fiercely, even in the face of death, because resurrection promises us that eventually life conquers death. We live with hope in a world that is hopeless because we know that, eventually, a new heaven and a new earth will come, and therefore our living hope is not held onto in vain.

~Prayer of Petition~

Evening

This Jesus God raised up. We are all witnesses to that fact. He was exalted to God's right side and received from the Father the promised Holy Spirit. He poured out this Spirit, and you are seeing and hearing the results of his having done so. (Acts 2:32-33)

Reflection

The resurrection is an event and a reality.

The event of Jesus's resurrection irreversibly changed the course of history. The early Christian confession, "Jesus is Lord," relies upon the conviction that the tomb is empty and that Jesus is alive and more powerful than Caesar. If Jesus is not risen, he is not Lord.

The reality of resurrection is experienced in the risen Lord's reign over creation, and made known through his appearing first to the apostles and now living within his followers through the Holy Spirit.

Peter's proclamation to the crowds on Pentecost that they were "seeing and hearing the results" (Acts 2:33) of Jesus's resurrection describes both the event and the reality.

The event of the resurrection is the empty tomb, the appearances of the living Lord, and the promise of the end times. The reality of the resurrection is fishermen turned into apostles, terrifying fear turned into unshakable faith, hatred and violence turned into love and sacrifice, and fear of death turned into confidence in eternal life.

The call of the Christian is to believe in the event of the resurrection and pray for the Holy Spirit's power to witness with our lives to the reality of resurrection.

~Prayer of Gratitude~

Day 3

Morning

As for the resurrection of the dead, haven't you read what God told you, I'm the God of Abraham, the God of Isaac, and the God of Jacob? He isn't the God of the dead but of the living. (Matthew 22:31-32)

Reflection

Have you ever known how something was going to turn out, but still had to go through the motions anyway? Often knowing the outcome can ease the burden that we often feel. Maybe you audited a class in school and knew that if you showed up, you were going to pass. With the outcome secure, you could handle the day-to-day with less stress, greater freedom, and reduced pressure. The resurrection offers us that same security with regard to our lives. We know the outcome of our lives and the world is renewal, new creation, and eternal life. The victory is secure. This doesn't mean that we get to skip grief and pain in our lives. The truth of resurrection doesn't mean that we won't make mistakes, disappoint people we love, or sin in ways that damage. It doesn't exempt us from working for reconciliation, challenging systems of oppression, or struggling for justice. The resurrection doesn't guarantee that life will always go how we expect. But resurrection does offer us a firm picture of where our lives are headed, and how the story ends. It ends with renewal, peace, reconciliation of relationship, and forgiveness of sin—it end with life. That foundation allows us to face our challenges in this life with greater courage, riskier love, and an inner peace that is only possible by knowing how the story ends.

~Prayer of Petition~

Evening

If we were united together in a death like his, we will also be united together in a resurrection like his. (Romans 6:5)

Reflection

We thought to find God where the body ends: and we made it suffer and transformed it into beast of burden, fulfiller of commands, machine for labor, enemy to be silenced, and we persecuted it in this way to the point of eulogizing death as the pathway to God, as if God preferred the smell of the tomb to the delights of Paradise.

—Rubem Alves, *I Believe in the Resurrection of the Body*

~Prayer of Gratitude~

Day 4

Morning

Look, the curtain of the sanctuary was torn in two from top to bottom. The earth shook, the rocks split, and the bodies of many holy people who had died were raised. (Matthew 27:51-52)

Reflection

In the accounts of Jesus death and resurrection, there are signs that what was happening was an extraordinary event. Earthquakes shook the land, solid rocks were split in two, and the sun grew dark. All of this reminds us that what was happening wasn't normal, it wasn't natural, and it didn't fit. And just in case you didn't get the hint, when Jesus died and was raised, Matthew tells us that holy people were raised up as well and started appearing. It was as if the death of Jesus led to an uncontrollable, unpredictable, and impossible explosion of life. This life was so forceful that the chains of the grave were broken, stones weighing tons were cast aside, and the foundations of the earth suddenly shifted. Resurrection meant that the rules of the normal no longer applied, that the predictable no longer would hold true, and that anything was possible. Scripture promises us that the same spirit that raised Christ from the dead—the same unpredictable, impossible, and uncontrollable spirit—is at work in our lives as well. And the result is the same. The normal doesn't apply, the immoveable can suddenly shift, and the impossible now becomes possible through Christ.

~Prayer of Petition~

Evening

The apostles continued to bear powerful witness to the resurrection of the Lord Jesus, and an abundance of grace was at work among them all. (Acts 4:33)

Reflection

Tis the spring of souls today; Christ has burst his prison,
And from three days' sleep in death as a sun hath risen;
All the winter of our sins, long and dark, is flying
From his light, to whom we give laud and praise undying.
Neither might the gates of death, nor the tomb's dark portal,
Nor the watchers, nor the seal hold thee as a mortal;
But today amidst the twelve though didst stand, bestowing
That thy peace which evermore passeth human knowing.
 —John of Damascus, "Come, Ye Faithful, Raise the Strain"

~Prayer of Gratitude~

Day 5

Morning

So if the message that is preached says that Christ has been raised from the dead, then how can some of you say, "There's no resurrection of the dead"? (1 Corinthians 15:12)

Reflection

What you believe about the resurrection of Jesus makes a difference. After all, it matters if someone is alive or dead. If a person is dead, you can remember them, be inspired by them, and even seek to live a life consistent with what they valued. But you can't sit down and have a cup of coffee with them, you can't have a conversation with them, and you cannot reasonably expect them to show up in a new and real way. The resurrection of Jesus means that he is alive. Jesus is living and therefore is active in our world and in our lives today. Jesus can guide, direct, rescue, and forgive right now. Jesus can speak to us in a real way today. Jesus's power is presently at work in the world, in our families, in our church, and in our lives. Jesus is alive and a God of the living and the active, the here and the now. To say Jesus is alive is at once to believe that he is still at work, not indirectly through memories or lessons passed down, but directly through the power of the Spirit at work in us.

~Prayer of Petition~

Evening

When they heard about the resurrection from the dead, some began to ridicule Paul. However, others said, "We'll hear from you about this again." (Acts 17:32)

Reflection

Empty, waiting to be fed;
first the water, then the bread
and the wine, God's offering:
Jesus Christ, the living spring.
As the ages come and go,
lives to you, like rivers, flow:
those who doubt and those who know,
nonetheless will find it so.
  —Daniel Charles Damon

~Prayer of Gratitude~

Eternal Life

Morning Prayer of Petition

Eternal God, I thank you for giving me your gift of eternal life beginning now. Help me to fully receive and stand in that gift. Help me to know that even now I have all I need to:

- find a sense of calm amid the chaos of life,
- pursue a call to live or serve in a new way,
- make wise decisions,
- claim the forgiveness and mercy you offer.

May your gift of life that is already given to me continue to grow until it matures in life eternal. Amen.

Evening Prayer of Gratitude

Holy God, despite your call to thanksgiving, I often choose to focus on the darkness around me. Lift the heavy clouds surrounding my head and heart, clearing my way to appreciate:

- moments of strength that steady me,
- small ways that I experience joy,
- people who surround and support me when I feel alone,
- new pathways that are being cleared for me.

Continue to clear my heart to receive the good gifts that you are giving to me even now. Amen.

Day 1

Morning

God so loved the world that he gave his only Son, so that everyone who believes in him won't perish but will have eternal life. (John 3:16)

Reflection

In the 1970s and 1980s it was hard to watch sports without, at some point, seeing the John 3:16 guy. There was a man (Rollen Stewart) who traveled around the country to major events and, standing in the most noticeable spot, held up a sign that simply had "John 3:16" on it. Although he later ended up in prison, people remember him for his several-decade mission to make sure everyone knew this famous verse of the Bible. As cliché as it may be to a longtime church person, it is worth considering anew, especially in the wake of Easter. Many of us confuse or unnecessarily complicate God's intention. We ascribe to God multiple motives and often mistakenly believe that everything from disappointment to pain, tragedy to loss is somehow a product of God's hand. But John reminds us that God is always and only working for one thing in the world—life. God's disposition toward you is one of love. And God is always working in and for you, that you might have life that is whole, rich, abundant, and eternal.

~Prayer of Petition~

Evening

The wages that sin pays are death, but God's gift is eternal life in Christ Jesus our Lord. (Romans 6:23)

Reflection

Crown him with many crowns,
the Lamb upon his throne.
Hark! how the heavenly anthem drowns
all music but its own.
Awake, my soul, and sing
of him who died for thee,
and hail him as thy matchless King
through all eternity.
    —Matthew Bridges, "Crown Him with Many Crowns"

~Prayer of Gratitude~

Day 2

Morning

A man approached him and said, "Teacher, what good thing must I do to have eternal life?" (Matthew 19:16)

Reflection

Many of us see eternal life as a prize to be earned rather than a gift to be received. While we may not admit this, we still operate out of a sense that Jesus awards life based on performance. For some of us this means a crushing self-imposed perfectionism. For others it means a destructive self-punishment for perceived shortcomings or sins. For leaders like pastors and church workers, it often means over-functioning and an inability to draw boundaries. For others it can look like a relentless pursuit to be the best student, parent, executive, or volunteer. We even do this with church and faith.

Easter

We want to know the expectations, the minimum requirements, and what is needed to be good with God. But eternal life isn't a reward for excellent performance. It isn't a merit badge for the religiously faithful. It is a gift that only needs to be asked for and received. A free gift that is available equally to those who've done well, and those who've screwed up, those whose life is put together and those whose life is a mess, those who have cleared every hurdle in life and those who have failed miserably. It is a gift that is offered and available to you.

~Prayer of Petition~

Evening

Simon Peter answered, "Lord, where would we go? You have the words of eternal life." (John 6:68)

Reflection

Crown him the Lord of life,
who triumphed o'er the grave,
and rose victorious in the strife
for those he came to save.
His glories now we sing,
who died, and rose on high,
who died, eternal life to bring,
and lives that death may die.
    —Matthew Bridges, "Crown Him with Many Crowns"

~Prayer of Gratitude~

Day 3

Morning

Compete in the good fight of faith. Grab hold of eternal life—you were called to it, and you made a good confession of it in the presence of many witnesses. (1 Timothy 6:12)

Reflection

If eternal life isn't something we earn, why compete in the good fight of faith? Why do we have to grab ahold of eternal life? Is it a limited time offer or in short supply? No. Think about gifts that you get. Someone can give the gift, but you must receive it, take it, open it, and use it. Similarly God offers us eternal life. Jesus comes to give this life to us. But we still have to receive it, grab ahold of it, and begin to live that life eternal. What does that look like? It means living as if death has no final sway. It can be living with courage and uncommon strength. At times it means claiming permission to be joyful and free, remembering that you are loved, and internalizing your inherent worth as a child of God. Grabbing ahold of eternal life can empower you through struggle, and give you a resilience to persevere through suffering. Eternal life is given, but it is yours to receive, to grab ahold of, and to begin living, beginning right now.

~Prayer of Petition~

Evening

Many of those who sleep in the dusty land will wake up—some to eternal life, others to shame and eternal disgrace. (Daniel 12:2)

Reflection

Much of Christianity has been reduced to the concepts of heaven and hell. The fear about where we will spend eternity can consume the Christian imagination. We get so preoccupied with what happens after death that we often can forget about what happens on this side of death.

There are many people who are living in hell, right here on earth. Poverty, war, racism, abuse of power, loneliness . . . these all are the opposite of shalom. They are in direct contrast to the wholeness and fullness that God so desires for us.

It is easy to become numb to the troubles of the world. We are constantly bombarded with news from around the world, across the nation, throughout our communities, and even in the midst of our personal affairs.

But Jesus tells us that the kingdom of God is here, among us. It is not yet here completely, but it is here. We might experience these kin-dom moments when we put our children to sleep, when we have a good cry alone in our car, when we do something kind for someone, or when we watch the birds dancing circles in the sky. These moments are here, just begging to be noticed.

Let us turn our attention to the kin-dom moments that are popping up all of the time.

~Prayer of Gratitude~

Day 4

Morning

I assure you that whoever hears my word and believes in the one who sent me has eternal life and won't come under judgment but has passed from death into life. (John 5:24)

Reflection

We usually think of eternal life in terms of quantity. That is to say, eternal life is everlasting life, that life that exists on the other side of death. And this is part of the promise that God offers through Christ. But eternal life is also a gift not just of quantity but quality. Jesus doesn't only want us to have life everlasting, but he wants us to have a fuller, holistic, and more abundant life right now. This promise has both a future hope and present gift. When we invite Jesus into our lives, and when we take steps to grow closer to Christ, it isn't for some future payoff. Jesus promises us transformation here and now. Jesus can guide us when we are uncertain where to go in life, offer us forgiveness so our past mistakes do not define our future potential, reconcile broken relationships, and rescue us from grief or despair. Life with Jesus is fuller and more abundant, and those gifts are immediate. Today is a day Christ can do something powerfully new in your life. Today is a day full of possibility and promise. Today you can pass from death to life.

~Prayer of Petition~

Evening

So, since we have been made righteous by his grace, we can inherit the hope for eternal life. (Titus 3:7)

Reflection

Crown him the Lord of peace,
whose power a scepter sways
from pole to pole, that wars may cease,
and all be prayer and praise.
His reign shall know no end,
and round his pierced feet
fair flowers of paradise extend
their fragrance ever sweet.

Crown him the Lord of love;
behold his hands and side,
those wounds, yet visible above,
in beauty glorified.
All hail, Redeemer, hail!
For thou hast died for me;
thy praise and glory shall not fail
throughout eternity.
  —Matthew Bridges, "Crown Him with Many Crowns"

~Prayer of Gratitude~

Day 5

Morning

This is the promise that he himself gave us: eternal life. (1 John 2:25)

Reflection

We have all been on the receiving end of broken promises. Someone tells us they will do something, we believe them and act as if they will keep their word, and then they disappoint us. Stack up enough of these disappointments and it begins to change us. Over time, it is tempting to no longer believe the promises people make. With the passing years, we stop trusting anyone beyond ourselves. The best way to not be disappointed is to not believe the promises of others in the first place and to rely only on what we can deliver. When we stop trusting and depending on others, our lives contract to what we reasonably believe that we alone can achieve or attain. This leads to a life that is safe but small. It is secure but predictable. We can slip into living this way with God. We say that we believe God, but we don't live as if we trust God's promises. But trusting God can change our capacity to live. When we trust God, and believe in God's promises, our lives take on new shapes and forms. We can live larger, take greater risks, expect bigger breakthroughs, endure more disappointment, and ultimately love more deeply. God enables in us a life that is far beyond the the one we alone could live.

~Prayer of Petition~

Evening

This is eternal life: to know you, the only true God, and Jesus Christ whom you sent. (John 17:3)

Reflection

The biggest star in the universe, currently known to scientists, is called UY Scuti. This extreme, red hypergiant is estimated to have a radius of 1,708 solar radii. In other words, it has nearly five billion times the volume of our sun. The sun is a mere speck in comparison.

What we think of as so absolute and knowable is actually a mere speck in comparison to the unknowability of God. Sometimes we come across people who stake a claim to ultimate truth, especially when it comes to the afterlife. There is an insistence that they know who will be in heaven and who will be in hell, who will be in and who will be out. In this assertion, they are declaring that God's love is knowable, confined, and conditional.

However, God's love is bigger than UY Scuti. It is bigger, wider, and deeper than we can ever fully comprehend.

The joy of Easter shows us the great lengths God will go to put this love on full display. We, like the disciples, may not recognize or believe it at first. But the risen Christ shows up to remind us that love knows no boundaries. May we allow our preconceived notions of who is in and who is out to dissolve in comparison.

~Prayer of Gratitude~

Grace

Morning Prayer of Petition

Gracious God, though you offer me endless grace, I find it hard to be patient with others. Shift my heart to a place of compassion so that I can better show grace to:

- those who have disappointed me,
- people who anger me,
- friends who have betrayed or neglected me,
- persons who see things very differently from me,
- those I'd prefer not to talk to or interact with.

May I mirror in my relationship with others the grace you give to me. Amen.

Evening Prayer of Gratitude

Good and gracious God, because I am challenged to show grace, I now remember those who have shown grace to me:

- pastors, spiritual mentors, and those who have shared your love with me,
- teachers who have shaped my understanding of the world,
- parents, friends, and family who have cared for me,
- co-workers, coaches, and colleagues who have invested in me.

Thank you for surrounding me with your grace through the people you place in my life. Amen.

Day 1

Morning

But I am loyal and gracious to the thousandth generation of those who love me and keep my commandments. (Exodus 20:6)

Reflection

Even when we forgive, we rarely forget the hurts others cause us. Once a person disappoints or betrays us, our views of that person are irrevocably altered. We see them differently. And even if we reconcile and continue in relationship, human nature is such that the specter of that past sin lingers. Against that backdrop it is remarkable to think that God does not hold our sin against us. God does not hold our unfaithfulness against us after the time of forgiveness. In fact, it is God's graciousness that is permanent. God's grace is what is remembered, what lingers, and what is passed down generationally. As we consider our lives, we often look back with regret on the moments that we didn't get it right, and often remember those moments with shame. We worry that we will be remembered by our worst moments because that is so often how we see others. But alongside our life's mistakes and sins is also a legacy of grace. What if instead of being remembered for our sins, we were remembered for the grace and transformation we receive? We all have a testimony about God's faithfulness to us, and God's ability to forgive and transform us. That is a legacy that is greater than our sin, and one that can be passed down from generation to generation.

~Prayer of Petition~

Evening

You are saved by God's grace because of your faith. This salvation is God's gift. It's not something you possessed. It's not something you did that you can be proud of. (Ephesians 2:8-9)

Reflection

At the heart of the Christian faith is the idea that God has saved us without us in any way deserving it. "This is not your own doing . . . so that no one may boast," the Apostle Paul bluntly tells us (Ephesians 2:9 NRSVUE). Christians are not supposed to be people who go around with their chests puffed out, striding about in self-assurance and self-satisfaction. We have not earned forgiveness for our mistakes by our wit or our charm. God has given it by grace. We have not, by our wisdom, brought healing to the places we have caused harm. God has done it by grace. We have not secured the promises of eternal life by our valor. God has given them by grace. We have not turned mourning into dancing by our strength or brought joy out of despair by our cleverness. God has done it by grace.

The only possible response to all of this is gratitude. A humble heart is one that is thankful. Give thanks for the big and small ways you have experienced the unmerited favor of God today. Remember that God loves you without end.

~Prayer of Gratitude~

Day 2

Morning

From his fullness we have all received grace upon grace. (John 1:16)

Reflection

We are used to a finite world where goods are in limited supply. We fill up our car with gas or charge it electrically but, over time, we use that power up. We buy food but eventually the food is consumed. We earn money but quickly (sometimes too quickly) it is gone. Nearly everything we have is in limited supply. Because of this, it is easy to see God's grace in the same way. We may have access to it, but we often mistakenly treat it like something we can use up. When we sin, we struggle to accept that God will treat us graciously and forgive. That doubt and struggle only gets exacerbated if we are stuck in a cycle of sin. God may shower grace on us once or twice but eventually that grace will run out. God will not continue to forgive over and over. At some point, will God's grace turn to God's judgment? But grace isn't like a consumable good in our kitchen pantry. God's grace isn't something that can be used up. This isn't meant to make you complacent with sin, but it does free us from the trap of shame and guilt. God's grace doesn't run out, and God does not grow weary when we reach out to God in repentance. With God, it is grace upon grace.

~Prayer of Petition~

Evening

God is the one who saved and called us with a holy calling. This wasn't based on what we have done, but it was based on his own purpose and grace that he gave us in Christ Jesus before time began. (2 Timothy 1:9)

Reflection

Can you feel the season turning
as an age of listening starts,
tuned to cries of deepest yearning,
changing minds and lives and hearts?
Sisters, brothers, bound together,
joining hands through time and space,
can you feel the season turning
toward the tender green of grace?
　　—Mary Louise Bringle

~Prayer of Gratitude~

Day 3

Morning

Let my request for grace come before you; deliver me according to your promise! (Psalm 119:170)

Reflection

When we have screwed up, it is easy to believe we don't deserve favor, goodness, or even a second chance. We regularly struggle with "forgiving ourselves" and shame can lead us to believe that we not only deserve but need punishment to make up for our mistakes. Sin can warp how we think of ourselves, and what we believe about ourselves. When we are struggling with our sin, we can get stuck in that brokenness, and it is easy to believe that God would never grant our prayers. For these reasons, the psalmist's prayer is surprising. Not only is the author reaching out to God, but the person is praying for grace. Grace is popularly defined as getting what you don't deserve. This person doesn't pray for mercy or a mere exemption from punishment. This person is bold enough to pray for God's favor and blessing. Where does this boldness come from? It does not come from the person's worthiness, but from God's promise. God desires a relationship with you despite your sin. God wants to grant you goodness and favor even though you don't deserve it. We should approach God with repentance, yes. But we also can be bold enough to approach God with a desire for good things in our lives as well. You don't deserve them, but God wants to give them nonetheless. That is what makes it grace.

~Prayer of Petition~

Evening

But the LORD was gracious to Israel and had compassion on them, turning back to them because of his covenant with Abraham, Isaac, and Jacob; he didn't want to destroy them or throw them out of his presence until now. (2 Kings 13:23)

Reflection

When we come to the table of Holy Communion, we sometimes pray a prayer that includes the line, "When we turned away and our love failed, your love remained steadfast." This is not just a statement about something that happened once, but instead it is a summary of God's relationship with us throughout time. God made a covenant, first with Abraham, then Isaac, then Jacob, then their descendants forever. Over and over again, the people failed to love God. In response, God forgave, reconciled, and renewed the covenant.

Then God sent Jesus and made a new covenant that included everyone who would believe. But the story has not changed. We turn away from the covenant and fail to love God first and fully. We give our hearts to other things. And God forgives. God reconciles with us. God renews the covenant. God does this knowing that eventually we will fail to stay faithful again, and that the forgiveness, reconciliation, and renewal will need to happen all over again. This is what it means to be loved with an unending love. This is what it means to be the recipient of grace.

~Prayer of Gratitude~

Day 4

Morning

All these things are for your benefit. As grace increases to benefit more and more people, it will cause gratitude to increase, which results in God's glory. (2 Corinthians 4:15)

Reflection

Grace is something all of us want to receive, but many of us are slow to offer others. We want people to see us in the best light and to give us the benefit of the doubt. We hope that people will forgive us when we mess up, or offer us a second chance when we fall short. But when others miss expectations and make mistakes, we often don't reflect that grace. We want accountability, we leave little room for error, and we sometimes assume the worst about the motives of others. The proper response to God's grace is gratitude. Grace ought to remind us that we have not always gotten it right. Grace reminds us that we often are treated better by God than we deserve. Grace reminds us that favor and blessing has been shown to us. Out of gratitude we are to reflect and practice that same grace toward others. What could this look like in your life. Maybe it means assuming the best about people who disappoint you. Perhaps it means giving people in your life a little more margin when they don't perfectly live up to your expectations. Maybe it means patience when dealing with someone who is missing the mark. And sometimes it might mean the generosity to give people a second chance. The proper response to God's grace in our own lives is gratitude to God, expressed through a willingness to offer grace to those around us.

~Prayer of Petition~

Evening

The result is that grace will rule through God's righteousness, leading to eternal life through Jesus Christ our Lord, just as sin ruled in death. (Romans 5:21)

Reflection

Christ the Lord is risen today, Alleluia!
Earth and heaven in chorus say, Alleluia!
Raise your joys and triumphs high, Alleluia!
Sing, ye heavens, and earth reply, Alleluia!

Love's redeeming work is done, Alleluia!
Fought the fight, the battle won, Alleluia!
Death in vain forbids him rise, Alleluia!
Christ has opened paradise, Alleluia!

Lives again our glorious King, Alleluia!
Where, O death, is now thy sting? Alleluia!
Once he died our souls to save, Alleluia!
Where's thy victory, boasting grave? Alleluia!
　　—Charles Wesley, "Christ the Lord Is Risen Today"

~Prayer of Gratitude~

Day 5

Morning

I am what I am by God's grace, and God's grace hasn't been for nothing. In fact, I have worked harder than all the others—that is, it wasn't me but the grace of God that is with me. (1 Corinthians 15:10)

Reflection

It is dangerous when we begin to think that the world (or our church) owes us something. As leaders, many of us work tirelessly for the sake of the organizations that we lead, or for institutions that we are a part of. And over time, we can slip into believing that all of our hard work ought to merit something special from God. We can begin to believe that we deserve special treatment. But that is not why we serve. Reward is not the reason we seek to mature in faith, overcome sin, transform our lives, or tirelessly work on behalf of God. Leaders have to be careful of believing that God owes them something. In truth, we are undeserving recipients of God's grace. The work we do and the growth we pursue is all a response of gratitude, and an acknowledgement that we do not want God's gift to be wasted on us. We are what God has made us, and our growth, service, and work grows out of what God first did for us. God doesn't owe us anything, but we owe God everything.

~Prayer of Petition~

Evening

Our Lord Jesus Christ himself and God our Father loved us and through grace gave us eternal comfort and a good hope. (2 Thessalonians 2:16)

Reflection

Come, thou Fount of every blessing, tune my heart to sing thy grace;
Streams of mercy, never ceasing, call for songs of loudest praise.
Teach me some melodious sonnet, sung by flaming tongues above.
Praise the mount! I'm fixed upon it, mount of thy redeeming love.
    —Robert Robinson, "Come, Thou Fount of Every Blessing"

~Prayer of Gratitude~

Repentance

Morning Prayer of Petition

God of forgiveness and second chances, I confess that I do not always love you or love others as you would have me. With humility, I confess:

- for words of mine that have hurt other people,
- for the selfishness and greed that I cling to,
- for relying more on material wealth than on you,
- for the times I have chosen cynicism or negativity over hope,
- for ways that I have failed to help those around me.

Forgive me and stir up in me a desire to serve you with a new spirit. Amen.

Evening Prayer of Gratitude

Ever-present God, you are always ready to receive me, giving me new perspective on my life. Turn me around so that today I can:

- see where you are working in my life,
- notice the ways you are offering me opportunities,
- receive the ways you are seeking to help and heal me,
- reconnect with people who love me.

As I turn toward you, I pray that you would receive me once again and fill me with your spirit. Amen.

Day 1

Morning

Zion will be redeemed by justice, and those who change their lives by righteousness. (Isaiah 1:27)

Reflection

Redemption is the fruit of repentance. Redemption means to purchase or buy back something or, as is often the case in ancient times, someone. Theologically, redemption is salvific, rescuing a person from the bondage of sin, and delivering them to a place of freedom. But redemption does not happen without an authentic change of heart and life; that is repentance. Too often we want our lives to look different or to head in a new direction, but we are unwilling to do the work of reorienting our hearts, habits, and behaviors. We might feel stuck but we can tend to dig ourselves deeper in a hole by an unwillingness to change comfortable or familiar behavior. Just like changed outputs don't come without changed inputs, we do not see new outcomes in our lives without new habits, disciplines, and behavior.

~Prayer of Petition~

Evening

In those days John the Baptist appeared in the desert of Judea announcing, "Change your hearts and lives! Here comes the kingdom of heaven!" (Matthew 3:1-2)

Reflection

For John Wesley, faithful Christian life and practice included a strong commitment to self-denial. In Sermon 122: "Causes of the Inefficacy of Christianity," he urges readers to hold tight to faithful Christian belief and practices. He claims that the people called Methodist achieve these and yet are still lacking in effectiveness, and then he asks, Why? Wesley answers his own question by explaining that doctrine and discipline can be undermined without self-denial. To love things of the world is to allow that desire to eclipse our love for God and neighbor. Desire for money and its accumulation is a dangerous sin since all wealth comes from God and is meant to be shared with God's children. An attitude of self-denial, alongside faithful beliefs and practices, is an essential characteristic of authentic, vital Christianity.

— *The Wesley Study Bible*

~Prayer of Gratitude~

Day 2

Morning

Healthy people don't need a doctor, but sick people do. I didn't come to call righteous people but sinners to change their hearts and lives. (Luke 5:31-32)

Reflection

As people, we often do the exact opposite of what is good for us. When we get stuck in a bad habit or,when we are acting in a way that we know is contrary to God's desire for us, we begin to isolate from other people. As we do, we get more and more caught up in a cycle of guilt and shame, broken commitments and repetitive behavior. This only leads us to further distance ourselves from people who care about us. You would think that when we are in trouble, we would reach out for help. But we don't. Church is often the last place those of us in trouble feel like we belong. But the only way out of this cycle is to do the opposite of what seems natural. It is precisely when you are stuck in sin, or caught in shame, that Jesus invites you to turn toward him. The only way out of sin, the cycle of shame, and the isolation it engenders is to turn around toward Christ, and toward those whom God has placed in your life. It is this turning that is the first step toward help, healing, and authentic transformation.

~Prayer of Petition~

Evening

After John was arrested, Jesus came into Galilee announcing God's good news, saying, "Now is the time! Here comes God's kingdom! Change your hearts and lives, and trust this good news!" (Mark 1:14-15)

Reflection

Whereas, the General Conference acknowledges and profoundly regrets the massive human suffering and the tragic plight of millions of men, women, and children caused by slavery and the transatlantic slave trade; and

Whereas, at the conclusion of the Civil War, the plan for the economic redistribution of land and resources on behalf of the former slaves of the Confederacy was never enacted; and

Whereas, the failure to distribute land prevented newly freed Blacks from achieving true autonomy and made their civil and political rights all but meaningless; and

Whereas, conditions comparable to "economic depression" continue for millions of African Americans in communities where unemployment often exceeds 50 percent; and

Whereas, justice requires that African American descendants of the transatlantic slave trade be assured of having access to effective and appropriate protection and remedies, including the right to seek just and adequate reparation or satisfaction for the legacy of damages, consequent structures of racism and racial discrimination suffered as a result of the slave trade; and

Whereas, Isaiah 61:1-3 provides a model for reparations . . .

—*2016 Book of Resolutions*

Consider Zacchaeus's act of repentance.

~Prayer of Gratitude~

Day 3

Morning

The Lord isn't slow to keep his promise, as some think of slowness, but he is patient toward you, not wanting anyone to perish but all to change their hearts and lives. (2 Peter 3:9)

Reflection

When many of us make a mistake, we want to move on quickly from it. We want to put distance between us and that thing we did that is uncharacteristic, embarrassing, or shameful. In a relationship, if someone wrongs the other and admits it, they hope for swift forgiveness and to put the issue to rest as soon as possible. We often think that when we decide to repent, we should get to move on, forgive and forget. But repentance and the turn toward a new direction doesn't often work quickly. We can think we have changed, without really changing. In our rush toward something new, if we aren't careful, we can end up right back where we started. True repentance and transformation is a process that takes time. Changing your life doesn't happen overnight. New direction is a choice one must make each morning and hold tightly to each evening. New life that comes from repentance only emerges over time, as we hold fast to the change. There are no short cuts or ways to fast forward through this. And often, trying to move quickly and forget the awful thing we've done short circuits the real work of turning around, facing our sin, finding forgiveness, and walking on a new path. God can forgive us in an instant. But the full transformation that God is working in your life takes time. God is patient with us. Will we be patient with God?

~Prayer of Petition~

Evening

Therefore, say to the house of Israel, The LORD God proclaims: Come back! Turn away from your idols and from all your detestable practices. Turn away! (Ezekiel 14:6)

Reflection

"I have eyes in the back of my head." Maybe you once believed this deception, wondering how your parents always seemed to know when you did something wrong behind their backs. Maybe you've even used this same tactic on your own children, trying to convince them of some mythical powers of omniscience. We often rely on convincing our children that we can look both ways at one time. Sometimes, we even convince ourselves we have such powers, or that at the very least we can live going two directions at the same time. Our scripture today says, "turn away all your faces." The word *repentance* means to turn. Repentance is not only saying, "I'm sorry," but also turning away from the behavior, person, place, or thing that has caused us to sin. Just as parents cannot see both ahead and behind simultaneously, we too cannot give our attention to things that both lead us apart from God and draw us near to God. We will have to pick one direction, turn our faces that way, and move toward that horizon. Today, reflect on the places in your life that you need to turn away from and ask God for a new direction toward which to turn.

~Prayer of Gratitude~

Day 4

Morning

Godly sadness produces a changed heart and life that leads to salvation and leaves no regrets, but sorrow under the influence of the world produces death. (2 Corinthians 7:10)

Reflection

As kids, we are often taught that guilt, that inner sense of regret over something we've done wrong, can be a good thing. Guilt can shine a light on things we've done wrong and lead us to repent and seek forgiveness. But, unfortunately, sometimes guilt establishes a foothold in your heart, and it isn't easily evicted. As we grow up, many of us are handed feelings of guilt by other people or continue to pile it on ourselves until it threatens to crush us. Over time, this guilt creates shame. What is the difference? Guilt can allow us to see that we are people who do bad things. Shame often tells us that we are bad people, incapable of forgiveness, redemption, and new life. One can point us in the direction of repentance; the other can threaten to chain us up and hold us back. Shame whispers lies about who we are and blinds us from what is possible. Shame seeks to keep us from discovering the truth—that nothing we do will separate us from the love of God. You are never beyond redemption and it is never too late for repentance. Guilt is not some price you have to pay or punishment you must endure for sin. Instead, its presence is a sign that it is time to turn toward God and the salvation God offers to all people, including you.

~Prayer of Petition~

Evening

Or do you have contempt for the riches of God's generosity, tolerance, and patience? Don't you realize that God's kindness is supposed to lead you to change your heart and life? (Romans 2:4)

Reflection

Among the many forces that shape our lives, surely one of the most powerful is the "mom guilt trips." Shame and guilt are powerful weapons a mother can wield to make you show up for family events or even church on Sunday mornings after a late night. Although mom guilt may get you to church, it does not produce the deep love that leads you to say "I'm sorry" when you have done something wrong. Deep regret is often precipitated by deep love. The same is true in our relationship with God. God does not motivate us with fear, anger, shame, or guilt. Instead, God acts on us with kindness, forbearance, and patience. God loves us, and God's kindness and patience can incite in us a love for God in return. Our response to God's deep love brings repentance as we realize that we have separated ourselves from God whom we love. Wesley called this, "convincing" grace. God's profound love draws us to God and "convinces" us to change our lives as a response to God's grace. Today, reflect upon what parts of your life need to be different to join God in a greater way in God's love story for the world.

~Prayer of Gratitude~

Day 5

Morning

Peter replied, "Change your hearts and lives. Each of you must be baptized in the name of Jesus Christ for the forgiveness of your sins. Then you will receive the gift of the Holy Spirit." (Acts 2:38)

Reflection

When someone confronts you over something you've done wrong, how do you react? For most of us, not well. We usually make excuses, deflect blame, get defensive, or turn it around by blaming the one who confronts us. Facing one's own sin and shortcomings isn't fun. That is why we human beings have gotten so good at creative justifications and self-rationalizations. But this is a foolish way to live. Ignoring our mistakes doesn't make them go away. Instead, it robs us of an opportunity to change. Digging in your heels when you've hurt someone doesn't help you; instead it often allows a small incident to lead to a broken relationship. Using justifications and excuses only blinds us from seeing our lives in a new way and keeps us from growing. Wise people choose the path of repentance, which begins with a sober acknowledgement that we are not perfect and accepting responsibility for our own actions. Choosing this path may be hard, but it leads to forgiveness, growth, maturity, change, and ultimately to the gift of living in a new way.

~Prayer of Petition~

Evening

Produce fruit that shows you have changed your hearts and lives. (Matthew 3:8)

Reflection

This is thy will, I know,
That I should holy be,

Easter

Should let my sin this moment go,
This moment turn to thee:

O might I now embrace
Thy all-sufficient power;
And never more to sin give place,
And never grieve thee more!
        —Charles Wesley, "O That I Could Repent!"

~Prayer of Gratitude~

Mercy

Morning Prayer of Petition

Holy God, your mercies are new every morning. Allow me to receive and live in your mercy. Today, give me permission to claim:

- joy instead of shame or guilt,
- freedom instead of a sense of obligation,
- rest instead of frantic production,
- courage instead of debilitating fear,
- generosity instead of a mindset of scarcity.

May your mercy transform my heart that I may live more fully for you. Amen.

Evening Prayer of Gratitude

Ever-loving God, after a day of distractions and preoccupations, quiet the noise around me so that I can:

- appreciate the small moments when I felt your presence,
- name the people who bring me joy,
- notice the tasks that bring me life,
- receive the gifts that you are trying to offer me,
- see the ways my struggles are teaching me.

God, continue to work in my life, that I may love you with all my heart, mind, soul, and strength. Amen.

Day 1

Morning

Have mercy on me, God, according to your faithful love!
Wipe away my wrongdoings according to your great compassion! (Psalm 51:1)

Reflection

Hebrew has several words that are translated as mercy. One of the most frequent is *hesed*, which means steadfastness, faithfulness, and even loyalty. It is a relational word, meaning that mercy is an attribute of one person toward another. In the case of the Old Testament, relationships were often accompanied by covenants, by which certain people made promises to each other. If one person broke those promises, the covenant could rightly be dissolved and the relationship ended. This was true in friendships, marriages, and business arrangements. In this context, mercy is when one party who had the right to walk away from a relationship, doesn't. Instead, they choose to stay, to be faithful to the relationship even when they would be justified in breaking that relationship. Scripture tells us that God is merciful, full of *hesed*. Even when we drift, rebel, neglect, or break the promises we make to God, scripture tells us that God doesn't break the relationship. God doesn't leave; God doesn't throw in the towel; God stays loyal.

~Prayer of Petition~

Evening

But when the Pharisees saw this, they said to his disciples, "Why does your teacher eat with tax collectors and sinners?" (Matthew 9:11)

Reflection

How high are the standards you set for the people around you? Are your standards attainable, or rarely met? What about the standards you keep for yourself? Do you reach them, or regularly fall short? While we may be prone to believe we have to pull ourselves together before being worthy of spending time in Jesus's presence, the standards for who Jesus chooses to spend time with are quite low. Rather than Jesus dining with religious authorities, his preferred table was the one occupied by tax collectors and sinners. The seating arrangement was mindboggling to those who preferred certain requirements for access to Jesus. "Why does your teacher eat with tax collectors and sinners?" the Pharisees wanted to know (Matthew 9:11). How often do we do the same, actively forgetting how Jesus longs for his friends to embody steadfast love toward all—regardless of who they are, where they have been, or what they have done? What might happen if we simply focused on embodying mercy, the steadfast love we believe Jesus has for us, toward every person we encounter?

~Prayer of Gratitude~

Day 2

Morning

He says to Moses, I'll have mercy on whomever I choose to have mercy, and I'll show compassion to whomever I choose to show compassion. (Romans 9:15)

Reflection

Do you remember growing up and seeing people receive special treatment that they didn't deserve? Maybe it was a classmate who always seemed to be treated well by the teacher, or a co-worker who inexplicably seemed to get promoted. It is frustrating to see others receive benefits that they don't deserve, and it can lead to a kind of resentment toward the people around us. When it comes to faith, there are some of us who have worked hard to live in the way that God calls us to live. We go to church, read scripture, take our faith seriously, and try to treat others well. We volunteer, we pray, and we are generous with our money. Secretly, many of us think that such hard work ought to earn us a little extra credit with God. We can get resentful when we see others who so freely ignore God receive apparent blessings while we are struggling. While it is easy to get to a place of moral or religious superiority, be careful. It is dangerous when we begin to believe that God owes us something. God doesn't. We don't earn God's favor or mercy. Instead, it is given freely, surprisingly, and, at times, offensively. Take care not to grow deserving of God's blessing but, instead, celebrate God's gift of mercy, not just in your own life, but in the lives of those around you.

~Prayer of Petition~

Evening

Turn to me, God, and have mercy on me
because I'm alone and suffering. (Psalm 25:16)

Reflection

The greatest disease in the West today is not TB or leprosy; it is being unwanted, unloved, and uncared for. We can cure physical diseases with medicine, but the only cure for loneliness, despair, and hopelessness is love. There are many in the world who are dying for a piece of bread but there are many more dying for a little love. The poverty in the West is a different kind of poverty—it is not only a poverty of loneliness but also of spirituality. There's a hunger for love, as there is a hunger for God.

—Mother Theresa, *A Simple Path*

~Prayer of Gratitude~

Day 3

Morning

Let the wicked abandon their ways
and the sinful their schemes.
Let them return to the LORD so that he may have mercy on them,
to our God, because he is generous with forgiveness. (Isaiah 55:7)

Reflection

Since mercy plays out in a relationship it requires something from both parties. Before one person can show mercy, the other person must seek it. This usually means admitting wrongdoing, turning around, and asking for forgiveness. If you have someone in your life who continually hurts you or who takes advantage of your mercy, you would most likely end that relationship. God's mercy is real, lasting, and generous. But God's mercy isn't license to ignore God's instructions and wisdom. We shouldn't see mercy as an excuse to do what we want, content to know that, in the end, God will forgive. Mercy isn't blanket immunity to the consequences of wrongdoing, and mercy doesn't exempt us from the real harm that our sins can cause. Therefore, we shouldn't take advantage of God's mercy or take it for granted. Instead, mercy is something we must seek. This seeking requires something from us—a change in our hearts, a desire to return to God, and ultimately a commitment to live in a new way.

~Prayer of Petition~

Evening

However, God is rich in mercy. He brought us to life with Christ while we were dead as a result of those things that we did wrong. He did this because of the great love that he has for us. You are saved by God's grace! (Ephesians 2:4-5)

Reflection

To whom should thy disciples go,
Of whom should they be taught, but thee?
Thy Spirit must thy meaning show;
O might he show it now to me!
Blessings thou dost to sinners give,
Not sacrifice from us receive:
Thy grace to all doth freely move,
Thy favourite attribute is love.
    —Charles Wesley, "To Whom Should Thy Disciples Go"

~Prayer of Gratitude~

Day 4

Morning

God is famous for his wondrous works.
    The LORD is full of mercy and compassion. (Psalm 111:4)

Reflection

Studies show that when asked what they want to be when they grow up, increasingly young people are saying, "famous." There is a rise of people who are famous not because of some accomplishment. They are famous simply for being famous! With the rise of technology and social media, which allows anyone anywhere to begin posting online and amassing followers, being famous has become an end in and of itself. If pressed, many of us would say we want to be known for our work or our accolades. Maybe some of us aspire to be known for our wealth or possessions. Others of us want to have perfect families with high-achieving kids. But what if we strive to be known simply for the way we treated others? What if we work for a legacy defined by compassion, faithfulness, and kindness? Scripture warns us that treasure rusts, material possessions decay, accolades are forgotten, and kids go their own way. Sometimes the greatest difference we can make, and the most lasting impression we will leave, is how we treat others. Let our achievements and accomplishments be in the way that we love others.

~Prayer of Petition~

Evening

Happy are people who show mercy, because they will receive mercy. (Matthew 5:7)

Reflection

A small group was sharing in conversation following a lively discussion on how to embody justice and live fearlessly. "How might we teach our children how to courageously take a stand?" the pastor asked. One person quickly responded by naming how we have to start with small opportunities to make a difference. She then described a playground with what is known as "The Friendship Bench." When children are on recess and need someone to play with, they are instructed to go and sit on The Friendship Bench. Every child knows they are to look for classmates sitting on this bench and invite them to play. "Sometimes you are the person on the bench who is in need of a friend. Other times you are the one who goes to the bench to expand your community," she said. Mercy and kindness are seemingly multiplied when shared, creating an ongoing cycle of goodness. How, then, do we create communities where people of all ages are able to say, "I have a need," believing there will be someone in that community who responds, "I know your need, and I can help meet it"?

~Prayer of Gratitude~

Day 5

Morning

Once you weren't a people, but now you are God's people. Once you hadn't received mercy, but now you have received mercy. (1 Peter 2:10)

Reflection

Can you remember a time in your life when someone showed you mercy? Perhaps it was a friend who freely forgave you even when you let them down? Or an employer who had reason to lose faith in you but instead gave you a second chance? Maybe it was a family member who had every right to be mad at you but instead embraced you? What was the experience of receiving mercy like? How did it change you? Has the experience of needing mercy helped you to see others differently? Having been offered mercy yourself, do you find yourself more able to extend that mercy to someone else? As people who have received God's mercy, we are also called to reflect it. If we allow it, mercy can soften our hearts, open our eyes, and expand our perspectives. Mercy can allow us to see others more graciously, to extend the benefit of the doubt, or to give some space for others in our lives to be imperfect. Do not just receive God's mercy, but seek to reflect it to those around you.

~Prayer of Petition~

Evening

Lord, *listen to my voice when I cry out—*
have mercy on me and answer me! (Psalm 27:7)

Reflection

Have I been zealous to do, and active in doing, good? That is, have I embraced every probable opportunity of doing good, and preventing, removing, or lessening evil? Have I pursued it with my might? Have I thought anything too dear to part with, to serve my neighbor?
—John Wesley, *From John and Charles Wesley*

~Prayer of Gratitude~

Promise

Morning Prayer of Petition

Faithful God, you promise to hear us when we pray to you. With confidence and boldness, I offer up to you:

- places in my life where I need your guidance and direction,
- people in my life who need your healing,
- situations in my community that need transformation,
- leaders in my world who need courage and wisdom.

May your kingdom in heaven be made real on earth. Amen.

Evening Prayer of Gratitude

God of restoration and life, you are ever faithful to your promise to love me and watch over me. May your promises give me greater ability to:

- set aside my stress from today,
- give thanks for the joy of today,
- receive freely the gifts of today,
- deal wisely with problems from today,
- rest fully from the burdens of today.

As I sleep, may your Spirit renew and restore my soul. Amen.

Day 1

Morning

The LORD said to Abram, "Leave your land, your family, and your father's household for the land that I will show you. I will make of you a great nation and will bless you. I will make your name respected, and you will be a blessing." (Genesis 12:1-2)

Reflection

Many of us are rightfully skeptical of the promises people make. We usually want some assurance that a person is going to produce what they promise before we act or take a risk. We don't usually step out on a promise alone. We usually don't quit a job unless we know we have another lined up. We are often scared to end one relationship because we aren't sure there will be another person out there for us. Many of us have trouble making a risky move unless we have some reasonable assurance that it will

153

work out. We like certainty in our lives. But often God doesn't work that way. God promises Abram a blessing, but doesn't say exactly what that blessing will look like or when it will happen. Instead, God asks Abram to leave home, to start traveling, to "the land that I will show you." God was asking Abram to leave home without even knowing where he was going. He had to take a risk without any certainty it would work out. God's promises required Abram to trust God, with no assurances of how it would work out. This is often the way God works in our lives. God promises us blessing, but God doesn't usually show us what those blessings look like ahead of time. God promises us provision, but we don't often get to see those provisions unless we first step out. God promises us direction, but we often have to begin a journey without exactly knowing the destination. There is a reason for this. The promises of God are rock solid, but they require trust. You can't wait around for God to show you everything you need before you make a move. Instead, God calls us to follow before we fully see where following will lead.

~Prayer of Petition~

Evening

We know that if the tent that we live in on earth is torn down, we have a building from God. It's a house that isn't handmade, which is eternal and located in heaven. (2 Corinthians 5:1)

Reflection

We humans build to frame a life
with meaning, love, and feeling,
but time or hate can bring collapse
and loss can leave us reeling.
Let faithful souls from rubble rise
to find new ways from sorrow,
and slowly, slowly form a shape
to welcome God's tomorrow.
For ev'rything our hands construct
will one day fall and crumble.
The God who is a carpenter
creates from scrap and jumble.
And we can join the work of God
to raise a new creation,
that what we do will long endure
upon a firm foundation.
We dedicate ourselves today
amid life's change and danger
to build with God a house of peace

for friend and foe and stranger.
Here may the peoples come and go,
delight in shared endeavor,
set free from terror, hate and war,
alive in God forever.
 —Ruth Duck

~Prayer of Gratitude~

Day 2

Morning

Not one of all the good things that the LORD *had promised to the house of Israel failed. Every promise was fulfilled.* (Joshua 21:45)

Reflection

A promise is only as good as the one who makes it. If a person makes a promise to you, usually you judge that promise based on their past behavior. You think back, and if the person has tended to come through for you, then you are more likely to believe them. If they tend to flake out on you, then you are rightfully skeptical. When life gets difficult it is hard to always believe in the promises of God. When we experience pain it is hard to believe that God is working for our joy. Or when we experience hardship, it is hard to believe God is working for our prosperity. When we feel like the universe is against us, it is hard to believe that God is for us. In these times, it is important to remember. We often see God's faithfulness in retrospect. As we look back on difficult seasons of life, we see the way that God was working for us and watching over us. In looking back, we are able to see what we could not see in the moment. Remembering the ways that God acted for us in the past gives us greater assurance that God can and will fulfill God's promises for the future.

~Prayer of Petition~

Evening

He didn't hesitate with a lack of faith in God's promise, but he grew strong in faith and gave glory to God. (Romans 4:20)

Reflection

What really is the strength of a promise if not the strength of the relationship between the giver and receiver? That distance between the two is spanned by an intricate web of vulnerability and trust—the necessary infrastructure of any promise spoken or expected. A promise is an act of self-giving sacrifice that ultimately leaves the giver vulnerable. For the receiver, a promise is a dare to reject other potential sources of provision in order to trust the giver, this is itself an act of vulnerability. The stronger the promise, the stronger the vulnerability. And so, Abraham believed and Sarah laughed and Hagar persisted—entrusting themselves to a promise made strong through vulnerability. Lord, teach us the strength of your promise!

~Prayer of Gratitude~

Day 3

Morning

Now if you belong to Christ, then indeed you are Abraham's descendants, heirs according to the promise. (Galatians 3:29)

Reflection

In the Old Testament, promise and blessing are often understood as inherited, something that could be passed down from parent to child. Because of this, a promise or a blessing could also be withheld from a family member. While certain people received favor, many more were left on the outside looking in when it came to the promises of God. There was a select group of insiders, and a whole lot of outsiders. It is similar today. Even in the church, there are varying understandings of who is deserving of God's promise and blessing, and who is not. We still draw lines that include a select few and leave many others out. But Christ obliterates these dividing walls and gerrymandered boundaries. If you belong to Christ, then you are part of the family. If you draw close to Christ, then he overrules any earthly declaration of your status. You are in. You are an heir. This was radical to those who first heard it because it meant that no earthly group or institution could decide your destiny. No humanmade label can determine your inclusion. Christ decides who is in the family. The promises are Christ's alone to give. In Christ, there is no longer Jew or Greek, male or female, slave or free. We are all in, and therefore the promise is yours.

~Prayer of Petition~

Evening

Because God remembered his holy promise to Abraham his servant,
   God brought his people out with rejoicing,
   his chosen ones with songs of joy. (Psalm 105:42-43)

Reflection

And these words: *You will not be overcome*, were said very insistently and strongly, for certainty and strength against every tribulation which may come. [God] did not say: You will not be assailed, you will not be belaboured, you will not be disquieted, but [God] said: You will not be overcome. God wants us to pay attention to his words, and always to be strong in our certainty, in well-being and in woe, for [God] loves us and delights in us.

—Julian of Norwich, *Showings*

~Prayer of Gratitude~

Day 4

Morning

From Paul, an apostle of Christ Jesus by God's will, to promote the promise of life that is in Christ Jesus. (2 Timothy 1:1)

Reflection

Unfortunately there are many people who grow up in the church believing that Jesus is a divine judge and accountant. He sees everything you do wrong and keeps a detailed ledger of where you stand. Too many people grow up in a church that seems obsessed with telling you what you can't do, who you can't hang around, who doesn't belong, what you can't believe, and what is wrong to stand for. Many people develop an understanding of faith that is narrow and restrictive, a faith that is more interested in holding you down than setting you free, more interested in keeping you in line than in erasing the lines, and more interested in limiting your life rather than expanding it. But this isn't the Jesus of scripture. Jesus is one who wants to expand our understanding, not limit it. Jesus wants to bless our lives, not condemn them. Jesus doesn't want to hold us back but, rather, wants to do more in and through us than we could ask for or imagine. Life with Jesus is more, not less. It is better, not worse. It is freeing, not restrictive. The promise of Jesus is life, and life more abundant than anything we could create on our own.

~Prayer of Petition~

Evening

When you make a promise to the Lord your God, don't put off making good on it, because the Lord your God will certainly be expecting it from you; delaying would make you guilty. (Deuteronomy 23:21)

Reflection

Done made my vow to the Lord and I never will turn back.
I will go, I shall go to see what the end will be.
Done opened my mouth to the Lord and I never will turn back.
I will go, I shall go to see what the end will be. (Traditional Spiritual)

Every worthwhile adventure is made so not by the magnificence of its destination but by the wonder and effort it takes to get there. What if we considered the promises of

God as an invitation to adventure? What if we understood God's promises as a dare to wonder and actively risk the possibility that things will actually be OK, that peace can be attainable, that joy is renewable, that love can be unconditional, that ashes can manifest hope? What if we stop trying to be unafraid and just go, certain only that the journey of faith itself will be worth it?

~Prayer of Gratitude~

Day 5

Morning

God's Son, Jesus Christ, is the one who was preached among you by us—through me, Silvanus, and Timothy—he wasn't yes and no. In him it is always yes. (2 Corinthians 1:19)

Reflection

God makes promises to us, but God rarely tells us how, or when, or in what way those promises will be fulfilled. Therefore, we often mistakenly hear a "No" where God intends a "Not yet." Maybe you are looking for a relationship and no one you meet seems to be working out. Maybe you are dissatisfied with your job and are praying earnestly for something new to emerge, only to find yourself stuck. Maybe you are in a wilderness period searching desperately for greater clarity, only to find your future muddled and opaque. Maybe you are tirelessly working for change, only to see all that work making a minimal difference. In the midst of these moments, it can feel like God is far away. If God is hearing our prayers, then the answer seems to be a resounding "No." But remember, often God is working precisely when we cannot see or detect it. While we feel like we are circling the wilderness, God is hard at work preparing a future promise. While we wander in circles, God is forging and strengthening us for something new. God is not slow. God does not delay unnecessarily. God's promises are certain; God's timing is not. Don't mistakenly think the answer to your prayer is a "No," when it may be a "Not yet."

~Prayer of Petition~

Evening

My whole being yearns for your saving help!
    I wait for your promise. (Psalm 119:81)

Reflection

In the bulb, there is a flower
In the seed, an apple tree
In cocoons, a hidden promise
Butterflies will soon be free

In the cold and snow of winter
There's a spring that waits to be
Unrevealed until its season
Something God alone can see

There's a song in every silence
Seeking word and melody
There's a dawn in every darkness
Bringing hope to you and me
From the past will come the future
What it holds, a mystery
Unrevealed until its season
Something God alone can see

In our end is our beginning
In our time, infinity
In our doubt, there is believing
In our life, eternity
In our death, a resurrection
At the last, a victory
Unrevealed until its season
Something God alone can see
        —Natalie Sleeth, "Hymn of Promise"

~Prayer of Gratitude~

WEEK 27

Holy

Morning Prayer of Petition

Holy God, it is for freedom that you have set me free. Loosen my grip on:

- habits that lead me away from you,
- words that diminish other people,
- busyness that neglects your daily presence,
- selfishness that prevents generosity,
- behaviors that hurt others and myself.

Forgive me today and help me to live in your holiness. Amen.

Evening Prayer of Gratitude

Holy God, though high above all things, you enter into my life to save me and restore me to your goodness. Open my eyes to see:

- how you are guiding me,
- how you are speaking to me through others,
- how you are empowering me to leave behind old behaviors,
- how you are directing me to new things.

When I fail, I pray that you would pick me up and help me to walk in the way that leads to life. Amen.

Day 1

Morning

From now on, brothers and sisters, if anything is excellent and if anything is admirable, focus your thoughts on these things: all that is true, all that is holy, all that is just, all that is pure, all that is lovely, and all that is worthy of praise. (Philippians 4:8)

Reflection

What you focus on often becomes your reality. Where you focus your thoughts and energy shapes what you look for, what you see, what you choose to engage, what you experience in the world. If you want to change your life, change what you choose to think about, pay attention to, and dwell on. Many of us unintentionally allow our thoughts to be commandeered by technology, entertainment, tempting profanity, fear, or negativity. It is easy to slip into a habit of allowing unhelpful or destructive voices in. We give away the real estate in our heads and hearts to ideas, people, or agendas that are not of God. But we can change that and become more intentional about what we focus on. Our lives can look remarkably different when we focus on hope instead of cynicism, the beauty of the world instead of its ugliness, the things that are going right instead of all that is going wrong. Our lives are shaped in dramatically better ways when we allow in the truth instead of falsehood and what is worthy instead of what is worthless. Holiness is shaped not simply by what we do and how we behave. But holiness begins with what we focus on, what we listen to, and what we allow to dwell in our heads and hearts.

~Prayer of Petition~

Evening

You are the holy one, enthroned.
You are Israel's praise. (Psalm 22:3)

Reflection

Holiness is a state of soul in which all the powers of the body and mind are consciously given up to God; and the witness of holiness is that testimony which the Holy Spirit bears with our spirit that the offering is accepted through Christ. The work is accomplished the moment we lay our all upon the altar. . . .

Will you come, dear disciple of Jesus, and venture even now to lay your all upon this blessed altar? He will not spurn you away. No; "His side an open fountain is," "His nature and His name is love."

—Phoebe Palmer, in Amy Oden, editor, *In Her Words*

~Prayer of Gratitude~

Day 2

Morning

Don't give holy things to dogs, and don't throw your pearls in front of pigs. They will stomp on the pearls, then turn around and attack you. (Matthew 7:6)

Reflection

Have you ever received an heirloom that has been in your family a long time? The more valuable and irreplaceable the item, the more we tend to take care of it, protect it, and look after it. We wouldn't take a meaningful piece of furniture or a rare painting and just leave it to any person to handle. We wouldn't leave something highly important just laying around unprotected. Jesus likens the gospel, our faith, and the relationship we have with God because of it to a highly sought-after pearl or a valuable coin. It is worth protecting, caring for, and nurturing. For those of us who have been a Christian for a long time, it is easy to drift from our faith. We can set it aside for long periods, neglect it, and stop tending to it. We might assume it will always be there, but when we need it most, sometimes it is hard to find, or it needs to be cleaned up, dusted off, and revived. Once you receive it, don't leave the gift of the good news of Jesus just lying around. Don't cast it aside, neglect it, or stop nurturing it. Take care that all of your meaningful experiences of Jesus are not in the past tense. Rather, stay engaged in that relationship, keep active in wrestling with your faith, let Jesus continue to challenge you, try new ways to serve, and follow the small nudges that God gives you each day. This faith is valuable. Don't let it gather dust.

~Prayer of Petition~

Evening

Let my whole being bless the LORD!
Let everything inside me bless his holy name! (Psalm 103:1)

Reflection

Praise! The psalmist commands: with everything that we are, bless the Lord. Praise the Lord. Have you ever felt down, overwhelmed, or anxious? Are things moving too quickly, or are they too busy? Have you ever just felt stuck? What is the way out? Praise! Blessing the Lord will refocus our attention on the God who creates, the God who saves, and the God who sustains. When we bless God with our whole being, praise will remind us of the holy nature of God. Blessing God reminds us that nothing is out of God's purview or reach. Blessing God reminds us all that God has acted on our behalf before and will act on our behalf again. Breakthrough. Break out. Pause. Focus on our holy God. And bless the Lord—with everything that you are and deep down into your soul. Praise!

~Prayer of Gratitude~

Day 3

Morning

I made myself holy on their behalf so that they also would be made holy in the truth. (John 17:19)

Reflection

As the Last Supper was ending, Jesus prayed for his disciples. He was concerned that without him the world would swallow them up. Jesus knew the world was hostile to his message and would be hostile to the ones who followed him. Over time, much has been made about the danger of "the world" or the culture around us. Of course, the nature of this danger shifts over time. Not many of us who are reading this are in danger of dying for our faith. But we do live in a culture where our faith can easily become compromised, weakened, and eventually dissipate into a lifestyle and worldview that is no longer distinct. This isn't to say that everything about culture is bad, rather that many Christians don't look much different than the crowd surrounding them. But Jesus wants us to be different. We are called to be set apart. We should, at times, look as strange to the values of the world as Jesus did during his own time. In a world soaked in materialism, we are to live simply. In a world of violence, we witness to peace. In a world where gossip is sport, we refrain from words that hurt. In a world of self-centeredness, we are called to put others ahead of ourselves. It is hard. It doesn't always come easy. It leaves us exposed at times. But we are called to follow Jesus and to be set apart, just as he was.

~Prayer of Petition~

Evening

While physical training has some value, training in holy living is useful for everything. It has promise for this life now and the life to come. (1 Timothy 4:8)

Reflection

The fifty-day Easter feast reminds the people of God that God is holy and that we are called to be holy. The nature of God is holy—pure, blameless, perfect, and worthy of worship and praise because of the perfect nature of God. The resurrection and its aftermath call us into an even higher awareness of the holiness of God and challenge the people of God to choose holiness for themselves. As humans, we are confronted with the choice to be and act as holy beings every moment of our lives. Do our words and our actions prove that we are set apart, sacred, consecrated, and devoted to God? Do our choices, spending habits, and where we spend time point to our lives as an offering to our holy God? God does not call us to perfection. God calls us to journey toward holiness. How can we live, act, and love more like Jesus? How can you live, act, and love more like Jesus?

~Prayer of Gratitude~

Day 4

Morning

The angel replied, "The Holy Spirit will come over you and the power of the Most High will overshadow you. Therefore, the one who is to be born will be holy. He will be called God's Son." (Luke 1:35)

Reflection

Holy means to be set apart for a special purpose. From his birth, the scriptures declare that Jesus was holy. The church has long declared that Jesus is fully divine and fully human. Throughout the generations, Christians have usually had an easier time holding on to one of these characteristics but struggled with the other. Some find it easy to declare Jesus's divinity, but struggle with the idea that he is a human like us. Some find it much easier to believe in Jesus's humanity but scratch their heads at how he could be divine. But Jesus is both and, as such, is set apart from birth to accomplish something that we cannot. Do you ever struggle with the idea that Jesus is divine? Maybe it is easy to imagine Jesus as a teacher and a man who lived his values and principles perfectly. Maybe it is easy to picture faith as seeking to live in the way of Jesus and witness to the teachings of Jesus. But part of our faith should struggle with this truth—that Jesus is also set apart for a work that only he can do. Our call is not only to follow Jesus or spread his same message, but also to worship him. Jesus is set apart for a special purpose, and accomplishes something in his life, death, and resurrection that only he could accomplish. This holy work is a gift to us. We cannot mimic it or follow it, we can only receive it and seek to live in gratitude for it.

~Prayer of Petition~

Evening

But if part of a batch of dough is offered to God as holy, the whole batch of dough is holy too. If a root is holy, the branches will be holy too. (Romans 11:16)

Reflection

O consuming fire, Spirit of love, "come upon me," and create in my soul a kind of incarnation of the Word: that I may be another humanity for him in which he can renew his whole mystery. And you, O Father, bend lovingly over your poor little creature; "cover her with your shadow," seeing in her only the "beloved in whom you are well pleased."
— Elizabeth of the Trinity

~Prayer of Gratitude~

Day 5

Morning

It is because of God that you are in Christ Jesus. He became wisdom from God for us. This means that he made us righteous and holy, and he delivered us. (1 Corinthians 1:30)

Reflection

What makes someone or something holy? When we practice communion, ordinary bread and wine become the body and blood of Christ. When we participate in a baptism, ordinary water becomes a means of God's grace. We call these sacraments "holy mysteries" where ordinary things are set apart and infused with God's presence and grace. What makes them holy? It is nothing intrinsic to the elements. It isn't the special character of the pastor or priest. It isn't a set of magic words. It is the Holy Spirit that sets apart and infuses holiness. It is the Spirit of God that transforms ordinary things. The same is true for people. Holiness is not a quality of one's character, and it isn't achieved or maintained based on good behavior or perfect piety. Holiness is not moral perfectionism, never screwing up and never sinning. Rather, holiness is a gift that is given when the Holy Spirit comes upon us. We are set apart not by our works but by the gift that God gives us in the spirit that dwells in us. This doesn't mean we don't strive to live a life worthy of that gift. We should and we do. But this work is a response to the gift, our offering back to God out of gratitude for calling us out and setting us apart for something special.

~Prayer of Petition~

Evening

Magnify the LORD, our God!
Bow low at his footstool!
He is holy! (Psalm 99:5)

Reflection

Holy, holy, holy! Lord God Almighty!
Early in the morning our song shall rise to thee.
Holy, holy, holy! Merciful and mighty,
God in three persons, blessed Trinity!

Holy, holy, holy! All the saints adore thee,
Casting down their golden crowns around the glassy sea;
Cherubim and seraphim falling down before thee,
Which wert, and art, and evermore shall be.
        —Reginald Heber, "Holy, Holy, Holy"

~Prayer of Gratitude~

Pentecost

Faith

Morning Prayer of Petition

God, you are more ready to give than we are to receive. Help me have the faith that you can:

- move in situations that seem to be stuck,
- provide clarity where the future is uncertain,
- heal where there is hurt and pain,
- reconcile relationships that are broken,
- bring justice where inequity exists.

May I live with the faith that you can and will move in my life and the world today. Amen.

Evening Prayer of Gratitude

Steadfast God, calm my spirit when I become anxious about what might happen in the future, and give me eyes to see what you are doing right now in my life. I thank you for:

- family and others who love me unconditionally,
- meaningful opportunities to use my gifts and skills,
- material resources that provide for me,
- new opportunities on the other side of disappointments,
- simple gifts that I take for granted.

May the reminder and recognition of the way you are faithful strengthen my own faith in you. Amen.

Day 1

Morning

At that the boy's father cried out, "I have faith; help my lack of faith!" (Mark 9:24)

Reflection

Faith is not a light switch that is either on or off. We are not people who either have faith or don't have faith. It is not a binary in that way. It is often thought that the opposite of faith is doubt. But that doesn't seem to square with the Gospels. The scriptures are full of stories of people who are grappling with who Jesus is, following him with a mixture of wonder, amazement, hope, trust, insecurity, fear, and doubt. The presence of one of these doesn't negate the possibility of others. In fact, some see certainty as the opposite of faith. When we are certain, all mystery is gone, all wonder ceases, and all exploring is over. Certainty is static. But faith is dynamic. Faith is full of mystery and wonder, and faith is a journey that we are constantly on but never complete this side of heaven. If you have doubts about what you believe, then you are on the road to a stronger faith. Confess your doubts to Christ and bring your uncertainty to God. Lean in and not away, and these very doubts can become the seeds of a stronger and more mature faith.

~Prayer of Petition~

Evening

The apostles said to the Lord, "Increase our faith!" (Luke 17:5)

Reflection

Faith then means confident trust, courageous adventure, and an inflowing of God-given power. . . . It is faith that enables us to have eyes to see and ears to hear. It is faith as "insight" that quickens the mind to truer "sight." . . . Faith is the union of trusting confidence and courageous action with response to God's leading, and of all these with the insight that lights the way toward truth. It is this combination that makes Christian faith such a powerful force.

— Georgia Harkness, *Understanding the Christian Faith*

~Prayer of Gratitude~

Day 2

Morning

People brought to him a man who was paralyzed, lying on a cot. When Jesus saw their faith, he said to the man who was paralyzed, "Be encouraged, my child, your sins are forgiven." (Matthew 9:2)

Reflection

There is a debate among scholars about whether we are saved by our faith in Christ, or the faith of Christ. One interpretation focuses primarily on us. It is our faith in Christ that saves. The other interpretation focuses more on Christ, and the faith he demonstrated on the cross. One highlights our role in faith; the other highlights Christ's work. Neither is wrong. We need both. As the gospel story illustrates, faith is more than a solo act. The paralyzed man is healed after Jesus sees the faith of his friends. In our culture, so focused on the individual, this dependence on others seems surprising. But faith is not merely individual. It feeds into and off of the faith of others. When we make a decision to attend worship, to serve, to practice generosity, or to pray for others, our faith creates opportunities for God to change the life of another person. Likewise, many of us have been convicted by, converted to, and shaped in Christ because of the faithfulness of other people. We are not solo operators, and our decision to follow Christ in simple ways each week carries with it the potential to impact and change the life of another person. Every Sunday morning when you worship, or every time you choose to volunteer, or every time you decide to be generous, may not feel like a mountaintop moment of faith for you. You may feel little change afterward. But remember that each time you practice faith, you create the conditions for someone to have their mountaintop moment with Jesus.

~Prayer of Petition~

Evening

When Jesus saw their faith, he said to the paralytic, "Child, your sins are forgiven!" (Mark 2:5)

Reflection

Have you ever found yourself in a vulnerable position that caused your faith to be shaken? Have you ever needed a friend to enter the muck and mire of your life and intercede for you? Have you ever been in so much pain that you could not pray for yourself? In Mark's Gospel, there was a group of men who took the initiative to climb up on the roof of someone else's house and dig a hole in it so that their paralyzed friend could have an encounter with Jesus. And it was because of their faith that Jesus intervened in their friend's circumstances. We all need spiritual friendships. We need people who can call on the name of Jesus when our spiritual tanks are empty. We need people who can activate their faith until we can activate ours. We need people who are willing to risk something to place us at the feet of Jesus until healing can occur. Are you that friend? Who is that friend for you?

~Prayer of Gratitude~

Day 3

Morning

Be rooted and built up in him, be established in faith, and overflow with thanksgiving just as you were taught. (Colossians 2:7)

Reflection

Sequoias are among the largest trees in the world. Surprisingly, these huge trees do not have a single tap root. Their roots do not go all that deep. Instead, the relatively shallow root system spreads out intertwining with other redwood root systems. They derive their strength from one another. When a storm hits, they literally hold each other up. Many of us want to be self-sufficient. We want to be strong and capable enough to take care of ourselves, solve our own problems, and overcome our own challenges. When a crisis hits, we often try to go it alone, dealing with it all and not letting anyone else know what we are going through. But this isn't how we are created to live. We are made to derive our strength from a power outside ourselves. We are meant to be rooted in Christ and to establish our strength from a source beyond ourselves. When the storms of life hit, we can withstand them, not by the depth of our own roots, but by the strength of the one we are connected to. The bad news is that you can't do life alone. The good news is that you don't have to. Our strength comes from being rooted and connected to God and others.

~Prayer of Petition~

Evening

"Daughter, your faith has healed you," Jesus said. "Go in peace." (Luke 8:48)

Reflection

O to grace how great a debtor daily I'm constrained to be!
Let thy goodness, like a fetter, bind my wandering heart to thee.
Prone to wander, Lord, I feel it, prone to leave the God I love;
Here's my heart, O take and seal it, seal it for thy courts above.
    —Robert Robinson, "Come, Thou Fount of Every Blessing"

~Prayer of Gratitude~

Day 4

Morning

In Christ we have bold and confident access to God through faith in him. (Ephesians 3:12)

Reflection

Imagine this: you not only have a relationship with God, but you can also talk to God boldly, with confidence! This matters, especially if you have been told that you don't belong, that you don't act quite right or look the way a Christian is supposed to look. Some of us settle for simply being included. We are content with the idea that we barely made it in the club on the coattails of Jesus. And that is true. But get this: Jesus says that we do not have to be timid or afraid of God. We don't have to approach God nervously, wondering if God will notice us and ask, "Who let you in here?" No! We get to be and bring our whole selves. We get to stand up and claim our spot. We get to access God with boldness in our requests and confidence in our acceptance. And if this is true before God, then it is true about God's community, the church. Take up your space, claim your place, and use your voice. You belong there because it is Christ's invitation to give, and he has given one to you.

~Prayer of Petition~

Evening

Alongside Babylon's streams,
* there we sat down,*
* crying because we remembered Zion.* (Psalm 137:1)

Reflection

In everyday conversation, hope indicates a feeling that things are likely to turn out well. In Christian theology, hope is choosing to live in the light of God's eternal love. Hope, along with faith and love, is one of the three theological virtues. As a virtue, it's both a blessing from God and something humans must decide to do. It's both a noun and a verb, a gift and a practice. Faith in God is the root of hope, and hope is lived out in love. Faith affirms that the world is held in the hands of a God who is greater than any trouble and can conquer even death. This means the future can be different from the past, and the present—however grim—still opens to a future created by God's power and love.
  —Shannon Craigo-Snell, *The CEB Women's Bible*

~Prayer of Gratitude~

Day 5

Morning

You are all God's children through faith in Christ Jesus. (Galatians 3:26)

Reflection

Human beings seem to have trouble with the word *all*, at least when it appears in scripture. We believe the Bible is the inspired word of God, many even read it literally, but we still have trouble believing all means all. Certainly, God didn't mean *everyone* is a child of God? What about people who look different, act differently, love differently? What about sinners and tax collectors, those who previously didn't listen to God and didn't really care to? But the community of Jesus is radical in precisely this way, the only entrance requirement is faith in Christ. A lot of us would like to believe in "Jesus plus." What does that mean? Jesus *plus* the right beliefs, doctrines, behavior, or identity. But no, Paul says it is just faith. It is not race, creed, identity, marital status, sexual orientation, political party, stance on the issues, moral conduct, justice work, or service hours. You are a child of God simply and solely through faith. That is the entrance requirement, and that is what binds us together. That is why you are welcome and that is why you belong. Don't let anyone tell you differently.

~Prayer of Petition~

Evening

Faith is the reality of what we hope for, the proof of what we don't see. (Hebrews 11:1)

Reflection

The book of Hebrews was written as a sermon to encourage Jewish Christians. In Hebrews 11, the writer tells us that "faith is the assurance of things hoped for, the conviction of things not seen." Then the writer provides evidence of this statement by giving the history of faith from Genesis to the time of Jesus. The writer reminds us of how the Israelites were delivered from the oppressive rule of the Egyptians by crossing over the Red Sea. The author reminds us of how the walls of Jericho came tumbling down, after the army marched around them for seven days. We are reminded how a prostitute named Rahab will forever be remembered for welcoming and protecting the spies who came to the land that was promised. The writer continues to tell us how the Lord had given victory after victory to the hands of the Lord's warriors. But the author also names the reality of those who faced trials, those who were flogged and thrown into jail, and those who lost their husbands and sons. And yet, God's promise to those Jewish Christians, who were experiencing a crisis of faith, is the same promise God has for us. God will provide something better for us.

~Prayer of Gratitude~

Courage

Morning Prayer of Petition

Empowering God, remind me today that you have given me a spirit of power, love, and self-control. Help me to see that I have all that I need today to:

- face the unexpected with confidence,
- persevere through hardship with resilience,
- deal with difficult people with grace,
- act even when I am afraid.

Give me courage for living today and help me to remember that you are with me. Amen.

Evening Prayer of Gratitude

God of Abraham, Isaac, and Jacob, just as you have worked wonders for our ancestors in faith, so you are at work in my life. Slow my pace so that I can stop and recognize how you:

- surround me with help when I need it,
- provide moments of joy even in challenging situations,
- make a way forward when I see dead ends,
- encourage me through other people.

May I live unafraid, confident in your love and grace. Amen.

Day 1

Morning

Remember this and take courage;
*   take it to heart, you rebels.*
Remember the prior things—from long ago;
*   I am God, and there's no other.*
I am God! There's none like me. (Isaiah 46:8-9)

Reflection

What is the relationship between memory and courage? God tells us to remember prior things, and the act of remembering will give us courage for what we currently face. Throughout scripture, God urges God's people to not forget the past, to remember God's mighty deeds, to repeat stories of miracles and deliverance. As the people of Israel remember all that God has brought them through in the past, they are able to take heart that God will also get them through their present struggle. The same is true for us. Memory gives us perspective. Look back on some of the hardest seasons of your life. While you may not have been able to see it at the time, often in retrospect we can see how God worked in and through those hard seasons. Remembering what God has brought you through and how God has shown up for you in the past can give you greater courage to face your present struggle. God's past faithfulness to us creates a track record of dependability and confidence that helps us face the future. So, remember what God has done, and face your present situation with the courage and confidence that God will show up again.

~Prayer of Petition~

Evening

Hope in the LORD!
Be strong! Let your heart take courage!
Hope in the LORD! (Psalm 27:14)

Reflection

It takes courage to be present in our lives. It seems that the world is constantly trying to get us to hide, numb, or distract ourselves—to not face the very lives that God has given us.

It takes courage to sit with our emotions, to forgive our past mistakes, and to speak honestly about our relationships and vices with other people. Part of this is facing the unknown.

And being present with ourselves takes practice. The more we are able to open ourselves to the realities of life, the more fully we are able to participate in it.

As Brené Brown says, "We cannot selectively numb emotions, when we numb the painful emotions, we also numb the positive emotions."

What are those areas that we are working hard to avoid? What might they teach us if we had the courage to face them? How might we be freed by addressing them?

Courage comes from the same place as fear. Whatever it is we are afraid of might very well be the same thing that teaches us what we need to know. Let us summon that courage. Trusting that God is with us before, during, and after.

~Prayer of Gratitude~

Day 2

Morning

"Don't let anyone lose courage because of this Philistine!" David told Saul. "I, your servant, will go out and fight him!" (1 Samuel 17:32)

Reflection

We don't truly have courage until we face something that scares us. Courage is theoretical until we face a challenge great enough to produce fear and uncertainty in us. If we always play it safe, and we avoid risk at all costs, then we rob ourselves of the opportunity to grow in courage. When was the last time you tried something that truly frightened you? When was the last time you attempted something so audacious that, unless God showed up in a big way, you would almost certainly fail? It is okay to be uncertain in your leadership, fearful about failure, and scared that what you are doing may not work. But courage is the quality of trusting God enough to try it anyway. And when you step out even when you are scared, one outcome is certain. You will learn. You will change. You will grow. So, next time you face a huge challenge or encounter a risk that scares you, do not reflexively run for the hills. Fear is not necessarily a sign that you are moving in the wrong direction. It may in fact be a signal that you are following God.

~Prayer of Petition~

Evening

In Christ we have bold and confident access to God through faith in him. (Ephesians 3:12)

Reflection

How can we sing our love for God
when God seems far away,
and we are captive to the hate
that threatens us today?
How can we sing a song of hope
when fear is in the air,
and when we shake, like hollow reeds,
in streams of deep despair?
So cried the psalmist long ago
from exile in a place
where sinful people wept and mourned
their dreadful fall from grace.
Yet even in this sad lament,
the psalmist's faith is clear:
though we may suffer in strange lands,
our God is always near.
    —Mary Nelson Keithahn, "How Can We Sing Our Love for God"

~Prayer of Gratitude~

Day 3

Morning

I've commanded you to be brave and strong, haven't I? Don't be alarmed or terrified, because the LORD your God is with you wherever you go. (Joshua 1:9)

Reflection

It is funny that God commands Joshua and the Israelites to be brave and strong. It doesn't seem like the sort of attributes that one can simply muster up in order to be obedient. Parents can attest that it isn't very effective to simply yell, "Be brave!" when your kids are clearly scared. But God isn't commanding us to be brave and strong on our own. Insrtead, God reminds us that the reason we can operate from a place of courage and strength is because we are not alone! God is with us. To many of us forget that at work, in relationships, during times of illness, or in the midst of significant hardship, we have a power that is already present with us and available to us. God doesn't promise us an exemption from fear, or the circumstances that produce fear. God does tell us that God's presence, power, and strength is with us and in us. Therefore we do not have to be afraid. We can be brave and strong.

~Prayer of Petition~

Evening

Jesus looked at them carefully and said, "It's impossible for human beings. But all things are possible for God." (Matthew 19:26)

Reflection

I think our Master, Jesus Christ, showed how the use of [spiritual tools] in His life brought courage and determination and even the quality of righteous indignation, when it was necessary to call people to a sense of their duty. I have not cringed; I have been a fighter for the things that are just and fair for myself and for my people—yes for *all* [hu]mankind.

—Mary McLeod Bethune, "Spiritual Autobiography"

~Prayer of Gratitude~

Day 4

Morning

All you who wait for the LORD, be strong and let your heart take courage. (Psalm 31:24)

Reflection

Courage comes in a lot of different forms. Sometimes courage can look like pressing ahead, moving forward, taking a risk, or making a change. But sometimes courage is holding your ground and patiently persevering even though everything in you is telling you to run. Patience requires courage. Patience in a marriage during a time of struggle, patience in a church that is going through turmoil, patience in a role at work when it isn't comfortable, patience with other people whom you find difficult to be around, or patience during a particular season of life that seems to be going nowhere. There are so many times in life when the easy thing to do would be to leave. Often, moving on is the path of least resistance. But having patience through a period of turbulence can be the predecessor to a breakthrough. Just because we feel stuck doesn't mean God isn't at work. And sometimes courage means giving God time to do a work in us before God does something new with us.

~Prayer of Petition~

Evening

It is my expectation and hope that I won't be put to shame in anything. Rather, I hope with daring courage that Christ's greatness will be seen in my body, now as always, whether I live or die. (Philippians 1:20)

Reflection

Our culture (especially our church culture) has taught us that being nice is among the highest virtues. But there are many times when being nice comes at a cost. These costs can include truth, justice, and even our integrity.

We can often let the fear of being "not nice" keep us from doing or saying what we know to be the right thing. You might feel this in your body. Your heart beats faster, your adrenaline is pumping, the words are on the tip of your tongue, you're ready to speak and then . . . you suppress it at the altar of being nice.

Jesus wasn't nice. Yes, Jesus was compassionate, kind, and inclusive. But he also demonstrated courage when he was speaking truth to power, flipping tables in the temple, and marching to his death on the cross. None of that was easy and none of it was nice. Jesus showed us what courage looks like through these acts of love.

Love and courage go together. If you didn't love something or someone, you would have no desire to summon the courage to engage in vulnerable and authentic ways. What is it that you love? How might you demonstrate courage as an act of love?

~Prayer of Gratitude~

Day 5

Morning

On the contrary, we had the courage through God to speak God's good news in spite of a lot of opposition, although we had already suffered and were publicly insulted in Philippi, as you know. (1 Thessalonians 2:2)

Reflection

One of the most difficult things to do is step out, stand up, and speak out when everyone else is quiet. Maybe it is a work situation where everyone else is conveniently ignoring an obvious problem or failing to speak honestly for fear of reprisal. Maybe it is at church when you feel compelled to offer a minority viewpoint or speak against the prevailing beliefs of the rest of your group. Or maybe it is socially when your political, social, or moral viewpoint is a clear departure from the people around you. Maybe it is claiming your faith and sharing it, even though the culture around you is indifferent or hostile. Courage is not only about taking big risks or overcoming extreme fears. Each day presents opportunities for small moments of courage. Following Christ is made up of small moments like these.

~Prayer of Petition~

Evening

Stay awake, stand firm in your faith, be brave, be strong. (1 Corinthians 16:13)

Reflection

O God, our help in ages past, our hope for years to come,
Our shelter from the stormy blast, and our eternal home!
Under the shadow of thy throne, still may we dwell secure;
Sufficient is thine arm alone, and our defense is sure.
Before the hills in order stood, or earth received her frame,
From everlasting, thou art God, to endless year the same.
A thousand ages, in thy sight, are like an evening gone,
Short as the watch that ends the night, before the rising sun.
Time, like an ever rolling stream, bears all who breathe away;
They fly forgotten, as a dream dies at the opening day.
O God, our help in ages past, our hope for years to come,
Our shelter from the stormy blast, and our eternal home!
    —Isaac Watts, "O God, Our Help in Ages Past"

~Prayer of Gratitude~

Purity

Morning Prayer of Petition

Righteous God, my heart is often divided when it comes to serving you. Fill me with a spirit of purity so that I can:

- turn away from thoughts and behaviors that are set against you,
- be patient with people who frustrate me,
- respond with grace when things don't go as I expect,
- cultivate humility when my stubbornness gets in the way.

Shape my heart to be more like Christ's this day. Amen.

Evening Prayer of Gratitude

Good and gracious God, all day long you work for good in the world and in my life. Allow gratitude to well up in me that I may see how you:

- blessed me today in surprising ways,
- led me to moments that gave me life,
- strengthen me in challenging situations,
- cared for me through friends and family.

May gratitude continue to define my heart more and more each day, so that my focus might be on you and your will in my life. Amen.

Day 1

Morning

The LORD's promises are pure,
like silver that's been refined in an oven,
purified seven times over! (Psalm 12:6)

Reflection

When you were a kid did you ever make a promise while at the same time crossing your fingers behind your back? We say one thing but really know that we mean something else. Maybe it signifies a white lie, an exemption to what we just said, or our intention not to really keep a promise. We therefore learn to be at least a little skeptical of the words of other people, knowing that they aren't always dependable, and we aren't either. Sometimes this habit carries over to our relationship with God, but it shouldn't. God's promises are wholly different from those of other people. God's words and speech are not full of the mixed motives and intentions that often mark the speech of other people. We don't have to wonder if God *really* meant what God said. We don't have to be skeptical. God doesn't cross God's fingers behind the back. When God speaks, those words are dependable, timeless, and true. We can trust them, and therefore live in the confidence that God does what God says.

~Prayer of Petition~

Evening

Happy are people who have pure hearts, because they will see God. (Matthew 5:8)

Reflection

No one wants to drink cloudy water. Most of us don't care to swim in murky water. The problem with murky water is that you just cannot see what is in it. Light can't get through to help you see what's there. Water is not the only thing that can become murky. Our hearts, too, can become cloudy, muddy, and muted. What can dirty the heart, one might ask? Could it be anger? Possibly resentment and bitterness? An unclean heart is different than a heavy heart. A heavy heart might be sad and distressed. An unclean or impure heart is one that is fixated on revenge, hate, anger, deceit, jealousy, or any other disposition that draws us farther away from God. When our hearts are dulled and dim, we cannot "see straight" and we surely cannot "see God." Our scripture, today, reminds us that the primary way we see God is through our hearts. Today, check in with your heart. Ask God to help you process your anger, bitterness, and resentment. Ask God to help you find forgiveness and peace. Allow God's grace to cleanse your heart that you may see God anew today.

~Prayer of Gratitude~

Day 2

Morning

*All the ways of people
are pure in their eyes,
    but the LORD tests the motives.* (Proverbs 16:2)

Reflection

When our behavior hurts another person, our first reaction is to justify our behavior. We think our motives are pure, but they often are more multilayered and complex than we like to admit. We can be passive aggressive, manipulative, and self-serving in our behavior. We also can be performative, behaving in ways that are aimed at getting others to see us in a positive or admirable light. It is easy to act one way, but deep-down harbor conflicting motives. And, often, no one ever knows what we are really thinking, or why we are acting the way we are. But God is not fooled. God doesn't merely look at our outward behavior, but can see the motives of our hearts. God can see if our behavior is aligned with our motives. Part of maturity and sanctification is the work of closing the gap that might exist between your outward appearance and the state of your heart.

~Prayer of Petition~

Evening

The voice spoke a second time, "Never consider unclean what God has made pure." (Acts 10:15)

Reflection

Calling a game is hard, thankless work. There is rarely applause when you make the right call, and suddenly every spectator is calling for your death when you make a bad one—or even just one they don't like. The job of a referee or umpire is not for the weak of heart. Most of us wouldn't choose it for a profession, but we are glad to be hobbyist referees on the field of life. We can be quick to name who is right and who is wrong. We are happy to determine what is good and what is bad. But like referees on the court, we will sometimes make the wrong call. Our judgments, even more so than behind the plate or on the sidelines, can cause pain and hurt for many. Being the judge is simply not our job. God is the judge and it is God's job to judge what is good and bad, clean and profane. The good news is that we do not have to judge, we only have to receive what God brings to us and to love. Today, release your need to judge others and work toward loving them as God loves them.

~Prayer of Gratitude~

Day 3

Morning

The LORD's regulations are right,
gladdening the heart.
The LORD's commands are pure,
giving light to the eyes. (Psalm 19:8)

Reflection

Have you ever received advice or counsel that you thought was biased or maybe didn't have your best interests in mind? Most of us have. As a result, we have to sift that advice through our own mental filters and figure out what to listen to and what doesn't apply to us. We get into the habit of arbitrating what we will listen to and what we won't. When it comes to God's wisdom though, this habit can get us into trouble. God's wisdom and instruction are always biased toward our flourishing and for our good. God doesn't give bad advice or misplaced counsel. It is easy to hear something that scripture says and immediately sift out the stuff we don't want to hear or that we think doesn't apply to us. But, usually, the wisdom we resist is the wisdom we most need to hear. The instruction that we chafe at is often the instruction that is most relevant and useful to our lives. When you have the temptation to take something that God says and set it aside as not relevant to you, stop. Instead, consider that the wisdom you least want to hear is the wisdom that you most need to listen to.

~Prayer of Petition~

Evening

Do everything without grumbling and arguing so that you may be blameless and pure, innocent children of God surrounded by people who are crooked and corrupt. Among these people you shine like stars in the world. (Philippians 2:14-15)

Reflection

Lord we thy presence seek;
may Ours this blessing be:
give us a pure and lowly heart,
a temple meet for Thee.
    —John Keble, "Blest Are the Pure in Heart, For They Shall See Our God"

~Prayer of Gratitude~

Day 4

Morning

The goal of instruction is love from a pure heart, a good conscience, and a sincere faith. (1 Timothy 1:5)

Reflection

These days, there is one virtue or characteristic that seems to be more valued than almost any other—authenticity. Whether it is a friend, boss, teacher, politician, or pastor, people crave voices that are sincere and genuine. Why? Because the world is filled with so many people who say what they think others want to hear. There are plenty of people who have mixed intentions and opaque motives. Authenticity denotes a kind of transparency and honesty, a purity of motive and intention. Authenticity leads to an increased ability to be vulnerable with and trust another person. God calls us to treat others with this kind of quality; to let our "yes" be yes and our "no" be no; to be straightforward, clear, transparent, and authentic in our interactions. God calls us to mean what we say and say what we mean. This kind of purity of speech and action is a milestone of maturity and a mark of faithfulness.

~Prayer of Petition~

Evening

You are pure toward the pure,
but toward the crooked, you are tricky. (Psalm 18:26)

Reflection

I pray, O God, that I may know thee, that I may love thee, so that I may rejoice in thee. And if I cannot do this to the full in this life, at least let me go forward from day to day until that joy comes to fullness.
  —Anselm, An Address (Proslogion)

~Prayer of Gratitude~

Day 5

Morning

From now on, brothers and sisters, if anything is excellent and if anything is admirable, focus your thoughts on these things: all that is true, all that is holy, all that is just, all that is pure, all that is lovely, and all that is worthy of praise. (Philippians 4:8)

Reflection

What we focus on shapes what we think about, how we feel, and what we do. That seems obvious, but we often underestimate just how much the content we consume shapes the way we live and act. Focus on money and it is easier to become greedy. Focus on work and it is easier to become a workaholic. Focus on what others are doing and it is easier to constantly compare yourself. Focus on pornography and it is easier to have unrealistic and harmful views of sex. Conversely, focusing on good or virtuous things has an enormous power to shape our lives in positive ways. Focus on gratitude and it is easier to find joy. Focus on serving and our lives can look less selfish. Focus on contentment and we find ourselves more capable of generosity. If you want to change what you feel and how you act, consider where your focus is. Focusing on the things of God make us more likely to become the kind of people God desires us to be.

~Prayer of Petition~

Evening

How can young people keep their paths pure?
By guarding them according to what you've said. (Psalm 119:9)

Reflection

This life, therefore, is not godliness but the process of becoming godly, not health but getting well, not being but becoming, not rest but exercise. We are not now what we shall be, but we are on the way. The process is not yet finished, but it is actively going on. This is not the goal but it is the right road. At present, everything does not gleam and sparkle, but everything is being cleansed.

    —Martin Luther

~Prayer of Gratitude~

Timing

Morning Prayer of Petition

Eternal God, in your sight a thousand years are but a day. I'm learning more and more every day to trust your timing in my life. Cultivate in me:

- patience for that which I must wait for,
- closure for those things that are ending,
- expectancy for that which I hope for,
- resilience for living in the in-between time,
- persistence for the work that is not yet finished.

Holy God, help me to trust your timing and to know that the time spent working and waiting is not in vain. Amen.

Evening Prayer of Gratitude

Mighty God, each day you offer me a new perspective on my life. In this moment, enlighten my spirit that I may perceive the ways you are at work, even when the progress is not as fast as I may want. Thank you for working today:

- in my stresses and anxieties,
- in my frustrations and setbacks,
- in my relationships, even those that are hard,
- in my responsibilities and commitments.

God, give me patience to persist as I wait for life to unfold and develop for me. I have faith that you are with me. Give me a tangible sense of your presence in my life. Amen.

Day 1

Morning

*There's a season for everything
    and a time for every matter under the heavens.* (Ecclesiastes 3:1)

Reflection

If you live in a place with four distinct seasons, then you know that whether you like it or not, seasons change. You may have a favorite season, but you can't hold on to it. It will inevitably slide into the next season, whether you are ready for it or not. This can be frustrating. In fact, we are often pining for a different season than the one we are in.

In winter, we dream of being outside by the pool. In the summer, we might dream of a brisk fall day far from the heat. But we don't get to choose the seasons we are in. We only get to choose how we will live in them. The same is true in life. Seasons of life and leadership change. In one phase, you may be single and in school. In another, married with a first job. In yet another, busy with kids at home and multiple responsibilities at work. Sometimes work is flowing and natural. Other times it is contentious, ambiguous, and uncertain. It is easy to pine for a different season than the one you are in. Even worse, sometimes we fail to acknowledge and embrace the season we are in, trying to live in a way that is no longer fitting for where we are in life. We cannot control the season we are in. But we can and should recognize the season and live in alignment with where we find ourselves. And if you don't like it, rest easy. The seasons always change.

~Prayer of Petition~

Evening

Know this: What I have spoken will come true at the proper time. But because you didn't believe, you will remain silent, unable to speak until the day when these things happen. (Luke 1:20)

Reflection

Abide with me: fast falls the eventide;
the darkness deepens; Lord, with me abide.
When other helpers fail and comforts flee,
Help of the helpless, O abide with me.

Swift to its close ebbs out life's little day;
earth's joys grow dim, its glories pass away.
Change and decay in all around I see.
O thou who changest not, abide with me.

Hold thou thy cross before my closing eyes.
Shine through the gloom and point me to the skies.
Heaven's morning breaks and earth's vain shadows flee;
in life, in death, O Lord, abide with me.
　　—Henry Francis Lyte, "Abide with Me"

~Prayer of Gratitude~

Day 2

Morning

And in the morning you say, "There will be bad weather today because the sky is cloudy." You know how to make sense of the sky's appearance. But you are unable to recognize the signs that point to what the time is. (Matthew 16:3)

Reflection

There is a theory about the life of any organization that says the best time to change and reinvent is when the organization is at its peak. This seems counterintuitive. When everything is going great, why would you change it? The reason is because we rarely can hold on to a peak. At our high points, we are often blind to the emerging challenges. We rely on past successes to fuel future challenges. But this rarely works. What gets an organization to one place is often not what will take it forward into the future. One of the great challenges of leadership is being able to see what is coming and adapt now to that coming reality. It is hard and takes faith to begin changing and evolving now for the sake of something new, the exact shape of which isn't known and not predictable. But what got you here is not necessarily what will get you to where you are going. Past successes are not a guarantee of future results. When everything is going well and firing on all cylinders, this is the best time to use your resources and creativity—not to hold on to where you are, but to prepare for where you are going.

~Prayer of Petition~

Evening

I will give you rain at the proper time, the land will produce its yield, and the trees of the field will produce their fruit. (Leviticus 26:4)

Reflection

Even when God does not liberate us in the time or way we want, God encourages us to continue struggling for healing and wholeness from hatred and violence.
  —Karen Baker-Fletcher, *Dancing with God*

~Prayer of Gratitude~

Day 3

Morning

God says, "When I decide the time is right,
  I will establish justice just so." (Psalm 75:2)

Reflection

It is possible to do the right thing but at the wrong time, or to make the correct decision at the incorrect moment. What to do and when to do it are two different questions, and wisdom is understanding when these two intersect. Some of us are so anxious to do what we think is right that we end up sacrificing the desired result because we rush into the action. We mistakenly underestimate the importance of timing and foolishly move before conditions are ready. Similarly, some of us are too slow to make a decision when a window of opportunity opens for us. Nervous about failing, or fearful about the uncertainty, we stall a decision until it is too late. Again, we mistakenly underestimate the importance of timing and pass up the perfect opportunity to make a move. God nudges us in certain directions and provides us windows of opportunity at the right time. Wisdom is understanding both what God is calling you to do and when God is calling you to do it.

~Prayer of Petition~

Evening

In fact, if you don't speak up at this very important time, relief and rescue will appear for the Jews from another place, but you and your family will die. But who knows? Maybe it was for a moment like this that you came to be part of the royal family. (Esther 4:14)

Reflection

It is part of God's infinite wisdom that, when things happen in God's timing, it is always the right timing. Paradoxically, it can be the right timing and also a timing we do not like at all. This was probably true for Esther, who had to summon incredible courage to risk her life at the right moment to save her people. It was with fear and trembling that she accepted the opportunity brought about by God's timing. It was not fun, but it was right.

Embracing God's timing can be hard, it can be complicated, and it can often mean letting go of our own plans in order to follow the road God has created. God's timing can be slower than we want, or it can feel like an interruption. God's timing can even bring us grief, like the peaceful death of someone whom we have loved.

But God's timing is always the right timing. It has blessings, gifts, and goodness that come with it, which we could never find following our own timing and plans. God's timing brings redemption, restoration, and deep joy. God's timing is resurrection timing. It saves us and saves the world.

~Prayer of Gratitude~

Day 4

Morning

Let the Israelites keep the Passover at its appointed time. (Numbers 9:2)

Reflection

Rituals are important because they automate the practices that are important. Rituals at appointed times take the guesswork out of what to do and when to do it, and ensure that important practices turn into habits. We can have a commitment to pray each day but, without a ritual of where and when, we are much less likely to keep that commitment. We can have a desire to be generous, but without a ritual that automates the practice, we likely will not follow through. If you want to be shaped and formed over time, then your commitments have to be converted to practices that eventually evolve to habits. A ritual is a consistent time and place for the practices that help this evolution along. Some see rituals as rote and unemotional, but they don't have to be. Instead, rituals are the way that we ensure that our priorities turn into actions.

~Prayer of Petition~

Evening

But know this, if the homeowner had known what time the thief was coming, he wouldn't have allowed his home to be broken into. You also must be ready, because the Human One is coming at a time when you don't expect him. (Luke 12:39-40)

Reflection

In several places in the Gospels, Jesus suggests that one thing we can count on about God's timing is that it will be a surprise. We can completely trust God to do what God has promised, but we, apparently, have little ability to predict when God's promises will be fulfilled. The proper response to this unknowing is to stay alert.

Staying alert means staying focused on the activity and movement of God. It means not letting other things distract us or take so much of our attention that we are as good as asleep to the work of God in the world. Staying alert means keeping our focus on loving God and loving our neighbor and not letting the stress of our job, chores, or family obligations close our eyes to the beautiful and surprising things God is doing around us.

The surprising nature of God's timing is not meant to be stressful but, rather, delightful. God wants to surprise us with joy, love, peace, healing, and wholeness. For us to discover these gifts, we must be open and alert.

~Prayer of Gratitude~

Day 5

Morning

Let me know my end, LORD.
How many days do I have left?
I want to know how brief my time is. (Psalm 39:4)

Reflection

If you could live completely healthy but die at 75, or if you could live until 90 but with uncertain health, which would you choose? The question doesn't just cause us to think about how long we have on this earth, but also what we want to do with that time. Some people get consumed with the question of how long their lives will be. We can obsess over health metrics, eating habits, exercise, and best practices to ensure that we can live as long as possible. These are good things to be concerned about. But life is about more than quantity; it is also about quality. What good is a long life if we are not using that life for a faithful and impactful purpose? We cannot control how long life is, and we will never know the answer to "When?" but we do get to control how we use the life God has given us.

~Prayer of Petition~

Evening

As you do all this, you know what time it is. The hour has already come for you to wake up from your sleep. Now our salvation is nearer than when we first had faith. (Romans 13:11)

Reflection

There isn't time, so brief is life, for bickerings, apologies, heartburnings, callings to account. There is only time for loving, and but an instant, so to speak, for that.

   —Mark Twain

~Prayer of Gratitude~

Obedience

Morning Prayer of Petition

Holy Wisdom, you offer me a pathway that leads to life but in stubbornness, I consistently choose my own way. Turn me around and loosen my grip on:

- the false belief that I must do everything myself,
- the hard-heartedness that keeps me from reaching out to others,
- the selfishness that prevents me from serving others,
- the materialism that lulls me away from faith in you,
- the myth that busyness is a badge of honor.

Help me to be more obedient to your teaching and wisdom so that I may walk the narrow path that leads to life. Amen.

Evening Prayer of Gratitude

Loving God, you are always at work for my well-being, not harm. Help me to trust that your commandments are for my good. Prick my consciousness so that I may see:

- the people to whom you are calling me to be more attentive,
- the areas of my personal life that I too often neglect,
- your nudges and promptings that I am ignoring or neglecting,
- the joy and rest that you are offering to me.

Shape in me a spirit of obedience to you and help me to remember that your precepts are perfect. Amen.

Day 1

Morning

So obey the LORD your God's voice. Do his commandments and his regulations that I'm giving you right now. (Deuteronomy 27:10)

Reflection

Obedience is not a popular word these days. It seems to be from a bygone era when institutions were more valued, authority more respected, and top-down instruction more in vogue. Obedience is set in opposition to freedom, individual expression, and making one's own decisions. It takes effort to sort through all of this and return to an appreciation for what the Bible might mean when it instructs us to obey. Maybe the best pathway into the wisdom of obedience begins with humility, or with a recognition that we are not quite as capable of self-direction as we like to think we are. Left to our own devices, we have a propensity to make decisions that often aren't best for us. We make short-term decisions without a proper view of the long-term. We make decisions that feel right, but that do not have the desired outcome in our lives. We justify and deceive ourselves instead of always seeing life in a clear-eyed way. We need a wisdom beyond ourselves. When the Bible asks us to obey God, it is because God knows that, left on our own, we can get lost and make a mess of life. God's instructions aren't forced upon us, and obedience isn't a punishment. Instead, they are an invitation and a pathway to not do life alone; they are given so that we might have a life that is far beyond what we can come up with on our own.

~Prayer of Petition~

Evening

The news of your obedience has reached everybody, so I'm happy for you. But I want you to be wise about what's good, and innocent about what's evil. (Romans 16:19)

Reflection

Obedience to God has consequences. The Bible is full of stories of people maintaining obedience to God, even unto death. History is full of the same stories. Growing up, when I heard these stories, I wondered if I would ever be in a position to have to make the ultimate sacrifice. Thank God I live in a country where I am free to practice my faith without fear of actual persecution. However, these stories of radical obedience still have much to teach us.

There are times when faithfulness to God runs counter to human desires. The spiritual fruit of generosity, for instance, runs counter to the desire to collect as much stuff as possible. The command to love God with all your heart, soul, mind, and strength does not say to love with "most of your heart and soul," but all of it. There are days when this level of obedience seems impossible, but the history of the church is full of stories of radical obedience, stories that teach us that such obedience is possible. And no story of obedience is as powerful as the story of the life, death, and resurrection of Jesus himself.

~Prayer of Gratitude~

Day 2

Morning

Does the LORD want entirely burned offerings and sacrifices
 as much as obedience to the LORD?
Listen to this: obeying is better than sacrificing,
 paying attention is better than fat from rams. (1 Samuel 15:22)

Reflection

Blind obedience is doing something even when you know it is wrong. It happens when we follow the orders of someone around us without thinking about the deeper meaning of the actions. This kind of obedience is problematic. It doesn't lead to growth and doesn't invite probing and questioning. Ultimately, it can do a lot of harm. Blind obedience is not what God desires of us. God doesn't want us to thoughtlessly and robotically fulfill a list of rules and rituals without connecting with the heart of God's instruction. Real obedience, the kind God desires, makes room for doubting, questioning, and probing. Real obedience makes room for difference, has grace for mistakes, and allows for growth. Real obedience is when we are asked not just to do something but to know and wrestle with why doing it is important. Real obedience leads to flourishing, for us and those around us. When it comes to our faith, God wants us to listen, obey God's instructions, and live aligned with God's will. But God also wants us to ask questions, wrestle with obedience, and, ultimately, understand the heart of why God desires this life for us.

~Prayer of Petition~

Evening

You saw what I did to the Egyptians, and how I lifted you up on eagles' wings and brought you to me. So now, if you faithfully obey me and stay true to my covenant, you will be my most precious possession out of all the peoples, since the whole earth belongs to me. (Exodus 19:4-5)

Reflection

Why, from seven years old, (the first time I felt a spark of faith,) my conviction was,—not to be conformed to the customs, fashions, and maxims of the world; and my frequent prayer was, as a little manuscript now by me proves,—Lord, bring me out from among the ungodly. Cast my lot with the poor who are rich in faith; and make me to have my delight with the excellent of the earth; and then I will not complain for toil, poverty, or reproach.

—Mary Bosanquet Fletcher

~Prayer of Gratitude~

Day 3

Morning

An eye that mocks a father
and rejects obedience to a mother,
may the ravens of the river valley peck it out,
and the eagle's young eat it. (Proverbs 30:17)

Reflection

Conflict among people of differing generations has a long history. Older people often think younger people are entitled, don't value experience, and aren't interested in persisting in work long enough to make a real difference. Younger generations often imagine older people as stuck in their ways, unimaginative, and not in touch with the way culture is shifting and changing. As a result, we often talk past one another, neither valuing what the other has to offer. When you were younger, did you have a tough time believing that the adults around you knew what they were talking about? I did. In my first job, I often scoffed at older leaders and was quick to point out the ways they didn't seem to get it. But I soon discovered that many older leaders had wisdom that I needed to make my ideas better, stronger, and more effective. Similarly, as an aging leader, my work has been revitalized by listening to younger people and their perspectives, instead of scoffing at their inexperience.

~Prayer of Petition~

Evening

As you set yourselves apart by your obedience to the truth so that you might have genuine affection for your fellow believers, love each other deeply and earnestly. (1 Peter 1:22)

Reflection

Listen carefully, my daughter to the master's instructions, and attend to them with the ear of your heart.
　　—*Rule of St Benedict*, Prologue 1

It is often forgotten that the root of the word *obedience* is found in *audire*, "to listen." When St. Benedict begins the Rule with the exhortation, "Listen," he emphasizes the stance of obedience required of all who seek wisdom. . . . For the monastic, obedience is putting into practice what is learned by listening to the other "with the ear of the heart" (RB Prol. 1). Centuries of Benedictine experience show that such listening requires a willingness to submit to imperatives outside of the self, something that is never easy to do, but that is deeply rewarding.
　　—"The Ten Hallmarks of Benedictine Education"

~Prayer of Gratitude~

Day 4

Morning

Be very brave and strong as you carefully obey all of the Instruction that Moses my servant commanded you. Don't deviate even a bit from it, either to the right or left. Then you will have success wherever you go. (Joshua 1:7)

Pentecost

Reflection

Do you trust God? No really, do you trust God and the way of life that God commands us to live? For example, God instructs us to live generously and to have a loose relationship with material possessions. But do you live generously, not seeing your money as yours but, instead, choosing to give some of what you have away for the sake of others? God also instructs us to be patient with one another, forgiving others. But are you as gracious with other people as you expect them to be with you? God instructs us on sexual ethics and how to be in relationship with others, but do you actually seek to live in the way God instructs? The question really comes down to trust. Do you trust that God's way of life is better than the one you can come up with on your own? In all honesty, most of us don't—at least not always. But when God instructs us, we should remember that it is for our good, for our success. Therefore, when God's instruction and your own desire clash, and when your instinct is to go your own way, try trusting and listening to God.

~Prayer of Petition~

Evening

As the Father loved me, I too have loved you. Remain in my love. If you keep my commandments, you will remain in my love, just as I kept my Father's commandments and remain in his love. (John 15:9-10)

Reflection

Let my spirit always sing,
though my heart be wintering,
though the season of despair
gave no sign that you are there,
God to whom my days belong,
let there always be a song.
Let your wisdom grace my years,
choose my words and chase my fears,
give me wit to welcome change,
to accept, and not estrange,
let my joy be full and deep
in the knowledge that I keep.
Let my spirit always sing,
to your Spirit answering,
through the silence, through the pain
know my hope is not in vain,

like a feather on your breath
trust your love, through life and death.
   —Shirley Erena Murray, "Let My Spirit Always Sing"

~Prayer of Gratitude~

Day 5

Morning

It is better to obey the reprimand of the wise
   than to listen to the song of fools. (Ecclesiastes 7:5)

Reflection

We all obey something or someone. Some of us listen to authority figures in our lives—parents, bosses, institutions, and authorities. Some of are especially drawn to the voices and opinions of our colleagues or friends. For others, we seek out and listen to the voice of experts and thought leaders. Some of us eschew outside voices and prefer to listen to our own instincts and desires. To whom do you find yourself listening? What voices do you spend time around and allow in? We are all influenced by the information we consume and the voices we spend time listening to. Over time, these voices begin to impact our decision-making, whether consciously or not. As the proverb makes clear, rebelling is never really an option. We all obey something or someone. The only question is, do we listen to voices that are wise or foolish?

~Prayer of Petition~

Evening

Those who obey me will dwell securely,
   untroubled by the dread of harm. (Proverbs 1:33)

Reflection

It can be difficult to recognize when God is active in your life, at least as it is happening. It is often only in retrospect that we can see how God has fit the pieces of our lives together in ways that set us up to thrive. Consider the high moments in your life. In the moment, perhaps none of these things felt entirely God-inspired. In retrospect, of course, they snugly fit together like pieces in a jigsaw puzzle. It is particularly important to schedule time to take a walk, or to soak in a pool, even to sit and to intentionally remember.

Pentecost

Obedience to God is not about blindly following just for the sake of doing so, or to stay out of trouble. Obedience is the response we are to offer God because of the ways that God has been faithful to us. And God has been faithful! When we think about it in this way, it becomes easier to see obedience less as an obligation and more of a gift: from us to God in response to God's goodness, from God to us in consideration of our best interests as humans.

~Prayer of Gratitude~

Sin

Morning Prayer of Petition

Holy One, each day you invite me to turn around, confessing my sin, and allowing you to forgive and redeem me. Today I ask you to help me with those places in my life where I harbor sin, forgetting to trust and follow you:

- in my personal habits and behaviors,
- in my relationship to money and material things,
- in my commitment to justice and equity,
- in the way I treat others, even those I don't know well,
- in my faith, when I neglect to make time for you.

Forgive me this day, and free me to live more fully in the freedom and goodness that you offer. Amen.

Evening Prayer of Gratitude

God of new beginnings, every time I make a mistake, there is an opportunity to learn. Every time I fail, there is a chance to grow. Every time I fall short of what you want for me, I experience more sharply your mercy. Call to mind for me the ways that today you:

- showed me grace through other people,
- strengthened me to do what was right and good,
- prompted me to take responsibility for my behavior,
- opened my eyes to a reality I was neglecting to see,
- freed me to live without guilt.

As you heal and restore me, may I be molded more and more in the likeness of Jesus. Amen.

Day 1

Morning

Because I know my wrongdoings,
my sin is always right in front of me. (Psalm 51:3)

Reflection

Sin sounds like the most negative aspect of the Christian faith. "Why," some ask, "do Christians focus so much on shortcomings and sins?" It is a question asked anew each generation, not just by those outside of the church but even by those inside. Wouldn't life be better and faith more inspiring if we stopped dwelling on the negative? The scriptural answer is "No." In a profound way, sin is our only hope. Genuine faith cannot start with an idealized version of the self or with wishful thinking about who we are and what we are capable of. Instead, faith begins with complete honesty and utter transparency about who are, not who we want to be. We are imperfect, finite human beings who want to get it right but who regularly get it wrong. We fail to do what we should and often do what we shouldn't. Pretending otherwise only keeps us from the mercy, grace, forgiveness, change, and growth that God has in store for us. But when we come to God as we truly are, we realize it is a gift to not have to pretend. It is inspiring to know we are loved, not for an idealized version of ourselves, but for the real thing. And it is in this acknowledgment of our sin, that God's true restorative work can begin.

~Prayer of Petition~

Evening

Happy are those whose sin isn't counted against them by the Lord. (Romans 4:8)

Reflection

I never fully understood the power of confession until I accompanied my husband to receive what is embraced as a sacrament at his Catholic church. "You stay here. I'll be back in a few minutes," he said as we parked the car in front of the church. I watched him approach the church's red doors as my mind pondered what he might share with the priest, who was waiting for him on the other side of the screen. Fifteen minutes later, my husband reappeared with a lightness that had not been present before. He was no longer walking with his head held low, but was seemingly being carried by an invisible wind. Is it any wonder that David used the word *blessed* to describe one whose iniquities are forgiven and whose sins are covered? How might the winds of the Holy Spirit be pushing us toward an experience of God's sanctifying grace today, as we turn toward God, name the places where we have fallen short, and stand in need of forgiveness?

~Prayer of Gratitude~

Day 2

Morning

And if your right eye causes you to fall into sin, tear it out and throw it away. It's better that you lose a part of your body than that your whole body be thrown into hell. (Matthew 5:29)

Reflection

There is a tension in our faith. We are finite, sinful humans. There is power in acknowledging that. And yet, with God's help, we can turn away from sin and seek holiness in our hearts and lives. Sin is a real part of who we are, but not an essential part. There are some people who assume that, because sin is part of being human, there is nothing they can really do about it. This can lead to a passive attitude in the face of sin, or a capitulation to it. We can grow complacent, and even comfortable, with our sin, forgetting that we are called to resist it and overcome it. Sin has found a home in all of our hearts, but we need not throw up our hands and assume there is nothing we can do about it. Instead, God's grace empowers us to work against the sin in our lives. This working against is not something that earns us God's love, but rather it is work empowered by God's love. God welcomes us as we are, but God doesn't leave us there. God works in our lives, helping us to root out sin. This is the work of faith.

~Prayer of Petition~

Evening

I don't do the good that I want to do, but I do the evil that I don't want to do. (Romans 7:19)

Reflection

John Wesley asked his mother Susanna Wesley for a definition of *sin*. She wrote back these words:

Take this rule: whatever weakens your reason, impairs the tenderness of your conscience, obscures your sense of God, or takes off your relish of spiritual things; in short, whatever increases the strength and authority of your body over your mind, that thing is sin to you, however innocent it may be in itself.

—Susanna Wesley

~Prayer of Gratitude~

Day 3

Morning

The next day John saw Jesus coming toward him and said, "Look! The Lamb of God who takes away the sin of the world!" (John 1:29)

Reflection

Christians have become known more for what they are against that what they are for. Listening to some Christians, you would think Jesus came to shout at us about our sin. Pastors and churches take up that cause and feel as if it is their duty to hold up a mirror to the culture, pointing out each flaw and evil. But as Christians—and especially as leaders—we must take care to tell the whole story. Jesus did talk about sin, and he often called it out among his followers. But Jesus always did this toward a particular end. Jesus did not come to condemn the world and he didn't come to condemn you. Jesus came not just to point out sin, but to take it away, to forgive it, and to give us a second chance. Pointing out sin is part of our faith, but if sin takes up a majority of our preaching, teaching, and public witness, and if we dwell there, or stop there altogether, we do not deliver the good news. The good news is this: Jesus is the one whom God sent to take away our sin, to forgive it, and to offer us a new start.

~Prayer of Petition~

Evening

But can anyone know
*   what they've accidentally done wrong?*
*   Clear me of any unknown sin.* (Psalm 19:12)

Reflection

The following excerpt is from a letter that had been typed and addressed to a pastor, and it began with the writer describing how he had been a member of the pastor's church sixty years ago. The brief introduction was followed by this detailed confession: "When I was about 10, I took a $5 bill off the altar rail during a communion service. It has bothered me from time to time for years, and a few days ago I woke up thinking about what I had done and decided it was time to clear my mind of this childhood act. Enclosed is my check in the amount of $20 which should cover the theft with compound interest."

The individual had carried the burden of knowing he had done something he should not have done for six decades! Realizing the grip of shame had not let him go, he discerned it was time to release himself from bondage. I like to imagine the man smiling as he wrote the letter, tucked a check inside it, and walked lightly to the mailbox. What baggage are we carrying, which could be checked with Jesus once and for all?

~Prayer of Gratitude~

Day 4

Morning

Yes, I was born in guilt, in sin,
*   from the moment my mother conceived me.* (Psalm 51:5)

Reflection

There is a debate in our culture: Are people born basically good or basically bad? Of course, most want to claim we are born good. We may make some mistakes along the way, but the intrinsic and natural desire of our hearts is toward noble ends. Christian doctrine has traditionally said the opposite. We are born sinful, with a heart that, when left alone, will tend toward that which is selfish and evil. One seems positive and hopeful. The other pessimistic and harmful. This broad set of ideas is often called original sin and, ironically, it has been a sign of hope for many Christians. It has taken a few forms throughout time, but the core of the idea is that we are born sinful. How can it be hopeful? First, if we are sinful, then it means that we won't and can't always get it right in life. We don't need to be perfectionists or over-achievers, judging our relative worth by how well we do. Instead, we need help and we need grace, as does everyone else. Secondly, an awareness of our propensity for sin ought to guard us against over-relying on ourselves or, worse, growing arrogant about our abilities. It engenders a humility and sober self-awareness that leads to growth and development. Finally, our sinfulness reminds us daily that we cannot do life alone and that we don't have to. We need a savior, someone to walk along side and guide us. We need Jesus.

~Prayer of Petition~

Evening

Once those cravings conceive, they give birth to sin; and when sin grows up, it gives birth to death. (James 1:15)

Reflection

Throughout its history, the church has been concerned with the sin of people, but has largely overlooked an important factor in human evil: the pain of the *victims* of sin. The victims of various types of wrongdoing express the ineffable experience of deep bitterness and helplessness. Such an experience of pain is called *han* in the Far East. *Han* can be defined as the critical wound of the heart generated by unjust psychosomatic repression, as well as by social, political, economic, and cultural oppression. . . . Sin and han must be treated together, if we are to grasp a more comprehensive picture of the problems of the world than that delineated by the doctrine of sin alone. In brief, the traditional doctrine of sin has been one-sided, seeing the world from the perspective of the sinner only, failing to take account of the victims of sin and injustice.

    —Andrew Sung Park, *The Wounded Heart of God*

Andrew Sung Park suggests that the experience of salvation, which is jubilee, begins at different points for folks in historically marginalized groups. The parallel journey to Wesley's path of salvation, which begins with prevenient grace, is followed by justification by faith. It leads to a life of sanctification as follows: acknowledgment of being sinned against, receiving the healing of the spirit, then being empowered to channel *han* into resistance to forge paths for jubilee.

—Hyemin Na

~Prayer of Gratitude~

Day 5

Morning

My little children, I'm writing these things to you so that you don't sin. But if you do sin, we have an advocate with the Father, Jesus Christ the righteous one. (1 John 2:1)

Reflection

If you're a parent, then you know the tension involved in teaching your kids to avoid wrongdoing, and yet recognizing that you will love them even if they screw up. We are often worried that stressing the forgiveness message too much might give them license to misbehave more freely. But if we emphasize avoidance of wrongdoing and the consequential nature of sinning, then young people often grow up worried that any infraction or mistake will be met with judgment and alienation. So, parents are often caught in between, wanting kids to know that their love is unconditional, while also stressing the importance of not sinning. We even see God walk this line with us in scripture. God gives us instruction, commandments, and a way of life urging us not to deviate from it. God isn't trying to scare us but also knows that, left on our own, we will not choose healthy and wise paths. God doesn't want us to sin because God loves us and wants a holistic and healthy life for us. This is why God stresses not sinning. But God also loves us unconditionally. Therefore, when we do sin, God does not cast us out, give us the cold shoulder, or withhold love. Instead, God embraces us fully in Jesus, forgiving our sin, setting us back on our feet, and giving us another chance. Both God's emphasis on sin and God's free forgiveness are signs of one unified impulse: to love us.

~Prayer of Petition~

Evening

As far as east is from west—
*   that's how far God has removed our sin from us.* (Psalm 103:12)

Reflection

O God, our help in ages past, our hope for years to come,
Our shelter from the stormy blast, and our eternal home!
Under the shadow of thy throne, still may we dwell secure;
Sufficient is thine arm alone, and our defense is sure.

Before the hills in order stood, or earth received her frame,
From everlasting, thou art God, to endless year the same.
A thousand ages, in thy sight, are like an evening gone,
Short as the watch that ends the night, before the rising sun.
Time, like an ever rolling stream, bears all who breathe away;
They fly forgotten, as a dream dies at the opening day.
O God, our help in ages past, our hope for years to come,
Our shelter from the stormy blast, and our eternal home!
    —Isaac Watts, "O God, Our Help in Ages Past"

~Prayer of Gratitude~

Security

Morning Prayer of Petition

Everlasting Lord, at the sound of your voice creation came into being and with your command the winds and waves obey. May your strength be a source of comfort for me today so that I:

- may not be controlled by my anxieties,
- do not succumb to fear,
- rely on your love instead of my performance,
- am free to be generous instead of defensive and protective

May I operate from the security that comes from knowing that you created me, you redeem me, and you love me unconditionally. Amen.

Evening Prayer of Gratitude

Strong God, you hold the world and me in your hands, and in that strength there is peace, confidence, and an ability to live unafraid. Let gratitude well up in me, that I may see:

- the ways you are protecting and providing for me,
- your Spirit guiding and prompting me,
- the people you are using to encourage me,
- the resources of help with which you surround me.

May I rest secure in the knowledge that you want what is best for me, are going before me, and are watching over me. Amen.

Day 1

Morning

He will stand and shepherd his flock in the strength of the LORD,
in the majesty of the name of the LORD his God.
They will dwell secure, because he will surely become great
throughout the earth. (Micah 5:4)

Reflection

Have you ever thought about what gives you a sense of security? Is it having enough money saved up so that you can weather whatever life might throw at you? Is it the stability and predictability of the job you have? Did you find security in relationships and family? Or maybe your security is rooted in a sense of control over the various aspects of your life. Whatever it is, we all find security in something. The challenge is that many of the places we look to for our security are circumstantial and fleeting. We can never have enough money, a job won't always be there, we never are really in control of life, and even relationships eventually end. That is why God invites us to find our security in Christ, one who is the same yesterday, today, and forever. It is in and through Christ that we find a security that is permanent, dependable, and unchanging.

~Prayer of Petition~

Evening

A person's steps are made secure by the LORD
when they delight in his way. (Psalm 37:23)

Reflection

Here I raise mine Ebenezer; hither by thy help I'm come;
And I hope, by thy good pleasure, safely to arrive at home.
Jesus sought me when a stranger, wandering from the fold of God;
He, to rescue me from danger, interposed his precious blood.
—Robert Robinson, "Come, Thou Fount of Every Blessing"

~Prayer of Gratitude~

Day 2

Morning

So Israel now lives in safety—
Jacob's residence is secure—
in a land full of grain and wine,
where the heavens drip dew. (Deuteronomy 33:28)

Reflection

Think about where you have felt safest. Maybe it was a time as a kid when you had no real stressors or fears, and the adults in your life provided everything you needed. Maybe it was the first time you were in a relationship where you could fully be yourself with another person. Perhaps it was on the other side of a stressful season of life, and you could finally sit back and truly relax. Try to remember. What did that time feel like? Where were you? Who was around you? What did it allow you to do? Security allows us to be safe enough for our true selves to emerge. Security provides the conditions for many of us to begin using our voices, taking risks, or stepping out in faith. Safety frees our minds to think more broadly and to feel more deeply. God doesn't just desire to be present with you, but wants you to know that you are secure. God wants to provide us a sense of security and safety, not that we may sit on our hands, but to provide us with the conditions to think, feel, and act more fully and authentically.

~Prayer of Petition~

Evening

So I'll keep reminding you about these things, although you already know them and stand secure in the truth you have. (2 Peter 1:12)

Reflection

Be at peace with your own soul; then heaven and earth will be at peace with you. Enter eagerly into the treasure house that is within you, and so you will see the things that are in heaven; for there is but one single entry to them both. The ladder that leads to the kingdom is hidden within your soul. Flee from sin, dive into yourself, and in your soul you will discover the stairs by which to ascend.

    —Isaac the Syrian

~Prayer of Gratitude~

Day 3

Morning

However, may King Solomon be blessed and David's throne be secure before the LORD *forever.* (1 Kings 2:45)

Reflection

We are to be humble before God, recognizing that we do not deserve the grace and mercy that is shown to us. But this humility shouldn't turn to insecurity. Pastors often encounter people who have trouble believing that God loves them. Perhaps you feel that way. Maybe there is something in your past that keeps you from fully trusting that God would welcome you into a relationship. Or, sometimes, once in a relationship with God, we can constantly question our standing, wondering if the most recent mistake we made has jeopardized our standing as a child of God. But through Christ, our relationship with God is secure. This doesn't give us free license to sin and doesn't exempt us from the work of repentance and sanctification. It does mean that we do not have to question God's presence and willingness to receive us when we turn to God.

~Prayer of Petition~

Evening

This hope, which is a safe and secure anchor for our whole being, enters the sanctuary be-hind the curtain. (Hebrews 6:19)

Reflection

There exists a pervasive separation of sacred and secular in our world that was not by God's design. We remember from the witness of scripture that sacred breath intermingles with mud and dust from the earth, forming a living being and healing the body. There is also an imposed separation in the human condition—a distancing of head from the heart—meant for survival, for resisting emotions that threaten to break us, for maintaining a mental story convenient to tell.

This is the chasm in creation, which Jesus broke into human history to mend; to integrate; to reconcile; and to bridge the echoing, cavernous gap found in between. Our savior pulls away the curtain separating us from the fierce, alluring, enigmatic presence of God veiled in each precious moment of this life. Our high priest's atoning ministry reaches past our own projected appearances to bring the very presence of God as close as our breath.

It is in this intimate presence where we find our foundational security to cross the divide and see what happens when we show up in the world as whole—open-minded and open-hearted, authentic and vulnerable, unburdened and free.

~Prayer of Gratitude~

Day 4

Morning

Watch your feet on the way,
and all your paths will be secure. (Proverbs 4:26)

Reflection

Did you ever have a parent tell you, "Pay attention to where you are going"? It may start with looking both ways when you cross the street, looking ahead when riding your bike, or driving defensively when you were learning to be behind the wheel. This advice is predicated on the idea that sometimes we can make mistakes that cause harm. But sometimes there is danger out in the world, and we need to be careful. Security comes from both controlling our own behavior as well as paying attention to the pitfalls around us. When it comes to our spiritual lives, the same is true. Sometimes we get into trouble because of our own bad actions. But sometimes we get into trouble not because we overtly sin, but because we don't pay attention to the situations that we put ourselves in or to the people with whom we are associating. Often, we do not set out to intentionally hurt people we love, make bad decisions, or put our lives, literal or spiritual, in danger. But often, your path leads to circumstances, situations, people, and compromises that cause hurt. Pay attention to the path you are walking. It will help your life to stay on secure and solid ground.

~Prayer of Petition~

Evening

Let your servants' children live safe;
> *let your servants' descendants live secure in your presence.* (Psalm 102:28)

Reflection

We live in a challenging world. Messages of fear threaten our peace of mind, rob us of joy, and attempt to defer our dreams. It's easy to allow our fears to paralyze our potential and whittle away our sense of worth. Repeatedly the Bible cautions us not to fear but to put our faith in God. Prayer reminds us that we do not overcome fear by our own power, but with trust in God we are victorious. Through God's infinite love and compassion, we exchange fears for faith, our weaknesses become strengths, and surrender empowers our belief. While the world may crumble around us, the assurances of God never fail. In Christ we discover abundant life as we surrender our fears to trust in God.
—Monica Moss, *The CEB Women's Bible*

~Prayer of Gratitude~

Day 5

Morning

In that way, the promise is secure for all of Abraham's descendants, not just for those who are related by Law but also for those who are related by the faith of Abraham, who is the father of all of us. (Romans 4:16b)

Reflection

The word *security* has two meanings. The more familiar one is to be safe from harm. The other comes from the financial world. A security is something pledged to guarantee a future outcome. If you borrow money, you usually have to put up an existing asset to secure that loan. It shows that you intend to fulfill your obligation to repay. Spiritually speaking, God makes us a promise about our future. God tells us that, despite the sin and brokenness of the world and the chaos of life, God has something better and more lasting in store for us. God has a future for us and it is one that not even death can spoil. But how are we to trust this, to feel secure in this promise? The answer is simple: because God has shown us proof, made a down payment, secured this promise, if you will. In the resurrection of Jesus, we not only have a savior who is alive and at work in our lives, but we also have a model of what will be true for all of us. We can be secure about our futures, and trust that God is at work for our good because God has already shown us God's power over death.

~Prayer of Petition~

Evening

Then my people will live in a peaceful dwelling,
*   in secure homes, in carefree resting places.* (Isaiah 32:18)

Reflection

Come, Almighty to deliver, let us all thy life receive;
Suddenly return and never, never more thy temples leave.
Thee we would be always blessing, serve thee as thy hosts above,
Pray and praise thee without ceasing, glory in thy perfect love.
    —Charles Wesley, "Love Divine, All Loves Excelling"

~Prayer of Gratitude~

WEEK 35

Fear

Morning Prayer of Petition

Perfect God, your love casts out all fear. In your love, may I face a new day unafraid of:

- the challenges and obstacles before me,
- people seeking to hold me back or rob my joy,
- sin that clings close and threatens to hold me back,
- injustice that seems to be permanent and unchanging.

Allow me to live courageously and powerfully in the face of all the forces that seek to instill fear in me. Amen.

Evening Prayer of Gratitude

Great God, your good news always includes a call to fear not. I pray that I would operate less from a place of timidity and more from a place of assurance. You surround me with signs of your presence and providence over me. I recognize today:

- the ways you provide for me,
- opportunities that have been given to me,
- moments that turned out better than I thought,
- hard situations that you brought me through.

May I more and more live out of a sense of assurance in your promises to me and your presence in my life. Amen.

Day 1

Morning

Don't fear, because I am with you;
don't be afraid, for I am your God.
I will strengthen you,
I will surely help you;
I will hold you
with my righteous strong hand. (Isaiah 41:10)

Reflection

There is power in knowing you are not alone. Consider any trial you've been through—losing a job, divorce, flunking out of school, battling an addiction, or dealing with depression or anxiety. In these kinds of situations there are rarely quick fixes or magic solutions. When we are in one of these situations and seek out help from a friend, counselor, or pastor, sometimes the best thing these people can do is to be with us in the pain. Sometimes, we even find someone else who has been through exactly what we are going through. Even though they cannot solve our challenges, it helps just knowing that others have walked this road as well. There is power is knowing you are not alone. When you face challenges in life and are scared about the future, remember one of the foundational promises of scripture: that you are not alone. God's presence is with you and God's power is at work for you. These truths can sustain us, even when we cannot see a way forward.

~Prayer of Petition~

Evening

Even when I walk through the darkest valley,
I fear no danger because you are with me.
Your rod and your staff—
they protect me. (Psalm 23:4)

Reflection

The GREAT FATHER above a SHEPHERD CHIEF is.
I am His and with Him I want not.
He throws out to me a rope
and the name of the rope is love
and He draws me to where the grass is green
and the water is not dangerous,
and I eat and lie down and am satisfied.
Sometimes my heart is very weak and falls down
but He lifts me up again and draws me into a good road.
His name is WONDERFUL.
Sometime, it may be very soon, it may be a long long time,
He will draw me into a valley.
It is dark there, but I'll be afraid not,
for it is between those mountains
that the SHEPHERD CHIEF will meet me
and the hunger that I have in my heart all through life will be satisfied.
Sometimes he makes the love rope into a whip,
but afterwards He gives a staff to lean upon.
He spreads a table before me with all kinds of foods.
He put His hand upon my head and all the "tired" is gone.
My cup he fills till it runs over.

What I tell is true.
I lie not.
These roads that are "away ahead" will stay with me
through this life and after;
and afterwards I will go to live in the Big Teepee
and sit down with the SHEPHERD CHIEF forever.
— Isabel Crawford, "A Native American Interpretation of the 23rd Psalm"

~Prayer of Gratitude~

Day 2

Morning

Just then Jesus spoke to them, "Be encouraged! It's me. Don't be afraid." (Matthew 14:27)

Reflection

Jesus was constantly reminding his followers not to be afraid. From the angelic announcement to the shepherds to the post-resurrection appearances, the followers of Jesus were reminded not to fear. Why? Because God is with us. While fear is part of the gospel story from start to finish, it isn't the only story. Alongside it, throughout the gospel, is the story of Jesus as God's presence with us. Think about it. At his birth, Jesus was given the name Emmanuel, which means God with us. Throughout his ministry, Jesus reminded the disciples that he was with them. The last promise Jesus made to his disciples before his ascension was that he will be with them always. From beginning to end, the story of Jesus is a story of God's presence with us. Fear is woven into the fabric of what it means to be human. But, in that fear, Jesus breaks through, reminding us that he is with us, his presence and power are at work right now for us, and that we are not alone. This promise does not eliminate fear, but it does encourage and embolden us to continue on, even in the midst of it.

~Prayer of Petition~

Evening

Peace I leave with you. My peace I give you. I give to you not as the world gives. Don't be troubled or afraid. (John 14:27)

Reflection

It is a natural temptation to accept the unfinished nature of a "false peace" in our lives. This "false peace" shows up in myriad ways. We delay conversations that need to happen, leaving truth unspoken. We allow analysis and rationality to cover a vast current of emotion suppressed in the heart for momentary survival. We endure this for a whole host of reasons: for the sake of institutional preservation; a desperate need for job security; or a hesitation to risk the cherished bonds of a partner, co-worker, friend, or family member.

Fear makes us settle for less than the deeper love and experience of belonging, which is eternally meant for us. This is the reality the Holy Spirit came to break, to heal, and to call us toward that love, no matter the risk or consequence. A life in the spirit offers a renewed trust in God's provision, a fresh wave of courage, and a release of attachment to particular outcomes. In this, we can be open to pursue for ourselves and for others a true, abiding peace.

~Prayer of Gratitude~

Day 3

Morning

Wisdom begins with the fear of the LORD,
*   but fools despise wisdom and instruction.* (Proverbs 1:7)

Reflection

We usually think of fear as a bad thing. We don't want to be scared, and Jesus reminds us not to be afraid. We even read that perfect love casts out all fear. Why, then, does scripture so frequently tell us to fear the Lord? An older meaning of the word *fear* is to have awe or wonder at something or someone. We fear something that is powerful and majestic, something or someone that we are not. When scripture tells you to fear the Lord, it is reminding you that God can do things you can't do, knows things you don't know, can see things you can't see, and can make pathways where you see no way forward. Therefore, God is worthy of awe and wonder. Fearing the Lord means that, when God's wisdom and our own instinct collide (an inevitability in life), it is better to choose God.

~Prayer of Petition~

Evening

The LORD is my light and my salvation.
*   Should I fear anyone?*
The LORD is a fortress protecting my life.
*   Should I be frightened of anything?* (Psalm 27:1)

Reflection

A mighty fortress is our God, a bulwark never failing;
Our helper he amid the flood of mortal ills prevailing.
For still our ancient foe doth seek to work us woe;
His craft and power are great, and armed with cruel hate,

On earth is not his equal.
That word above all earthly powers, no thanks to them, abideth;
The Spirit and the gifts are ours, thru him who with us sideth.
Let good and kindred go, this mortal life also;
The body they may kill; God's truth abideth still;
His kingdom is forever.
 —Marth Luther, "A Mighty Fortress Is Our God"

~Prayer of Gratitude~

Day 4

Morning

Overcome with terror and dread, they fled from the tomb. They said nothing to anyone, because they were afraid. (Mark 16:8)

Reflection

Psychologists say there are at least three responses to fear—fight, flight, or freeze (some add fawn or overcompensating to make others happy). While we may use each of these strategies, most of us have a default response to stressful and dangerous situations. It is helpful to know how you instinctually react to fear because while those responses are natural, they may not be ideal. While these reactions may make sense in pure evolutionary terms, they often don't work when it comes to our spiritual and emotional lives. They are all defense mechanisms meant to resolve the danger as quickly as possible. But sometimes God calls us to act in the face of fear. Sometimes, God calls us to move forward faithfully and calmly, trusting that the fear we feel can sometimes be a sign that we are progressing, changing, or being challenged. While fear can mean danger, fear can also mean growing. Fighting that growth, running away from these opportunities, or freezing in the face of them might lead us to an immediately calmer place, but it will not lead us to the long-term maturity and adventure that God has in store for us.

~Prayer of Petition~

Evening

The fear of the LORD is wise instruction,
*   and humility comes before respect.* (Proverbs 15:33)

Reflection

I learned to put my trust in God and to see Him as my strength. Long ago I set my mind to be a free person and not to give in to fear. I always felt that it was my right to defend myself if I could. I have learned over the years that when one's mind is made up, this diminishes fear; knowing what must be done does away with fear.

—Rosa Parks

~Prayer of Gratitude~

Day 5

Morning

Even the hairs on your head are all counted. Don't be afraid. You are worth more than many sparrows. (Luke 12:7)

Reflection

If you are around young kids, then you know there are times when they think they are all alone, out of the reach of any adults. They often will begin to test limits, try new things, and even get themselves into a dangerous situation. Maybe they are playing in the yard and begin to get a little too close to water, to the edge of a trail, or to a busy street. Maybe they are inside and beginning to watch something they aren't supposed to watch, or getting into a drawer that is off limits. In such situations, parents often swoop in to pick them up, correct an action, keep them from the dangerous situation, or set them on the right path. Kids may think they are always alone, but good parents are usually watching over them. Jesus says something similar about us. We often feel alone in our lives. We can get lost in our own thoughts, believing that we are the only ones experiencing something. We even make decisions in life that are unhealthy, a little too close to danger, or misaligned with God's will for our lives. We do all this, believing no one will notice or care. But God is like a parent, watching us more closely than we could ever imagine, knowing more about our lives than we would ever guess, and often moving and nudging us at just the right time to remind us that we are never truly alone.

~Prayer of Petition~

Evening

The angel said, "Don't be afraid! Look! I bring good news to you—wonderful, joyous news for all people." (Luke 2:10)

Reflection

I am not lonely. God is here.
Hand at my shoulder. Word in my ear.
The Lord is the shepherd who leads me down
to quiet pools and a soft green ground.
He feeds, restores, beholds, relieves me,

Shows the right road, then precedes me.
I am not lonely. God is here.
Strength for my going. Song in my ear.
Yea, though I cross the valley of dying,
I do not fear. I am not crying.
Thy rod for the beast, thy staff for my leaning,
thou art my comfort and thou my redeeming.
Thou art my present, beginning and ending,
the oil that I feel on my forehead descending,
the goodness that follows my every endeavor,
the temple I'll dwell in forever and ever—
O lord, I am not lonely now,
for thou art with me, my shepherd—thou!
  —Walter Wangerin, *The Book of God: The Bible as a Novel*

~Prayer of Gratitude~

Sow

Week 36

Rest

Morning Prayer of Petition

God, today I make the active choice to receive your gift of rest. To join you in delighting in the world you made. Help me to be obedient to your command by naming:

- what is clattering in my life, distracting me from you,
- what feels like toil and work, draining my energy,
- what I am trying to control that I can let go of,
- what is betraying my ability to feel joy.

Today help me to remember that my life is more than what I produce, to be aware of what distracts and drains me, and to find opportunities to rest in you. Amen.

Evening Prayer of Gratitude

God, as the day draws to a close, I stop to see and name where you have been at work in my day:

- for the moments of surprise,
- the moments of learning,
- the moments of assurance,
- the moments of relief and help.

Thank you for being present with me even when I am not present with you. Help me to trust you more fully, and to find my rest in you. Amen.

Day 1

Morning

Six days you may work and do all your tasks, but the seventh day is a Sabbath to the LORD your God. Don't do any work on it. (Deuteronomy 5:13-14a)

Reflection

In my first job, I struggled to ever take a vacation day. While I knew that I was allowed a certain number of days off, I felt guilty stepping away from my work and lazy for taking time to simply relax. Amid this struggle, a mentor and boss told me to think of it this way: "Think of vacation days as times when we pay you to relax." Some of us are such over-achievers that rest just feels wrong. We mistakenly believe that we must always be productive and never be idle, and that recreation is for the lazy. But, here, we find Jesus asking, indeed commanding, his disciples to come away to a secluded place and rest. This is not optional. It is a direct request by Jesus to them. To fail to do it would be disobedience or worse, a dereliction of discipleship. For followers of Jesus, rest is not optional; it is part of the expectations of the one who leads us.

~*Prayer of Petition*~

Evening

Many people were coming and going, so there was no time to eat. He said to the apostles, "Come by yourselves to a secluded place and rest for a while." (Mark 6:31)

Reflection

Sometimes I have loved the peacefulness of an ordinary Sunday. It is like standing in a newly planted garden after a warm rain. You can feel the silent and invisible life.
　—Marilynne Robinson, *Gilead*

~*Prayer of Gratitude*~

Day 2

Morning

If you stop trampling the Sabbath,
*　　stop doing whatever you want on my holy day,*
*　　and consider the Sabbath a delight,*
*　　sacred to the LORD, honored,*
*　　and honor it instead of doing things your way,*
*　　seeking what you want and doing business as usual,*
*　　then you will take delight in the LORD.* (Isaiah 58:13-14a)

Reflection

I regularly "trample on the Sabbath." Recently, I had a major project due, but I had procrastinated and filled my week with other work. Left with no choice, I spent my Sunday working instead of resting, enjoying family, and connecting with those I care about. I convinced myself that this was necessary, just this one time. But that was a lie. It was neither necessary, nor unavoidable. It was a choice. It is tempting to justify our regular trampling of the Sabbath by convicing ourselves we have no choice. But that is rarely true. Breaching the Sabbath and failing to take a day of rest is almost always a result of us doing things our own way instead of God's. But here Isaiah reminds us that when we stop trampling on the Sabbath, then we are able finally to take delight in God and the gifts God has given us.

~Prayer of Petition~

Evening

I am the LORD your God! Follow my regulations! Observe my case laws and do them! Make my sabbaths holy, and let them be a sign between us that I am the LORD your God. (Ezekiel 20:19-20)

Reflection

There is a realm of time where the goal is not to have but to be, not to own but to give, not to control but to share, not to subdue but to be in accord. Life goes wrong when the control of space, the acquisition of things of space, becomes our sole concern. . . .

The Sabbath is no time for personal anxiety or care, for any activity that might dampen the spirit of joy. The Sabbath is no time to remember sins, to confess, to repent or even to pray for relief or anything we might need. It is a day for praise, not a day for petitions. Fasting, mourning, demonstrations of grief are forbidden.

—Rabbi Abraham Heschel, *The Sabbath*

~Prayer of Gratitude~

Day 3

Morning

So you see that a sabbath rest is left open for God's people. The one who entered God's rest also rested from his works, just as God rested from his own. (Hebrews 4:9-10)

Reflection

Anyone with a laptop knows that, while battery life seems to get better each year, even the best computers can't last long without regularly and consistently connecting back to a power source. In fact, the kind of batteries in most computers function better and last longer if you keep them above a 50 percent charge. Draining the battery all the way will reduce its capacity and shorten its overall life. Though we have a tough time admitting it, we do not have endless supplies of physical, emotional, mental, or spiritual energy. Part of being human means that we are finite. We wear out. We get tired. We grow weary. We have to regularly connect back to a power source. And while it is tempting to do this only when you absolutely have to, you will work better, stay healthier, and live longer if you regularly allow God to strengthen and renew you.

~Prayer of Petition~

Evening

I will strengthen the weary
and renew those who are weak. (Jeremiah 31:25)

Reflection

Again I resume the long
lesson: how small a thing
can be pleasing, how little
in this hard world it takes
to satisfy the mind
and bring it to its rest.
      —Wendell Berry, *Sabbaths*

~Prayer of Gratitude~

Day 4

Morning

Unless it is the Lord *who builds the house,*
*   the builders' work is pointless.*
Unless it is the Lord *who protects the city,*
*   the guard on duty is pointless.*
It is pointless that you get up early and stay up late,
*   eating the bread of hard labor*
*   because God gives sleep to those he loves.* (Psalm 127:1-2)

Reflection

No one likes to think that their work is pointless. In fact, we often act as if the exact opposite is true. We get tempted to think the role we play or the work we do is absolutely essential. We treat our meetings as if they are tackling the most pressing concerns of the day. We are tethered to our devices, checking them obsessively, lest some critical matter pops up. We struggle to take a day, much less a week, off. There is something almost offensively sobering about the scripture telling us that what we think is so important is actually pointless. That isn't to say that what we do doesn't have value. But the value of our activity is compromised if we fail to recognize God's ultimate power in and over it. When we make ourselves out to be so important, we forget who is actually important. When we think that the world (or our workplace or family) will fall apart if we take a break, we fail to recognize by whose power the world is actually sustained. We may think that things in life depend on us, but they don't. What we do is always done in cooperation with, and under the power of, one who is ultimately in control. Recognizing and remembering that not only adds value to what we do but also allows us the ability to step away from it.

~Prayer of Petition~

Evening

Come to me, all you who are struggling hard and carrying heavy loads, and I will give you rest. (Matthew 11:28)

Reflection

Come unto me Jesus says.
Like a grandmother who always has a jug of iced tea and freshly baked cookies ready.
Like a dear friend who is always there to pick up the phone and listen to your troubles.
Like a church where the doors are wide open, and a friendly face is there to welcome you:
Come in, just as you are.
Jesus invites us to come to him. He sees our struggles and the weights of the world we are carrying. He knows our pain and our worries. We don't have to explain anything to him. He already knows, and he welcomes us in love to come, and sit a spell. Just rest.
Leave your shoes by the door, he says, *and stay a while. Here's a blanket and a glass of cold water. Let me take your coat. Have a seat here, on this comfortable sofa. There now.*
You are safe. Close your eyes, if you want. Let me lay a soft blanket over you.
Shhh. All is well. All is well. All will be well.

~Prayer of Gratitude~

Day 5

Morning

News of him spread even more and huge crowds gathered to listen and to be healed from their illnesses. But Jesus would withdraw to deserted places for prayer. (Luke 5:15-16)

Reflection

Every excuse we have for not being able to honor the Sabbath, to rest, and to take time for being instead of doing withers with this passage. Here, Jesus himself models rest, and at the expense of life-saving work. News about Jesus spread primarily because he was miraculously healing people. Just prior to his withdrawal to the desert, he cured a man's skin disease with a simple touch. And, immediately after this time of prayer, he was nearly trapped in a house by a crowd of people who wanted him to heal them. Every minute of every day could have been spent addressing eminently important work—the physical, emotional, and mental needs of people who were suffering. And yet, Jesus withdraws to pray. Many might read this and wonder what Jesus was thinking and can reasonably speculate on an answer. But, regardless, the story serves as a challenge, as an indictment of any excuse we have not to take a

Sow

break, not to rest, and not to prioritize connecting with God. If Jesus can make the time to pray, then so can we.

~Prayer of Petition~

Evening

Remember the Sabbath day and treat it as holy. (Exodus 20:8)

Reflection

There is an Orthodox synagogue in my neighborhood and many of my neighbors are observant Jews. On Saturdays I see them walking to temple with their families and going to one another's homes on Friday night for Shabbat. When it's raining, they don raincoats because they are not permitted to carry umbrellas on the Sabbath. Once, some neighbors had blown a fuse on a Saturday morning, and had to ask the Catholics next door to come and flip the breaker. From the outside, it's easy to see this strict observance of the Sabbath as a bunch of silly rules—a list of "thou shall nots"—that make little sense in our modern world. But part of me is a bit envious of my neighbors and their community's commitment to dedicating twenty-four hours each week to God. I wonder what my life might be like if I were to take a day each week and resist the urge to fill it with activities? What might my life be like if I were to log off my email on Friday nights and simply spend time with my family or friends? How might my relationship with God change with fewer distractions? I think there is something I can learn from my neighbors' practice of honoring God by "keeping the Sabbath holy."

~Prayer of Gratitude~

Fruit

Morning Prayer of Petition

Mighty God, for everything there is a season. In our life, there is a time to sow and a time to harvest. Today, help me to plant seeds that:

- lay the groundwork for my future,
- begin a process that I have put off,
- make room for rest and restoration,
- blossom in new relationships with others.

Guide my steps today and help me to remember that seeds planted now will bear fruit in the future. Amen.

Evening Prayer of Gratitude

God of growth, every day you provide for me. Give me pause to make the connections between your work over time and the blessings I experienced today. Thank you for:

- long-standing relationships that now support me,
- meaningful work that provides for me,
- persistent effort that is changing me,
- moments of insight and encouragement that bless me.

May I continue to see the fruit that is borne in my life through faith in you. Amen.

Day 1

Morning

Either consider the tree good and its fruit good, or consider the tree rotten and its fruit rotten. A tree is known by its fruit. (Matthew 12:33)

Reflection

People are like billboards. We all walk around advertising something. When people see you or spend time around you, they see something in you. Whether you realize it or not, you have a certain impact on the people who spend time around you. It is worth considering what is it, exactly, that you advertise? What happens to people who spend time with you? Do they get frustrated? Are they more creative and innovative? Maybe they get scared or nervous, or perhaps they smile and express gratitude. There is a practice in management called a "360 review." This kind of review solicits feedback not just from those you work for, but from those you work with, and even from those you supervise. This kind of review is hard and soul-baring because it shows someone how others experience them. The same kind of exercise can be used in other areas of life. The impact we have on people when no one else is looking says a lot about what is happening in our own hearts. Are you bearing good fruit or bad fruit in the lives of others around you?

~Prayer of Petition~

Evening

Produce fruit that shows you have changed your hearts and lives. And don't even think about saying to yourselves, Abraham is our father. I tell you that God is able to raise up Abraham's children from these stones. (Luke 3:8)

Reflection

It is easy to think of ourselves as right with God or, at least, right enough with God because of a status conferred upon us by humans or earned by our own efforts. How often we smugly assume God is on our side because of our church membership, our leadership roles, our education, our denomination, our hard work, our family, or our resources!

Jesus's teachings in Luke 3:8 outline an entirely different way of seeing our relationship with God:

> *Produce fruit that shows you have changed your hearts and lives. And don't even think about saying to yourselves, Abraham is our father. I tell you that God is able to raise up Abraham's children from these stones.*

According to Jesus, the only permissible evidence of our relationship with God is the fruit we produce. If our beliefs do not change how we behave, they are nothing more than theological musings. If our worship does not change the way we work, we are not praising God. We are just enjoying fine music and motivational speaking.

Our fruit does not justify us. God's grace does that. Our fruit indicates whether we are drawing close to our Redeemer or hiding from our Creator.

~Prayer of Gratitude~

Day 2

Morning

I assure you that unless a grain of wheat falls into the earth and dies, it can only be a single seed. But if it dies, it bears much fruit. (John 12:24)

Reflection

One of the more counter-intuitive ideas in nature is that for some species and ecosystems to grow stronger and healthier, they first have to be cut back, go dormant, or even die. Maybe the best example of this is natural forest fires. There are several species, both plants and animals, that have come to depend on fire in order to survive. Fire rids an ecosystem of organic material, releases nutrients into the soil, and even melts the pitch on certain pinecones so that the seeds inside may begin to germinate. What looks destructive can lead to greater life. The same is true in us and in our churches. Sometimes, people and organizations need to stop certain habits, end certain practices, and even let certain things die as a first step toward health and new life. It is hard to grab hold of something new when our hands are firmly grasping something old. Sometimes, to move forward we have to leave certain things behind and let them die. When we do, we are more ready for the new life that now has space to take root.

~Prayer of Petition~

Evening

We're praying this so that you can live lives that are worthy of the Lord and pleasing to him in every way: by producing fruit in every good work and growing in the knowledge of God. (Colossians 1:10)

Reflection

The fruit of silence is prayer, the fruit of prayer is faith, the fruit of faith is love, the fruit of love is service and the fruit of service is peace.
 —Mother Theresa, *A Simple Path*

~Prayer of Gratitude~

Day 3

Morning

As for the seed that was spread among thorny plants, this refers to those who hear the word, but the worries of this life and the false appeal of wealth choke the word, and it bears no fruit. (Matthew 13:22)

Reflection

Have you ever thought about why New Year's resolutions usually don't lead to any lasting change? It is because intentions are easy, but new habits are hard. Resolutions usually fail not because we don't care passionately about the intent or the goal, but because we neglect to actually change our behavior long enough for it to form into a new habit. We over-emphasis the important *what* we want to change. Yet we underestimate *how* we intend to reorder our lives so that we can turn that intention into reality. Habits are quite powerful in leading us to a new reality overtime. If you do ten push-ups every single night before bed, after a year you will look differently. Read a chapter of a book each morning before your cup of coffee and, in a year, you will have become a reader. Transformation does not usually happen all at once, but it forms slowly, over time, and with a persistent dedication to new habits. So, if there is a change you want to see in your life, figure out what new habit will lead you there. Then, dedicate yourself to it. Pick a consistent time, place, and space for it. Only when we make it routine will it withstand the daily distractions of life that can so easily choke it out.

~Prayer of Petition~

Evening

The seed that fell on good soil are those who hear the word and commit themselves to it with a good and upright heart. Through their resolve, they bear fruit. (Luke 8:15)

Reflection

If we illuminate with Christian hope our intense longings for justice and peace and all that is good, then we can be sure that no one dies forever. If we have imbued our work with a sense of great faith, love of God, and hope for humanity, then all our endeavors will lead to the splendid crown that is the sure reward for the work of sowing truth, justice, love, and goodness on earth. Our work does not remain here; it is gathered and purified by the Spirit of God and returned to us as a reward.

—Óscar Romero, "The Final Homily of Archbishop Romero" *(Note: Archbishop Romero was assassinated during this, his final service.)*

~Prayer of Gratitude~

Day 4

Morning

But the fruit of the Spirit is love, joy, peace, patience, kindness, goodness, faithfulness, gentleness, and self-control. There is no law against things like this. (Galatians 5:22-23)

Reflection

We have all met people who claim the identity of being a Christian, but who look and act nothing like what we would expect of a Christian. Followers of Christ are filled with the Holy Spirit in such a way that certain behaviors and characteristics begin to show in their lives. While some claim it is enough to believe the right things or fulfill the right rituals, people who follow Jesus are to demonstrate certain virtues in their life. If you believe in Jesus but are angry all the time, it should raise alarm. If you claim Christ but aren't patient, feel a need to react to everything you see on social media, or are judging those around you (even if just in your head), it should raise questions. If you think your job is to "confront" others, speak the truth without any grace or compassion, or to stir up controversy with your thoughts and ideas, then you should take notice. Scripture tells us what it looks like when one is authentically and genuinely growing in the Spirit. Be careful of those who claim the name, but do not bear the fruit consistent with it.

~Prayer of Petition~

Evening

Therefore, I tell you that God's kingdom will be taken away from you and will be given to a people who produce its fruit. (Matthew 21:43)

Reflection

Whether you teach or live in the cloister or nurse the sick, whether you are in religion or out of it, married or single, no matter who you are or what you are, you are called to the summit of perfection: you are called to a deep interior life perhaps even to mystical prayer, and to pass the fruits of your contemplation on to others. And if you cannot do so by word, then by example. Yet if this sublime fire of infused love burns in your soul, it will inevitably send forth throughout the Church and the world an influence more tremendous than could be estimated by the radius reached by words or by example.

— Thomas Merton, *The Seven Storey Mountain*

~Prayer of Gratitude~

Day 5

Morning

Jesus told this parable: "A man owned a fig tree planted in his vineyard. He came looking for fruit on it and found none. He said to his gardener, 'Look, I've come looking for fruit on this fig tree for the past three years, and I've never found any. Cut it down! Why should it continue depleting the soil's nutrients?'" (Luke 13:6-7)

Reflection

Anyone who enjoys gardening and landscaping knows that after a particularly cold winter, it is hard to tell which trees or shrubs have made it through the cold, and which ones have not. As spring emerges, though, the evidence begins to reveal itself. Some trees, bare and brittle as they may appear, start to form bud, leaves, and eventually flowers. Other trees produce nothing. Whether or not they are alive only reveals itself over time, as the shrubs either produce the signs of life or don't. Perhaps one of the hardest parts about leadership in the current church is the obsession with results and numbers. These metrics often measure the wrong things or are reductionistic in the outcomes they look for. But we should abandon the idea that what we produce says something about our vitality, or the vitality of the organizations we are a part of. Over time, our lives, our work, our money, our ministries, and our organizations are called to bear fruit. That is to say, that healthy things change, grow, develop, and eventually make a difference in the world in a visible and noticeable way.

~Prayer of Petition~

Evening

I am the vine; you are the branches. If you remain in me and I in you, then you will produce much fruit. Without me, you can't do anything. (John 15:5)

Reflection

All we must do to bear fruit for the kingdom of God is remain in Christ. Christ is the vine. We are the branches.

The health of the fruit of the vine depends upon weather, insects, and a host of factors beyond the control of the branches. The health of the branches, which produce the fruit, depend solely on staying well-connected to a healthy vine.

One year may produce a bumper crop. Another year, the fruit may shrivel and rot. Yet, if the branch stays connected to the vine, it will bear fruit again and again, year after year.

One year, our ministry may bring hundreds or even thousands to faith. The next year we may notice fewer and fewer people worshipping in our sanctuaries. One year our ministry may birth works of mercy and justice that transform communities. The next year, ministries may close for lack of servants to lead them.

The health of the fruit depends upon the health of the branch and the conditions of the atmosphere. The health of the branch depends only on staying connected to the eternal vine.

If we remain in Christ, we will bear fruit!

~Prayer of Gratitude~

Justice

Morning Prayer of Petition

God of the universe, your word created the world, your Son redeemed the world, and your Spirit is making all things new. Yet there is still brokenness, sin, and injustice. I pray for:

- division among your people that keeps us separated,
- economic disparity that leaves so many of your children in need,
- broken systems of education, healthcare, and political leadership that unequally impact people,
- victims of violence and those who live in fear on a daily basis,
- those who are excluded, rejected, or cast aside because of who they are or what they've done.

As I pray, may I also be moved to action and see the opportunities you offer to be salt and light in this broken world. Amen.

Evening Prayer of Gratitude

Just God, you are working all things together for good, including the brokenness of my life and the world. Raise my awareness to the places where you are:

- bringing strained relationships back together,
- producing progress towards justice,
- moving in the hearts of resistant people,
- bridging divides between factions.

Help me not only to see where you are at work but also to join you in that work, that your justice may be made real in this world. Amen.

Day 1

Morning

Remember the wondrous works he has done,
all his marvelous works,
and the justice he declared. (1 Chronicles 16:12)

Reflection

There is a connection between persevering in the face of injustice and finding hope in remembering God's past deeds. The present chaos and evil of the world can make it seem as if God is absent, God's promises are moot, and God's goodness is compromised. When those thoughts creep in, remembering the way God has acted during past periods of injustice, violence, and evil can offer a hope that the present circumstances don't afford us. God has made ways where there were no ways, turning seas into highways, dead bones into living armies, and desert wilderness into a highway to salvation. God has shown up for us in the past, and that offers us a hope that the present injustice, though real and pervasive, is not permanent.

~Prayer of Petition~

Evening

Establish justice for me, LORD,
>*because I have walked with integrity.*
>*I've trusted the LORD without wavering.* (Psalm 26:1)

Reflection

What I am looking for is some sort of balance in my life—a balance "so delicate, so risky, so creative," as Maria Boulding puts it, that she likens it to a bird in flight, a dancer in motion. One of the favorite words in the Rule is "run." St Benedict tells me to run to Christ. If I stop for a moment and consider what is being asked of me here, and what is involved in the act of running, I think of how when I run I place first one foot and then the other on the ground, that I let go of my balance for a second and then immediately recover it again. It is risky, this matter of running. By daring to lose my balance I keep it.

>—Esther de Waal, *Living with Contradiction*

~Prayer of Gratitude~

Day 2

Morning

How terrible for you Pharisees! You give a tenth of your mint, rue, and garden herbs of all kinds, while neglecting justice and love for God. These you ought to have done without neglecting the others. (Luke 11:42)

Reflection

The tendency of those who are comfortable is to advocate for peace in the face of unrest. It is convenient and compelling for those not currently bearing the brunt of injustice to urge others to calm down, be patient, and act orderly. In the face of great injustice, many people in places of relative safety default to a concern over small things while neglecting the big thing. Protest marches elicit outcries over blocked traffic or a broken window, while neglecting the underlying systemic injustices that lead protesters to the streets. In the wake of school shootings, politicians argue over marginal policies instead of confronting the injustice inflicted on others by those who so easily access guns. In the face of homelessness, we focus on rules about sleeping in parks or asking for money on the street, instead of asking deeper questions about why poverty is so persistent even in the wealthiest country in the world. While minor things matter, they cannot, and should not, be a shield protecting us from having to ask the systemic and major questions as well.

~Prayer of Petition~

Evening

He enacts justice for orphans and widows, and he loves immigrants, giving them food and clothing. (Deuteronomy 10:18)

Reflection

Distinguished professor Michael Eric Dyson suggests that "Justice is what love sounds like when it speaks in public." Love, then, sounds like people praying at a candlelight vigil for victims of gun violence in the evening before walking into a congressional office the next day to lobby for legislation that might curb senseless acts of gun violence in the future. Love creates a chorus from cans being sorted in a community food bank before the collective volunteers testify about the need for more affordable housing at a city council meeting later in the week. Love disrupts the silence of inaction, attracting voices from those who may think they do not have what it takes to speak aloud before revealing how every voice can be used, no matter one's age or experience. Love turns the tables over in the temple and then proclaims how God's kingdom is near. Where have you heard the sound of love? How are you called to speak this language as you sow seeds of justice in your community?

~Prayer of Gratitude~

Day 3

Morning

Instead, renew the thinking in your mind by the Spirit and clothe yourself with the new person created according to God's image in justice and true holiness. (Ephesians 4:23-24)

Reflection

Justice never seems as urgent for those who are comfortable as it is for those who are vulnerable. You see this play out in churches that differ widely on the role that justice work plays in their overall ministry. For some, it is central to who they are and how they understand serving God in the world. For others it is a small side ministry, led by a few passionate folks, but is otherwise on the margins of the church's overall work. A few churches even eschew such ministry as unchristian, as an intrusion from the cultural social justice movement that has no real place in a community that ought to be focused on personal souls. On a personal level, it is worth reflecting on our own commitment to seeking justice as part of our commitment to follow Christ. How central is this work to your own ministry? If the answer is, "Not very," then it is worth considering why something so critical to God is not critical for those in God's church.

~Prayer of Petition~

Evening

Get up, LORD; get angry!
Stand up against the fury of my foes!
Wake up, my God;
you command that justice be done! (Psalm 7:6)

Reflection

Abba, deliver us from evil—
people who shield our ears, eyes,
failing to see this world, so hostile;
failing to heed its anguished cries.
Amma, in mercy, hear our prayer.
Save all your children from despair.
—Mary Louise Bringle

~Prayer of Gratitude~

Day 4

Morning

Seek justice:
help the oppressed;
defend the orphan;
plead for the widow. (Isaiah 1:17)

Reflection

The church can complicate what God makes simple. When it comes to matters of mission and justice, we can overthink what we are called to do and unnecessarily complicate how we are called to engage. We shy away from justice work because we fear it is too political or divisive in our community. Meanwhile, God couldn't be clearer about what we are to do. In Isaiah, in one short verse, God gives four directives. These commands are not bogged down by disclaimers or conditional clauses. They are direct and unambiguous. Why then does the church struggle so mightily to listen to these commands? Why do some of us see this work as less of a priority than the work of worship, study, or prayer? What if instead of overcomplicating the work of justice, we began to engage in it earnestly? What if instead of talking too much and working too little, we began to seek the justice God cares so deeply about? When we do, we might be surprised by the way that God will meet us there.

~Prayer of Petition~

Evening

God says, "When I decide the time is right,
I will establish justice just so." (Psalm 75:2)

Reflection

To keep one's eye on results is to detract markedly from the business at hand. This is to be diverted from the task itself. It is to be only partially available to demands at hand. Very often, it causes one to betray one's own inner sense of values because to hold fast to the integrity of the act may create the kind of displeasure which in the end will affect the results. However, if the results are left free to form themselves in terms of the quality and character of the act, then all of one's resources can be put at the disposal of the act itself.

There are many forces over which the individual can exercise no control whatsoever. A man plants a seed in the ground and the seed sprouts and grows. The weather, the winds, the elements, cannot be controlled by the farmer. The result is never a sure thing. So what does the farmer do? He plants. Always he plants. Again and again he works at it—the ultimate confidence and assurance that even though his seed does not grow to fruition, seeds do grow and they do come to fruition.

The task of men who work for the Kingdom of God is to *Work* for the Kingdom of God. The result beyond this demand is not in their hands. He who keeps his eyes on results cannot give himself wholeheartedly to his task, however simple or complex that task may be.

—Howard Thurman, *The Inward Journey*

~Prayer of Gratitude~

Day 5

Morning

Establish justice for me, God!
Argue my case against ungodly people!
Rescue me from the dishonest and unjust! (Psalm 43:1)

Sow

Reflection

The world seems like an inherently unfair and unjust place. Bad things happen to good people, while good things happen to bad people. Systems of inequity may evolve, but they persist despite efforts to eradicate them. Every society in every place seems to divide people up into those who have and those who have not. If our hope is only in this world, then there is reason to despair. But our hope is rooted in something more than what human progress can accomplish on this earth. We believe in a God who is making all things new. Working for justice can often seem futile, and experiencing the inequities of this word can too easily lead to despair. No matter how hopeless or futile that work may seem this side of heaven, it is not. Bit by bit, piece by piece, God's justice is being established, and God's righteousness is being made real. Therefore as frustrating as the quest for justice may be, it is a pursuit we should always undertake and never expect to fully finish until God makes all things new.

~Prayer of Petition~

Evening

Those who make peace sow the seeds of justice by their peaceful acts. (James 3:18)

Reflection

When apartheid was the law of the land in South Africa, members of Central Methodist Church in Johannesburg anchored a large candle encircled by a string of barbed wire on a piece of shellacked wood and placed it on the altar. Each week, members of the congregation would light the candle during worship and read John 1:5, "The light shines in the darkness, and the darkness did not overcome it." Worshippers would then name the people who had been tortured, imprisoned, or killed during the week for seeking to end the government sanctioned racism. The act of lighting what became known as "The candle of peace, hope, and justice," offered an opportunity for people to collectively grieve before (re)committing themselves to the work of justice. When apartheid ended, many congregations continued to light the candle each week, reminding their members of how peace and hope are rarely possible without the work of justice. Peace, hope, and justice must always be cultivated, nurtured, and protected together. What victims of injustice are on your heart tonight? Take a moment to name them aloud. How could you play a role in setting them free as you become a visible reminder of how the darkness has not overcome the light?

~Prayer of Gratitude~

Week 39

Trust

Morning Prayer of Petition

Steadfast God, may your Spirit so fill me that every day I learn to trust you more. Call to mind today the assurance that you are worthy of my trust when:

- I am scared or nervous about what the future holds,
- I am overwhelmed and uncertain about a way forward,
- I am bored and life feels rote,
- my relationships feel strained or stuck,
- I doubt your presence in my life or in the world.

Strengthen within me a reliance on you and a strong belief that you are active and at work in me. Amen.

Evening Prayer of Gratitude

Almighty God, you are at once far above all creation and intimately close and present in my life. While I often neglect to pay attention to your work in my life, I know you are here. Let gratitude well up in me today as I name:

- the moments that were life-giving today,
- the interactions with others that reminded me I am not alone,
- progress I made in the challenges I am facing,
- signs of light and hope in my community, country, or world.

Thank you, God, for being ever present to me in Jesus and through the power of your Holy Spirit. Amen.

Day 1

Morning

Trust in the LORD with all your heart;
don't rely on your own intelligence. (Proverbs 3:5)

Reflection

We live in a culture that encourages us to listen to our gut, to go with our instincts, and to do whatever feels right to us in the moment. While it isn't wrong to consider what we want and what our instincts tell us, this way of living and making decisions is flawed. Relying solely on your own understanding is a limiting way to live life. Never trusting the wisdom and counsel of someone outside yourself will naturally shrink your life's possibilities to only those that you can see or imagine. Furthermore, our own instincts will eventually conflict with God's word or the wisdom that scripture offers us. We will read one thing but want to do another. In these situations, the proverbs encourage us to trust God, and to be skeptical of our own understanding. God sees things that you cannot see, knows things you don't know, and can do things you cannot do. Trusting God does not limit our choices but expands them beyond what we could do or even imagine on our own.

~Prayer of Petition~

Evening

Those who know your name trust you
  because you have not abandoned
  any who seek you, LORD. (Psalm 9:10)

Reflection

Great is thy faithfulness, O God my Father;
there is no shadow of turning with thee;
Thou changest not, thy compassions, they fail not;
as thou has been, thou forever wilt be.
    —Thomas O. Chisholm, "Great Is Thy Faithfulness"

~Prayer of Gratitude~

Day 2

Morning

"Now is the time! Here comes God's kingdom! Change your hearts and lives, and trust this good news!" (Mark 1:15)

Reflection

What is the difference between believing something and trusting in someone? The Greek word *pistos* (used here in Mark) is often translated in English as *believe*. This translation doesn't always get to the heart of what the original word means. When we hear the English word *believe*, we usually think of an intellectual agreement with some set of facts or a mental assent to certain propositions. But the word *pistos* usually doesn't indicate a belief in a set of facts or propositions, but instead a trust in someone. To trust in the good news of Jesus is different than simply believing it. Belief seems static while trust seems dynamic. Trust isn't so much to believe something but to believe in someone. Trust indicates that because of this good news one would be willing to change in response to it or live differently because of it. When Jesus asks us to trust the good news, he is asking us to rely on it, depend on it, and believe in it. Ultimately believing the good news is to believe in and trust the one who proclaims it.

~*Prayer of Petition*~

Evening

I trust in God; I won't be afraid.
  What can anyone do to me? (Psalm 56:11)

Reflection

I endeavored to speak as God gave ability. . . . I felt free, the tongue was loosed, the lip was touched, and the heart was warm. . . . The Lord owned the word, and the hearty Amens that went up caused the woods to echo.
  —Jarena Lee, *The Religious Experience and Journal of Jarena Lee*

~*Prayer of Gratitude*~

Day 3

Morning

Although you've never seen him, you love him. Even though you don't see him now, you trust him and so rejoice with a glorious joy that is too much for words. (1 Peter 1:8)

Reflection

We trust in all sorts of things that we do not fully understand. We get on planes having never met the pilot or knowing much about aerodynamics. We drive across bridges without a solid understanding of engineering. Most of us take medications without an advanced understanding of pharmacology. We trust in these things because of our history and experience of them being reliable and faithful in the past. Similarly, faith requires trust in God's presence and power. This isn't blind faith. We feel God's love, catch glimpses of God's presence, and experience signs confirming God at work in our lives. We can look back and see the way God has been reliable in our past. We know the history of God showing up for God's people. All of this allows us a greater confidence to trust God even with doubt and without an ability to fully see or understand.

~*Prayer of Petition*~

Evening

Some people trust in chariots, others in horses;
  but we praise the LORD's name. (Psalm 20:7)

Sow

Reflection

Never be afraid to trust an unknown future to a known God.
    —Corrie ten Boom

~Prayer of Gratitude~

Day 4

Morning

Trust in the LORD forever,
    for the LORD is a rock for all ages. (Isaiah 26:4)

Reflection

All of us trust in something. That is to say that we put our confidence in something or someone for security, comfort, and happiness. Some put their trust in wealth and savings, believing that when trouble comes their money can mitigate the impact or fix the problems. Some put their trust in other people, relationships, or family. Some of us put a lot of confidence in our careers to make life meaningful and to bring us joy. Yet others think that experiences will bring us a sense of satisfaction and happiness in life. But all of these have one commonality: they do not last. They are ultimately temporal realities, like grass that is here one day but can wither the next. Scripture instead invites us to put our trust in the Lord, who is like a rock—permanent and solid. If we build a sense of hope, security, and joy on this rock we can rest assured that nothing in this life can take it away.

~Prayer of Petition~

Evening

Don't be troubled. Trust in God. Trust also in me. (John 14:1)

Reflection

Everyone struggles with something at one time or another, because struggle is a fundamental part of life. Just as the hatchling struggles to break through the hardness of the egg, so, too, our lives can feel like we are constantly pecking against barriers that seem more designed for captivity than incubating freedom. And because struggle is hard and painful, with uncertain outcomes and utterly beyond our control, we can easily lose faith in a God who seems powerfully able to effect change but may not always appear willing. Jesus's words—"Believe in God; believe also in me"—invite us to see him as God's attempt to be with us in the struggle, to prove to us again that nothing can separate us from the love of God (Romans 8:32). Everything Jesus does, everything Jesus teaches, everything Jesus proclaims, everyone Jesus heals, and every miracle Jesus performs is meant to point to the promise that—no matter the struggle —God is with us and we are never alone!

What is Jesus doing in your life today? Could trusting in Jesus today help you see your past not as a record of your pain but as a testimony of God's faithful presence?

~Prayer of Gratitude~

Day 5

Morning

Trusting with the heart leads to righteousness, and confessing with the mouth leads to salvation. (Romans 10:10)

Reflection

Have you ever trusted someone else for something that you alone could not do? Perhaps you trusted a parent to take care of you when you knew that you could not do it yourself. Maybe you traveled on a trip trusting a guide when you would have been lost if left to your own devices. Maybe at work you have to trust a team of other people to come through if your project is to be a success. In life, we must trust others often because there are all sorts of things we cannot accomplish on our own. When it comes to faith, and having the ability to live the kinds of lives God wants for us, we cannot do it on our own. We cannot forgive ourselves, comfort ourselves, correct ourselves, or guide ourselves. When we try, we will inevitably grow frustrated and even disillusioned. Instead, our forgiveness, growth, healing, and salvation are gifts that come when we rely on and trust in God. It is precisely when we stop trying it alone, and begin to trust God and the people that God places around us, that we find the life we are looking for.

~Prayer of Petition~

Evening

Commit your way to the LORD!
  Trust him! He will act
  and will make your righteousness shine like the dawn,
  your justice like high noon. (Psalm 37:5-6)

Reflection

I hear the psalmist say, "Trust," and I want to say, "Amen"—but I have questions:
  What does trust really look like and how do I know when to do nothing or when to take action?
  Can I trust God without feeling vulnerable?
  Does "love others" also mean "trust others"?

What if I don't know how to do that? What if I don't want to do that?

Can I really trust God even if I don't trust people?

Can we create, nurture, and grow trust—even after we've lost it? I'll wait for answers.

In the meantime, let's rehearse again the stories of sign and symbol, full of promises of hope and the dawning of new life—and the faithfulness of a trustworthy God.

~Prayer of Gratitude~

Darkness

Morning Prayer of Petition

Holy One, you are light, and in your presence even night is as bright as day. During dark seasons of my life, help me to turn to you with:

- loneliness, in my life or in the lives of people I love,
- anxiety and mental health challenges that threaten my joy,
- grief in and around me over lost loved ones, relationships, or opportunities,
- anger that threatens to consume me or those I care about,
- addiction that menaces so many people including those I know.

May I learn to trust you as I walk through the dark, knowing that in it you are powerfully at work walking with us. Amen.

Evening Prayer of Gratitude

Creator God, with a word you called forth light and it shone. With that same word, you continue to shine light in the darkness of my life and the world. May my eyes be opened so that today I can see your light in:

- healing that is happening for people I love,
- new beginnings that spring up around me,
- moments of peace and calm when I am stressed and anxious,
- surprise encounters that give me perspective and assurance,
- positive news in a world that seems consumed by negativity.

Continue to help me trust and follow you, even in the dark. Amen.

Day 1

Morning

When God began to create the heavens and the earth—the earth was without shape or form, it was dark over the deep sea, and God's wind swept over the waters. (Genesis 1:1-2)

Reflection

Do you ever feel like your life is in chaos, the plans you make are not working out, and the goals that you make aren't getting any closer to reality? We can often feel like our lives are out of our control, like we are victims to our circumstances. It can seem like nothing about our lives is moving in the direction we expected or wanted. But in

Sow

seasons of chaos, uncertainty, or inactivity, God is not absent. In the beginning, when chaos seemed to reign, God's spirit moved to bring order to chaos, and shape to form-lessness. God filled the void and created something out of nothing. That same God is at work in our lives. God can work in the present chaos of your life to bring order, beauty, and form out of it. Precisely when we feel like we are getting nowhere, God leads us somewhere. When we feel like we are stuck, God provides a breakthrough. When life feels empty, suddenly God surprisingly and inexplicably can fill us up. God is in the business of bringing something out of nothing, not only in the beginning, but in your life as well.

~Prayer of Petition~

Evening

In addition, we have a most reliable prophetic word, and you would do well to pay attention to it, just as you would to a lamp shining in a dark place, until the day dawns and the morning star rises in your hearts. (2 Peter 1:19)

Reflection

You hardly imagined
standing here,
everything you ever loved
suddenly returned to you
looking you in the eye
and calling your name.

And now
you do not know
how to abide this ache
in the center
of your chest
where a door
slams shut
and swings open
at the same time,
turning on the hinge
of your aching
and hopeful heart.

I tell you
this is not a banishment
from the garden.

This is an invitation,
a choice,
a threshold,
a gate.

  —Jan Richardson, "The Magdalene's Blessing"

~Prayer of Gratitude~

Day 2

Morning

Do not rejoice over me, my enemy,
*   because when I fall, I will rise;*
*   if I sit in darkness, the LORD is my light.* (Micah 7:8)

Reflection

When I fall, I will rise. Has there been a time when God raised you up when you were at a low point? Was there ever a time when God powerfully wove together the mess of your life into something redemptive and beautiful? Has God ever taken your trials and used them to strengthen you? While God does not cause the seasons of struggle and suffering, God shows up in them, works through them, and is a source of light during them. In fact, sometimes God can do things in our darkness that God cannot do when all is well. You may wonder why you are struggling, or why you are in pain, or why disappointment continues for you. You can ask that question; there is nothing wrong with it. But there may be a more powerful and hopeful question. Even now, where might God be at work in my darkness, shining a light?

~Prayer of Petition~

Evening

From noon until three in the afternoon the whole earth was dark. (Matthew 27:45)

Reflection

In the darkness, God is working. If we cannot believe that, then we will struggle to understand the purpose of darkness. Theologian Barbara Brown Taylor reminds us that "new life starts in the dark. . . . Whether it is a seed in the ground, a baby in the womb, or Jesus in the tomb, it starts in the dark" (*Learning to Walk in the Dark* [HarperOne, 2014]). The Israelite people walked in the dark. Jacob wrestled in the dark. Jonah sat in the dark belly of the whale. Paul was blinded for three days. The "whole earth was dark" on Good Friday for three hours. Jesus was in the tomb for three dark days. And, every single time, God was at work. When it is dark, remember that God is at work. Deliverance starts in the dark. Healing starts in the dark. Peace starts in the dark. Resurrection starts in the dark. New life starts in the dark. In the darkness, remember that God was, is, and will forever be at work.

~Prayer of Gratitude~

Day 3

Morning

If I said, "The darkness will definitely hide me; the light will become night around me," even then the darkness isn't too dark for you! Nighttime would shine bright as day, because darkness is the same as light to you! (Psalm 139:11-12)

Reflection

There is a tendency to think of darkness as bad. Darkness masks, cloaks, and hides. We use darkness as a metaphor for evil. We are afraid of the dark. But seasons of darkness can be powerful and transformative for us. The night is a time of rest and rejuvenation. The night can be a time of respite and calm. Seasons of darkness where we cannot see exactly where we are going can challenge us to think creatively, see our life differently, and trust in God more fully. There are opportunities for God to uniquely work in the dark. God can teach us, mold us, lead us, and change us during times of darkness. Right now, you may be in a season that feels like darkness. Maybe you are questioning your work, frustrated in your relationships, waiting impatiently for change, or anxious about the uncertainty of the future. But God does some of God's best work in the dark. In God, there is no difference between night and day.

~Prayer of Petition~

Evening

The light shines in the darkness, and the darkness doesn't extinguish the light. (John 1:5)

Reflection

This is an invitation,
a choice,
a threshold,
a gate.

This is your life
calling to you
from a place
you could never
have dreamed
but now that you

have glimpsed its edge
you cannot imagine
choosing any other way.

So let the tears come
as anointing,
as consecration,
and then
let them go.
     —Jan Richardson, "The Magdalene's Blessing"

~Prayer of Gratitude~

Day 4

Morning

You've made my loved ones and companions distant.
   My only friend is darkness. (Psalm 88:18)

Reflection

There are some scriptures that you can feel, that you instantly know are true because they name something deep within you. Any of us who have suffered from depression know the deep truth of this psalm. In the pit of despair or hopelessness, everything and everyone seems distant. More so, as a person of faith, despite desperate prayers, the loneliness and isolation don't magically subside. Even worse, in the face of unanswered prayers, it can feel as if the distance is caused by God. In the pit of depression, grief, and sadness it seems as if darkness is our only companion, our only dependable presence, and our only friend. When you are in this place, it can feel like you are the only one, and that no one, especially church folk, could understand what it is like. But the scriptures name this place as one that many before us have walked. Like a cave with marks left by those who've gone before us, we are not the first ones who have been here. And, even now, others sit with us, even though we cannot see them. There is no redeeming the feeling of being in the dark, but there is power in knowing that you aren't alone there, that others have been, and are, there. There is also hope in knowing that many before us, like the psalmist, have come through it to write these words of encouragement and hope, reminding us that the dark is not permanent.

~Prayer of Petition~

Evening

The people walking in darkness have seen a great light.
   On those living in a pitch-dark land, light has dawned. (Isaiah 9:2)

Sow

Reflection

Growing up, I was terrified of storms. The noise, the lightning, and the threat of darkness sent me running for a safe place to hide. As I grew older, the storms transformed into an invitation to be still. To listen. To pray. Our human reaction is to try to eradicate darkness. Turn on the lights. Light candles and lanterns. Do everything we can to make the darkness disappear. We are the same way in our everyday life, coming and going—we do everything we can to run the darkness off. Humans do everything possible to skip human darkness—grief, difficulty, and pain. Yet, for a healthy sleep cycle, your body needs darkness. To see the stars in their glory, darkness is required. Even plants and animals cannot thrive in total and constant light. The Old Testament prophets and Jesus remind us that there will be darkness in this life. It's up to you what you do with it. Will you sow into the darkness and see what harvest will be reaped? What can you hear? What can you learn? Take a deep breath . . . the darkness is here to teach us.

~Prayer of Gratitude~

Day 5

Morning

Early in the morning of the first day of the week, while it was still dark, Mary Magdalene came to the tomb and saw that the stone had been taken away from the tomb. (John 20:1)

Reflection

In 1996, a photographer named Charles O'Rear was driving in Napa Valley, California. A storm had just passed through, one of many that seemed to darken the landscape that year for this otherwise sunny spot. But on this day, O'Rear noticed how green the landscape had become because of the rain. He stopped and took a photograph that would become famous. Entitled *Bliss*, it became the iconic default wallpaper image for Microsoft Windows and is one of the most viewed photographs in the world. On most days, the hillside in the picture doesn't look nearly as green and idyllic as it did that day in the wake of the storms. It is during the dark storms of your life that God is often at work preparing something beautiful to emerge. While it is still dark, when it still feels hopeless, or when it seems dire—God is present and bringing about something new. This hope has its start in the dark. Your low point is not your last point, but in this place of darkness, when you can't even see it, something new and beautiful is emerging.

~Prayer of Petition~

246

Evening

What I say to you in the darkness, tell in the light; and what you hear whispered, announce from the rooftops. (Matthew 10:27)

Reflection

Let this blessing
gather itself around you.

Let it give you
what you will need
for this journey.

You will not remember
the words—
they do not matter.

All you need to remember
is how it sounded
when you stood
in the place of death
and heard the living
call your name.
   —Jan Richardson, "The Magdalene's Blessing"

~Prayer of Gratitude~

Patience

Morning Prayer of Petition

Forgiving God, you are evermore patient with me when I frustrate, neglect, or disobey you. Foster in me that same patience in my life towards:

- my family, children, and those close to me,
- co-workers or classmates with whom I am angry or disappointed,
- those with whom I disagree and who seem to work against the very things I value,
- myself, when I fail to do what I want or intend to do.

Help me to be as patient with others in my life as you are with me. Amen.

Evening Prayer of Gratitude

God of the still small voice, my life is so filled with activity that sometimes it I hard to see you at work. Quiet my heart, and give me an ability to see:

- the ways that you are guiding and caring for me,
- the progress being made in my life and relationships,
- the promising changes that are happening in my family, community, and world,
- the small ways you bring joy into my life.

Strengthen in me the ability to stop and notice the ways that my life is growing and developing despite my frequent inability to see it. Amen.

Day 1

Morning

Therefore, brothers and sisters, you must be patient as you wait for the coming of the Lord. Consider the farmer who waits patiently for the coming of rain in the fall and spring, looking forward to the precious fruit of the earth. (James 5:7)

Reflection

Nothing tests one's patience more than gardening and tending to plants. There is no real shortcut to get from seed to vegetable or from shrub to flower. You can prepare the soil, amend with fertilizer, and water fastidiously. You can get the right amount of light and sun and keep the temperature in an idea zone. You can try to control all the circumstances, but you cannot control the growth. For that, there is no substitute for waiting. In our lives, we often anxiously work to control all of the circumstances that can contribute to the outcomes we want. Whether it is at work, with our health, in relationships, or with our kids, there is so much that we try to control and manipulate to more quickly get the outcomes that we desire. While there is much we can control, we are wise to recognize what we can't. We might be able to manipulate all the conditions but there are some things in life that we cannot control. There are no shortcuts to the outcomes we want. Once all the conditions are ideal there is no substitute for waiting. Certain things take time, and we don't control the timing.

~Prayer of Petition~

Evening

But you, my LORD,
*   are a God of compassion and mercy;*
*   you are very patient and full of faithful love.* (Psalm 86:15)

Reflection

We hate to wait. We are hard wired to want resolution immediately, and we want to know what is ahead of us. God knows that as humans, patience is not something we come by naturally. But while patience is not natural to us, it is part of God's nature. God has all the time in the world, and God is patient with us as we fall down, or make a poor decision, or take the wrong turn, and patient when we try again. The psalmist reminds us that though God has plenty of reasons to be quick to judge, God's nature is to be patient with us and to extend grace to us time and again. Today, thank God for God's patience with you, and ask for God to convict you of your own need of patience with yourself and others.

~Prayer of Gratitude~

Day 2

Morning

Love is patient, love is kind, it isn't jealous, it doesn't brag, it isn't arrogant. (1 Corinthians 13:4)

Reflection

Love is a strange word in the English language. It is used to describe everything from the way we feel about our favorite food to the way we feel about our own children. Because of this, our culture has an expansive and muddy understanding of what love is and what love looks like. We use it to describe so much that it has lost much of what it truly means. For this reason, Paul's reflection on love in Corinthians is refreshing and helpful. Here, Paul tells us what Christ-like love is like. It is not only a compelling definition of love, but it is also a mirror that invites us to look to see how well we reflect it in the world. As you read the description of love throughout this chapter, you are invited to ask the question, "Do I love like this?" Undoubtedly the passage will challenge us with some aspect of love we neglect, correct some aspect of love we have warped, inspire us with some aspect of love that we have overlooked, and ultimately, invite us to love more faithfully and fully in the way of Christ.

~Prayer of Petition~

Evening

The LORD passed in front of him and proclaimed:
"The LORD! The LORD!
a God who is compassionate and merciful, very patient,
full of great loyalty and faithfulness." (Exodus 34:6)

Reflection

O Master, let me walk with thee
In lowly paths of service free.
Tell me thy secret; help me bear
The strain of toil, the fret of care.
Help me the slow of heart to move
By some clear, winning word of love;
Teach me the wayward feet to stay,
And guide them in the homeward way.
Teach me thy patience; still with thee
In closer, dearer company,
In work that keeps faith sweet and strong,
In trust that triumphs over wrong;
In hope that sends a shining ray
Far down the future's broadening way
In peace that only thou canst give,
With the, O Master, let me live.
   —Washington Gladden, "O Master Let Me Walk with Thee"

~Prayer of Gratitude~

Day 3

Morning

Patience leads to abundant understanding,
but impatience leads to stupid mistakes. (Proverbs 14:29)

Reflection

There is a quote that is often attributed to the poet Walt Whitman, "be curious, not judgmental." It is debatable that he ever said or wrote this, but regardless it resonates. We often quickly sum up other people, put them in a category, and form an opinion all before we ever really get to know them. Curiosity requires a patience to withhold judgment long enough to learn about another person. The same is true for many situations in life. In our anxiety or unease with difficult situations, we often rush to fix, address, confront, or solve perceived problems around us. In our impatience we often fix nothing, instead we add to the problem. But patience offers us an opportunity to be curious—to explore, learn about, and understand a situation more fully. This space usually leads to a better decision, a smarter choice, or a wiser approach. Next time you are tempted to act quickly and rush to judgment, practice the patience that can offer you a chance to be curious. It leads to more understanding and better outcomes.

~Prayer of Petition~

Evening

The LORD is very patient but great in power;
*   the LORD punishes.*
His way is in whirlwind and storm;
*   clouds are the dust of his feet.* (Nahum 1:3)

Reflection

There are countless ways in which this (spiritual journey) may happen: sometimes under conditions which seem to the world like the very frustration of life, of progress, of growth. Thus boundless initiative is chained to a sick bed and transmuted into sacrifice; the lover of beauty is sent to serve in the slum, the lover of stillness is kept on the run all day, the sudden demand to leave all comes to the one who least expects it, and through and in these apparent frustrations the life of the spirit emerges and grows.

    —Evelyn Underhill, *The Spiritual Life*

~Prayer of Gratitude~

Day 4

Morning

Hotheads stir up conflict,
*   but patient people calm down strife.* (Proverbs 15:18)

Sow

Reflection

If you spend any time around kids or teenagers, then you know that they rarely respond well to adult anger or yelling. Usually, emotional outbursts only beget more emotional responses until the situation spirals out of control. As angry as kids can make us, part of being an adult is keeping your cool. The same is true in all relationships, especially when it comes to leaders in a company, organization, social group, or family. Perhaps one of the most important qualities for leadership is the ability to be the least reactive and least anxious person in the room.

~Prayer of Petition~

Evening

The Lord isn't slow to keep his promise, as some think of slowness, but he is patient toward you, not wanting anyone to perish but all to change their hearts and lives. (2 Peter 3:9)

Reflection

If I did not simply live from one moment to another, it would be impossible for me to be patient; but I only look at the present, I forget the past, and I take good care not to forestall the future. When we yield to discouragement or despair it is usually because we think too much about the past and the future. . . . It is wrong to pass one's time in fretting, instead of sleeping on the heart of Jesus.
　　—St. Therese de Lisieux

~Prayer of Gratitude~

Day 5

Morning

Comfort the discouraged. Help the weak. Be patient with everyone. (1 Thessalonians 5:14b)

Reflection

Patience is not an instinct or a default ability for most of us. Instead, it is a discipline that has to be intentionally learned, deliberately practiced, and constantly refined. Patience is easy to have with people we love and appreciate. With those we trust, it is easier to assume the best and offer grace when they disappoint or fall short of our expectations. Where patience becomes a true discipline is with those who annoy or anger us. Maybe it is a coworker, certain family member, or a friend that rubs you the wrong way consistently enough for you to want to snap. This is where patience is practiced and perfected. What if we saw the people who annoy us the most as the very people who can best help us develop a discipline of patience? How would this approach help you to deal with those you must interact with, but who most frustrate you? After all, patience isn't developed with the easy people in our lives, but with the ones who are the most difficult.

~Prayer of Petition~

Evening

But if we hope for what we don't see, we wait for it with patience. (Romans 8:25)

Reflection

These words from Paul contain a challenge to us. It is hard to hope for something we have not yet seen. We have not yet seen the promised fulfillment of the new creation, or the world in the wholeness that God has in mind. We instead see the brokenness around us and experience the heartbreak of the world as it is. But Paul tells us that because what we are waiting on is the fulfillment of God's promise, we wait with patience. In other places in scripture, we are told that patience is a gift of the Spirit, and is a trait possessed by God that God shares with those who ask. Have you asked God for the gift of patience as we hope for what we cannot yet see? How might your prayer life be enriched by the gift of patience?

~Prayer of Gratitude~

Weakness

Morning Prayer of Petition

Powerful God, so often I intend and desire to obey you, but fail to live up to those intentions. As Jesus taught, my spirit is willing, but my flesh is weak. May your Spirit anoint me today and provide me strength:

- in areas of life where I am tired and burned out,
- to tackle the challenges and obstacles that I face,
- in situations that have no easy solution,
- to persevere when I feel like giving up,
- to love those around me, especially those whom I find it hard to love.

God, today may I remember that in and through your strength, I can do all things. Amen.

Evening Prayer of Gratitude

Heavenly Father, you remind me that when I am weak, there I'm strong. Each day I try to lean more into the truth of what this means. Help me not to hide from weakness but in gratitude to:

- claim the parts of me of which I am embarrassed or ashamed,
- see how weakness can be a source of strength,
- notice the help you provide in and around me,
- receive your permission to not be perfect all the time.

Work in my weakness, that your strength may be known in my life. Amen.

Day 1

Morning

Strengthen the weak hands,
and support the unsteady knees. (Isaiah 35:3)

Reflection

Babies are entirely dependent on others for their survival. But as they grow up, they begin to develop independence. Walking, feeding themselves, going to school, and eventually driving a car, having a job, and living on their own. Our culture often marks maturity with milestones of independence. The less we need others, the more grown up we are. But this way of thinking is dangerous when taken to the extreme. We aren't meant to be completely independent, but rather we need God and others. Weakness and the subsequent need for support are features of human living; they are not bugs to be fixed or extirpated. In order to live abundant and full lives, we will inevitably need help. Moments of weakness remind us that we are pushing ourselves, trying hard things, and taking risks. Weakness is not a sign of failure, but yet another milestone on the road to a purposeful and impactful life.

~Prayer of Petition~

Evening

If God dresses grass in the field so beautifully, even though it's alive today and tomorrow it's thrown into the furnace, how much more will God do for you, you people of weak faith! (Luke 12:28)

Reflection

Love has, at its core, vulnerability: the willingness to open yourself so radically that you might get hurt. For as much as the church sings of God's power, one of the most radical things God has ever done is to become weak, to be vulnerable. Think of the cross, that great matter of obedience, the Christ who was so vulnerable that he was willing to die. There is power in vulnerability.

Think of creation, the matter in which God said, "Let us create humankind in our image" (Genesis 1:26), a sharing of God's self with all of humanity. There is enough electricity in that statement to power of all of creation, to create something from nothing.

But vulnerability is not easy. Another account of creation shares that one of the first acts of humankind is to abuse that vulnerability, to strike God directly in the exposed area of God's deepest heart.

Still, knowing that the strike is possible, God shares that heart in an act of deep vulnerability, and it is a wonder that all of creation does not break down from the frequency of God's cries. Instead, God keeps calling out to us, pulling us closer to God's own heart.

~Prayer of Gratitude~

Day 2

Morning

In the same way, the Spirit comes to help our weakness. We don't know what we should pray, but the Spirit himself pleads our case with unexpressed groans. (Romans 8:26)

Reflection

When we falter is when God shows up. Moments when our strength runs out are moments when we more clearly sense God's strength at work. When our efforts fail and fall short, we are more able to see God's capacity to redeem and make a way. Therefore we shouldn't be afraid or embarrassed when we find ourselves in over our heads, unable to move forward, or not knowing what to do next. In moments of weakness is when the Spirit shows up and when God's fingerprints on your life become evident. Remember this. That we live with a power that is not our own. That when we fall, God catches. When we get nervous, God stays steady. When we do not know the way, God provides clarity and direction. When we do not know what to say, God gives words. When we hit our limits, we are finally in a position to see God's power most at work.

~Prayer of Petition~

Evening

God guides the weak to justice,
teaching them his way. (Psalm 25:9)

Reflection

All cruelty springs from weakness.
— Seneca, *Seneca's Morals: Of a Happy Life, Benefits, Anger and Clemency*

~Prayer of Gratitude~

Day 3

Morning

This is because the foolishness of God is wiser than human wisdom, and the weakness of God is stronger than human strength. (1 Corinthians 1:25)

Reflection

It is precisely when God makes little sense to us that we ought to pay the most attention. When God's actions, nudges, teachings, or commandments do not seem logical or preferable to us is the moment that God has the greatest capacity to transform us. Therefore, it is important not to pursue a version of God that already agrees with everything that we believe and value. We have to leave room for God's wisdom to contradict our own—to seem silly or unwise. We must pay attention when God's actions in Christ seem weak. It is in these moments that God challenges and indicts human wisdom and shows us a different way. If we are open, it is in these moments of contradiction that God has the greatest ability to change us.

~Prayer of Petition~

Evening

When my heart is weak,
*   I cry out to you from the very ends of the earth,*
Lead me to the rock that is higher than I am. (Psalm 61:2)

Reflection

Prayer is not asking. It is a longing of the soul. It is daily admission of one's weakness. It is better in prayer to have a heart without words than words without a heart.
   —Mahatma Gandhi

~Prayer of Gratitude~

Day 4

Morning

I stood in front of you with weakness, fear, and a lot of shaking. (1 Corinthians 2:3)

Reflection

When is the last time you tried something that had a good chance of failing? When is the last time you took a risk outside your comfort zone? When is the last time you tried something big enough that, unless God showed up, you would almost certainly fail? This is the zone that courageous discipleship lives. Feelings of weakness and fear aren't signs that you are going down the wrong road. Instead, they can be signs that you are finally trying something out of your comfort zone. When we stretch our abilities and try something that requires help, that is when we are trying something worthy of the calling to which we have received. Feeling weak and inadequate is a mark of discipleship in the way of Jesus. We ought to feel this way. We ought to need Jesus. If your answer to the above questions is, "I can't remember," then it is time to reassess. Do not narrow your goals to that which you can only accomplish confidently and safely on your own. Rather, try something that makes you feel weak. These are the moments when God breaks in and we often break through.

~Prayer of Petition~

Evening

But the weak will inherit the land;
*   they will enjoy a surplus of peace.* (Psalm 37:11)

Reflection

In his book, *Jesus and the Disinherited*, Howard Thurman explores what the Gospels have to say in support of people "with their backs against the wall." He writes, "it cannot be denied that too often the weight of the Christian movement has been on the side of the strong and the powerful and against the weak and oppressed—this, despite the gospel." I suspect that what Thurman means is that many of the Gospel accounts demonstrate Jesus's teaching that there is great power in powerlessness: blessed are the poor, the meek, those who are persecuted. And, yet, the church remains enamored with power. Jesus is for all people, of course, but the consistent narrative of the Bible is that God sides with the weak over the strong, the poor over the powerful. As I am someone who is neither poor nor weak, I am left to wonder: What does it mean that God identifies with a group that does not include me? How can I concern myself more with being on God's side?

~Prayer of Gratitude~

Day 5

Morning

Stay alert and pray so that you won't give in to temptation. The spirit is eager, but the flesh is weak. (Matthew 26:41)

Reflection

Have you ever been in a job interview where someone asks you to talk about your weaknesses? None of us like this question. In fact, we usually answer with a weakness that ends up making us look as good as possible. But we all have areas of temptation and weakness in our lives. Jesus warns his disciples to be self-aware enough to know that they aren't perfect and that, despite their best intentions, temptation has a way of preying on these areas of weakness. He encourages them to be alert, to know and notice where they are susceptible to temptation. We do not like to dwell on our temptations or weaknesses. We especially do not like to consider where we morally and ethically are most susceptible. But discipleship and leadership require us to be aware of areas of weakness. The more we know ourselves, and the more we understand our vulnerabilities, the more we can stay alert to those forces that seek to exploit them.

~Prayer of Petition~

Evening

All my bones will say, "LORD, who could compare to you?
You rescue the weak from those who overpower them;
you rescue the weak and the needy from those who plunder them." (Psalm 35:10)

Reflection

My Lord God, I have no idea where I am going. I do not see the road ahead of me. I cannot know for certain where it will end. Nor do I really know myself, and the fact that I think that I am following your will does not mean that I am actually doing so. But I believe that the desire to please you does in fact please you. And I hope I have that desire in all that I am doing. I hope that I will never do anything apart from that desire. And I know that if I do this you will lead me by the right road though I may know nothing about it. Therefore will I trust you always though I may seem to be lost and in the shadow of death. I will not fear, for you are ever with me, and you will never leave me to face my perils alone.

—Thomas Merton, *Thoughts in Solitude*

~Prayer of Gratitude~

Belonging

Morning Prayer of Petition

God of all people, you not only created all that is, but you sustain the whole with your love and grace. Today, prick my conscience and consciousness so that I am fully aware of:

- those around me who are feeling alone and isolated,
- people who are overlooked or ignored,
- people who are difficult to love,
- words and conversations that tear others down instead of building them up.

As you extend a place for me to belong, help me to be a person who draws others in and creates space for them. Amen.

Evening Prayer of Gratitude

Holy God, like a mother hen you long to gather your children under your wing. I resist and doubt my place in that family and yet you continue to welcome me back to you. Even today, I see the ways that you:

- surround me with support systems,
- take care of me materially and spiritually,
- supply opportunities for me to learn and grow,
- provide me with friends who walk with me,
- welcome me back to you even when I sin.

Grow in me a sense of gratitude for your provision and give me a sense of assurance that I have a place in your family. Amen.

Day 1

Morning

So now you are no longer strangers and aliens. Rather, you are fellow citizens with God's people, and you belong to God's household. (Ephesians 2:19)

Reflection

Have you ever been in a new environment where everyone around you seems to already have a group of friends? It is lonely. There is an incredibly uplifting feeling when someone calls over to you and says, "Join us." The feeling of belonging somewhere and with someone is powerful. When it comes to faith, there are so many voices that proclaim to know who is in and who is out, who is included and who is not. Voices of exclusion are prevalent and loud, leaving many of us feeling isolated. Even walking into many churches, we visibly sense that others belong there while we do not. But in a crowded cacophony of voices, this one is the loudest. The voice of God calls us from our place of isolation and loneliness and invites us in. The voice of God proclaims that we are part of God's family. God's voice says that we reside in God's household. God tells us that we belong and this is a voice we must listen to.

~Prayer of Petition~

Evening

But you belong to Christ, and Christ belongs to God. (1 Corinthians 3:23)

Reflection

Humans throughout time have found it difficult to accept the notion that standing before God is not a result of our own doing, but rather the work of God through Jesus Christ. But the acceptance of this reality is crucial to a true life of faith. Our faith grows out of grace that God has freely offered to us. Faith is a true expression of our calling as beloved children of God. We live out this faith through our love of God and our love of others.

— Cynthia Weems, *The CEB Women's Bible*

~Prayer of Gratitude~

Day 2

Morning

But now, says the LORD—
*   the one who created you, Jacob,*
*   the one who formed you, Israel:*
Don't fear, for I have redeemed you;
*   I have called you by name; you are mine.* (Isaiah 43:1)

Reflection

Have you ever poured your blood, sweat, and tears into creating or building something? Maybe it is a DIY house project that took countless YouTube videos, dozens of trips to the hardware stores, and hours of work. When you complete something that you have worked so hard on, you care about it exponentially more. You are even willing to overlook imperfections and apparent mistakes because the work is yours. You protect it, maybe even brag about it, and you want to show it off to your friends and family. Others may not be impressed but it doesn't matter. You love it. That is how God looks at you. God created you, designed and formed you with great care and intentionality. When sin threatened to distort and mar that creation, God redeemed you and restored you to God's original design. God has put countless hours into you and fussed over you with great attention. And because of this, you are God's. You belong to God. Nothing you are or do can erase that. Nothing anyone else says or does takes this truth away.

~Prayer of Petition~

Evening

Since we belong to the day, let's stay sober, wearing faithfulness and love as a piece of armor that protects our body and the hope of salvation as a helmet. (1 Thessalonians 5:8)

Reflection

Be serious and frequent in the examination of your heart and life . . . Every evening review your carriage through the day; what you have done or thought that was unbecoming your character; whether your heart has been instant upon religion and indifferent to the world? Have a special care of two portions of time, namely, morning and evening; the morning to forethink what you have to do, and the evening to examine whether you have done what you ought.

Let every action have reference to your whole life, and not to a part only. Let all your subordinate ends be suitable to the great end of your living. Exercise yourself unto godliness.

—John Wesley, *John and Charles Wesley*

~Prayer of Gratitude~

Day 3

Morning

The earth's depths are in his hands;
  the mountain heights belong to him. (Psalm 95:4)

Reflection

Jesus once told his disciples that it is easy to love people who love you. Similarly, it is easy to praise God when events in your life are going your way. When we are on those proverbial mountain tops, we find it more natural to thank God, praise God, and attribute the good things in our life to God's blessing. But what about those low points in life? What happens to our relationship with God when we find ourselves in the proverbial pit? It is easy to blame God, to question our faith, and to wonder why God isn't fixing the circumstances that swirl around us. It is okay to question God, and God can undoubtedly handle our questioning, and even our blame. But scripture reminds us that both the high points and the low points belong to God. In all circumstances, God is powerfully at work in our lives. God is able to bend all of the world's chaos toward his purposes and plans. While we are allowed to question and doubt God, we can instead choose to praise God even in the low points. We can expect God to be working even when we can't see it or detect God. It is easy to praise God on the mountain, but can you also do it in the depths of the pit?

~Prayer of Petition~

Evening

Little children, let's not love with words or speech but with action and truth. This is how we will know that we belong to the truth and reassure our hearts in God's presence. (1 John 3:18-19)

Reflection

Today, John tells us that "talk is cheap." John reminds us that the way we love one another is through actions and in truth, not merely with words of affirmation or public speech. What we do and how we behave is all part of belonging to one another and belonging to God. Francis of Assisi supposedly said, "Preach the gospel at all times. If necessary, use words." Like John before him, Francis reminds us that how we love each other is not only a practical guide for a life lived together well, but is also a witness to those around us. The way you treat your spouse tells the world about God. The way you run your business reflects how you love others. Today, reflect upon what your actions and behaviors are telling the world about God and God's love.

~Prayer of Gratitude~

Day 4

Morning

Don't you know that you have the Holy Spirit from God, and you don't belong to yourselves? (1 Corinthians 6:19b)

Reflection

A seemingly unquestioned value of our culture is that you are your own person. You don't owe anybody anything. As long as you don't break the law or infringe on someone else, you can do what you want. That may be the prevailing ethos of our world, but it is not how God sees things. When we develop a relationship with God, make a commitment to follow Christ, and invite the Holy Spirit into our hearts, our very lives become collaborative. We find that our lives are not only our own, but that we cooperate with

Sow

God as we live and move and have our being. This means that we invite God into the decisions of our lives, big or small. It means we consult God when we determine a direction in our lives, even if we think we know the way. It means you surrender to God when your will collides with God's wisdom, especially when you feel like ignoring it. It means we listen to God when the Spirit nudges, calls, or prompts us. As a follower of Christ, your life is a group project, so make sure to make room for God in all aspects of it.

~Prayer of Petition~

Evening

When your words turned up, I feasted on them;
and they became my joy, the delight of my heart,
because I belong to you,
LORD God of heavenly forces. (Jeremiah 15:16)

Reflection

The scriptural witness challenges us to remember not only that we are loved and made in the image of God but that others are as well. We are of sacred worth and equal with everyone else because our primary "status" is as children of God. To be a follower of Christ places us among all the other adopted children of God and calls us to treat others as Christ did.

Imagine a world in which all people truly recognize each other as equal in value and dignity. Imagine a world in which all people truly live up to the gifts they have been given—the gift of being made in God's image, equally loved, one and all.

—Mireya Martinez, *The CEB Women's Bible*

~Prayer of Gratitude~

Day 5

Morning

The earth and all that is in it belong to the Lord. (1 Corinthians 10:26)

Reflection

It is troubling to think that earth and *everything* in it belongs to God. What about mosquitos? How about annoying people and terrible weather? What about natural disasters or the evil potential of a human heart? Does everything really belong to God? The answer is "Yes, but." Yes, but God does not cause all that happens. God created humans but does not create the evil we devise. God created the winds and sea, but not the natural disaster that takes lives and wreaks havoc on the world. To say that all things belong to God means that nothing is outside of God's power and purview. Nothing is independently powerful enough to challenge God. More simply, it means that God can and will bend all things toward God's will. It means that the earth and everything in it are ultimately subject to God's sovereignty, God's redemptive power, and God's will. This is true about the world, and true about your life. Everything in your life belongs to God, and nothing is beyond God's power to forgive, redeem, and make new.

~Prayer of Petition~

Evening

I know every mountain bird;
even the insects in the fields are mine. (Psalm 50:11)

Reflection

I wonder if you remember what it felt like to own your first car or your first house? Do you remember a strange mixture of excitement and fear? The home is yours, sure . . . but it's also up to you to maintain and fill with furniture and fix whatever breaks. When something belongs to us, we have a responsibility to it. The psalmist speaks in God's voice, naming the ways that God owns creation down to the smallest swallow or tiniest firefly in the fields. God invites us to call out to God, because God's ownership means that God claims responsibility over us. And God invites us to share in that responsibility—what divides the righteous from the wicked, the psalmist goes on to say, is how the wicked don't even care for their own siblings. Belonging means responsibility. What is something that belongs to you that requires you take greater responsibility? Today, let us be God's hands and feet by taking responsibility and caring for every good gift that God has given to us.

~Prayer of Gratitude~

Harvest

Strength

Morning Prayer of Petition

God of all, you uphold the world by your might, and in your wisdom, you work all things toward good. Call to my mind today the places and people in need of your strength, particularly those who:

- are hurting and suffering silently,
- are caught in a pattern of addiction,
- are actively sinning or moving away from you,
- are seeking healing in body or spirit.

May your strength be with me and all those who need you this day. Amen.

Evening Prayer of Gratitude

God Most High, you hold the world in the palm of your hand, and there is not a hair on our head that is not counted by you. Raise in me an awareness of your strength at work in my life, and thank you for:

- your forgiveness made real for me today,
- your love made known to me today,
- your conviction felt by me today,
- your joy encountered by me today,
- your strength given to me today.

Help me to live out of a sense of gratitude to you and live boldly empowered by your strength. Amen.

Day 1

Morning

All you who wait for the LORD,
be strong and let your heart take courage. (Psalm 31:24)

Reflection

We usually think of waiting as a passive posture. When we can't *do* anything more, we resort to waiting. But waiting is an active spiritual practice that requires courage and strength. Most great endeavors include seasons in which it is easier to walk away. Whether it is marriage, a vocation, a personal commitment, or a new direction in life—most activities worth doing require a strength to hang on, even when throwing in the towel is more tempting. Sometimes the easy thing to do, the less risky action, is to quit, to move, or to give up. But staying committed to a place or relationship that God calls you to is an act of great courage. It requires the kind of strength to continue to move forward, to press on in a consistent direction, trusting that God is indeed working.

~Prayer of Petition~

Evening

The LORD is my strength and my power;
  he has become my salvation.
This is my God, whom I will praise,
  the God of my ancestors, whom I will acclaim. (Exodus 15:2)

Reflection

The Lord was pleased to strengthen us, and remove all fear from us, and disposed our hearts to be as useful as possible.

   —Richard Allen and Absalom Jones (This pamphlet is a rebuttal by Allen and Jones to false accusations—they cared for persons regardless of race during an epidemic in Philadelphia.)

~Prayer of Gratitude~

Day 2

Morning

Stay awake, stand firm in your faith, be brave, be strong. (1 Corinthians 16:13)

Reflection

Have you ever put up a tent but ignored the need to thoroughly stake it to the ground? Or maybe you've put an umbrella or shade canopy up on the beach but bypassed the sandbags that are suggested to weigh it down. These structures are fine until a storm comes. Strong wind gusts can pick up even the sturdiest tent and move it effortlessly if it isn't tethered to something. What seems optional in good weather becomes essential during a storm. Life is similar. Building strength spiritually requires cultivating and developing your faith, even when everything is going smoothly. We have a temptation during good times to drift from God, to neglect the practices that bolster our faith, and to drift from prayer. But our strength is built day-by-day, week-by-week, as we tether our lives to something solid and certain. When the storms come, that strength of faith will allow us to stand firm amid the wind.

~Prayer of Petition~

Evening

You've given me the shield of your salvation;
your strong hand has supported me;
your help has made me great. (Psalm 18:35)

Reflection

The image of the shield of salvation is a defensive one. The shield is used in battle for protection and coverage, not necessarily for charging forward or mounting an attack. Our greatness and strength come from the protection and coverage that are offered by God's salvation. Shielding ourselves with God's salvation makes us great. Paul will later write about the full armor of God and encourage readers to pick up the shield of faith. God never expects us to come up with our own protection or our own salvation; rather, our salvation comes from God. If we will pick up the shield God is giving us, we will find the protection we need to encounter every challenge.

~Prayer of Gratitude~

Day 3

Morning

Don't think to yourself, My own strength and abilities have produced all this prosperity for me. Remember the LORD your God! He's the one who gives you the strength to be prosperous. (Deuteronomy 8:17-18a)

Reflection

When discussing generosity, it is common for someone to argue, "I have earned what I have, why should I give it to someone else?" This line of thinking extends to other areas of life. There is a strong tendency to believe that, when we succeed, we did it ourselves. We worked hard, we took risks, we used our abilities to get ahead. Life, though, is not a prize we achieve but a gift we receive. It is God who creates, God who pours out gifts and abilities, God who opens up opportunities we don't deserve, and God who provides strength that we cannot muster on our own. Working hard and building your own strength both matter. But they are a response to the gifts God has given, not a substitute for them. One day, our own efforts will run out, and it is then that we will most clearly see that God's strength and presence have been at work in our lives all along.

~Prayer of Petition~

Evening

Hope in the LORD!
Be strong! Let your heart take courage!
Hope in the LORD! (Psalm 27:14)

Reflection

I arise today
Through the strength of Christ's birth with his baptism,
Through the strength of his crucifixion with his burial,
Through the strength of his resurrection with his ascension,
Through the strength of his descent for the judgment of Doom.
Through the strength of heaven:
Light of sun,
Radiance of moon,
Splendour of fire,
Speed of lightning,
Swiftness of wind,
Depth of sea,
Stability of earth,
Firmness of rock.
    —from St. Patrick's Breastplate

~Prayer of Gratitude~

Day 4

Morning

This is because the foolishness of God is wiser than human wisdom, and the weakness of God is stronger than human strength. (1 Corinthians 1:25)

Reflection

Most of us dislike failure. We struggle to admit fault, we shirk responsibility for events that don't work out, and we avoid calling attention to our shortcomings. But, in a great irony of faith, we see God most at work when we are at our weakest. Why? When we are operating out of perceived strength, we become susceptible to dangerous tendencies. We don't ask for help, we don't collaborate or let others contribute, we think more highly of our abilities than we ought, and, maybe most importantly, we are less reliant on God. But when we are weak, we are more open to the work of God. We accept help more readily, admit shortcomings and therefore address them more honestly, and we invite God into the work knowing that we cannot accomplish it alone. While our culture may tempt us to always present strength and confidence, God encourages us not to fear shortcomings or despair in seasons of weakness. It is at these times that God can do some of God's most transformative and powerful work in and through us.

~Prayer of Petition~

Evening

I've commanded you to be brave and strong, haven't I? Don't be alarmed or terrified, because the LORD your God is with you wherever you go. (Joshua 1:9)

Reflection

God spoke these words to Joshua after the death of Moses, as Joshua was preparing to step into leadership and bring the people into the promised land. These words feel like the kind of thing Joshua needed to hear at such a moment. God sensed that and gave Joshua the assurance that God would be with him wherever he went and whatever he faced. The source of Joshua's strength was not his own might, or the power of the Israelite army; rather, the source of Joshua's strength was God's presence with him. So often we believe we must rely on our own cleverness, intellect, abilities, or capacities to move forward. The words of God to Joshua are a clear reminder to us that we stand not in our own strength, but in God's.

~Prayer of Gratitude~

Day 5

Morning

I can endure all these things through the power of the one who gives me strength. (Philippians 4:13)

Reflection

Among many of the sayings often misattributed to scripture is, "God never gives you more than you can handle." The Bible never says this, exactly. In fact, if we rely solely on our own strength and ability, there is much in life that we can't handle. Longevity in marriage, mental and physical health, financial faithfulness, personal development, career accomplishments, faithful parenting, and spiritual maturity all require more capacity and ability than any one person has. All of these depend on help from a power greater than one's self. Scripture doesn't promise us that God won't give us more than we can handle. But scripture does tell us that we can handle anything thrown at us because of the power of the one whose strength rests on us, dwells in us, and operates through us. Our power comes not from our reliance on self, but from our connection to Christ.

~Prayer of Petition~

Evening

The LORD is my solid rock,
      my fortress, my rescuer.
My God is my rock—
I take refuge in him!—
      he's my shield,
      my salvation's strength,
      my place of safety. (Psalm 18:2)

Reflection

Be still, my soul: the Lord is on your side.
Bear patiently the cross of grief or pain;
Leave to your God to order and provide;
In every change God faithful will remain.
      —Katherina von Schlegel, "Be Still, My Soul"

~Prayer of Gratitude~

Calm

Morning Prayer of Petition

God of Peace, in you we can find a calmness that the world does not offer. In the chaos of our world, I pray for peace and a sense of deep calm for:

- friends who are lost and searching for a way forward,
- people who are suffering and hurting because of injustice,
- those battling physical and mental illness and disease,
- people stuck in places marked by violence, war, and death,
- family and friends who are far away from you.

Give me and all those who need you a day light on anxiety and rooted by and in your peace. Amen.

Evening Prayer of Gratitude

God who sees, you know all, are in all, and over all. Every day you walk in front of me and behind me, leading me toward still waters. May a sense of calm settle in my soul as I remember the ways that you:

- provided for me today when I was stressed or anxious,
- show your presence to me in surprising moments,
- lead me through difficult conversations or circumstances,
- calm my spirit when I get angry or frustrated,
- extend support through people in my life.

May I rest knowing that when life seems out of control, you are in control. Amen.

Day 1

Morning

Instead, make yourselves beautiful on the inside, in your hearts, with the enduring quality of a gentle, peaceful spirit. This type of beauty is very precious in God's eyes. (1 Peter 3:4)

Reflection

I once heard it said that leadership is the ability to be the least anxious person in the room. But a calm and peaceful spirit is not what we often associate with strong leadership. Instead, we think of things like tenacity, decisiveness, and confidence. Many of us are so concerned with what we can accomplish out in the world. We seek to influence others, try to control situations, desire to achieve certain outcomes. We work so hard to maintain control over the world around us that we neglect to shape what exists within us. And, yet, the only thing we can really control is ourselves. Spiritually mature leaders are those who have tended to the internal work of the spirit, allowing God to shape, mature, and develop what lies within. How you react in the face of disagreement, how you handle criticism, and how you show up in divisive and heightened situations will determine your success as much as any outward accomplishment. It is when we can show up with a calm and non-anxious presence that we are most able to influence, shape, and contribute to the team, organization, or church that we are tasked with leading.

~Prayer of Petition~

Evening

You calm the roaring seas;
*   calm the roaring waves,*
*   calm the noise of the nations.* (Psalm 65:7)

Reflection

It amazes me to think about how the God who created the heavens and the earth and everything in it, also shows God's power and might by bringing all of it—the natural world and humanity—down to a simple silence. It almost feels like the awesome chaos of establishing mountains is balanced by the silencing of the roaring seas.

I wonder if we allow ourselves that same balance? So often, our lives are on the run, on the go, moving from moment to moment, activity to activity, appointment to appointment. We build with our lives, and we forget that God is also in the silent spaces, in the calm seas, in the quieted hearts and minds. If we can find and enter into these moments with intentionality, perhaps we can have a connection with God that allows us simply to be. Perhaps then we can live more fully, more balanced, and into a holistic relationship with the God who silences seas.

~Prayer of Gratitude~

Day 2

Morning

The fruit of righteousness will be peace,
*   and the outcome of righteousness,*
*   calm and security forever.* (Isaiah 32:17)

Reflection

One of the greatest oxymorons is an angry, anxious Christian. Yet, Christ followers sometimes seem more known for what they are afraid of or against than what they are for. Preachers spend time bemoaning our culture and warning people about it. The message it sends is that Christians are angry, anxious, and fearful people. The world is full of enough anxiety, chaos, and anger. God does not need us to feed into it or mirror it. The fruit of a right relationship with God is not anger, but calm. It is not anxiety, but a peace that surpasses understanding. It is not an agitated and fearful disposition towards the world, but a sober-minded and gentle ability to build up the common good. Since following Christ, have you become more irritated with others or less? Do you find yourself more judgmental or more grace-filled toward people? Do you spend more time critiquing or building up? Are you more hopeful or less about the world around you? The answers will say a lot about what voices you are listening to and who you are really following.

~Prayer of Petition~

Evening

When my anxieties multiply,
your comforting calms me down. (Psalm 94:19)

Reflection

Breathe, O breathe thy loving Spirit into every troubled breast!
Let us all in thee inherit; let us find that second rest.
Take away our bent to sinning; Alpha and Omega be;
End of faith, as its beginning, set our hearts at liberty.
—Charles Wesley, "Love Divine, All Loves Excelling"

~Prayer of Gratitude~

Day 3

Morning

After the earthquake, there was a fire. But the LORD *wasn't in the fire. After the fire, there was a sound. Thin. Quiet.* (1 Kings 19:12)

Reflection

Have you ever wondered why God doesn't show up to you the way God showed up to so many people in the Bible? We often long for God to speak to us in a clear and audible voice, perform an undeniable miracle, answer our prayers directly and immediately, or unambiguously show us the direction we are to go. We want God to speak to us, and many people wonder why God seems to speak less today than God did in biblical times. But if you have trouble hearing God's voice, have you ever considered what the real problem might be? Maybe the problem is that God doesn't speak as much as God used to. Or maybe the problem is that we, as people, have a tougher time listening. Today, we have so much that distracts us and keeps our mind racing. From twenty-four-hour news to phones that constantly spit information at us, our minds and hearts rarely have time to be calm and quiet long enough to hear anything. But what if we worked to create patterns of disengagement and quiet in our life? What if we pursued a calm spirit as a spiritual discipline? Maybe then we would develop the ears to hear and the eyes to see the God who is desperately trying to speak to us.

~Prayer of Petition~

Evening

Lord, my heart isn't proud;
> *my eyes aren't conceited.*
> *I don't get involved with things too great or wonderful for me.*
No. But I have calmed and quieted myself
> *like a weaned child on its mother;*
> *I'm like the weaned child that is with me.*
Israel, wait for the Lord—
> *from now until forever from now!* (Psalm 131)

Reflection

How many decisions do you think you make in a day? In an hour? In a minute?

Many of us are confronted with a never-ending flow of decisions from the moment we wake in the morning until we lay ourselves to rest. Some may feel incredibly insignificant, while others carry the weight of the consequences that will be felt for the whole day, for years, or even for generations.

And in the midst of all that surrounds us, the busyness of our lives and all that we carry in our hearts and in our souls, when do we make time for God?

The psalmist sings this Song of Quiet Trust and invites us to do the same—to make space to calm and quiet our souls. Perhaps that means finding time away from the busyness that allows us to become more aware of God's presence all around us. Breathe. Breathe again. Calm your soul and trust that God is with you.

~Prayer of Gratitude~

Day 4

Morning

He got up and gave orders to the wind, and he said to the lake, "Silence! Be still!" The wind settled down and there was a great calm. (Mark 4:39)

Reflection

Have you ever spent time contemplating the power of Jesus to bring calm and order to chaos? In the creation story, the spirit of God took the deep and chaotic and brought forth life. Jesus demonstrated his power by bringing control and calm to the unpredictable and uncontrollable storm. This story, in particular, is ripe with symbolism, clearly making it about more than Jesus's meteorological abilities. The sea was an ancient symbol of chaos, the boat on the water an early symbol for the church. Amid the chaos and storms of life, the body of Christ is a protection, a bulwark, a place of safety. Jesus himself is the one who comes to calm the chaotic forces that threaten each of us. The gift Christ offers the disciples is the calm and assurance that no chaos is powerful enough to engulf us. Jesus is more powerful than the chaos of life. Your life will feel uncontrollable at times. Your life will be unpredictable, full of uncertainty. Life will sometimes be so overwhelming that you wonder if you can handle it all. But scripture reminds us that while following Jesus may not exempt us from life's chaos, it offers us the confidence that Jesus is more powerful than the circumstances around us.

~Prayer of Petition~

Evening

The LORD your God is in your midst—a warrior bringing victory.
   He will create calm with his love;
   he will rejoice over you with singing. (Zephaniah 3:17)

Reflection

Be still, my soul: the Lord is on your side.
Bear patiently the cross of grief or pain;
leave to your God to order and provide;
in every change God faithful will remain.
Be still my soul: your best, your heavenly friend
through thorny ways leads to a joyful end.
   — Katharina von Schlegel, translated by Jane Borthwick, "Be Still, My Soul"

~Prayer of Gratitude~

Day 5

Morning

Listen, Job; hear me;
   be quiet, and I will speak. (Job 33:31)

Reflection

You've heard it said that we have two ears and one mouth. We should listen more than we speak. But how often do you take this to heart when it comes to your relationship with God? Our prayers tend to be heavy on speaking and light on listening. We list off our petitions to God, giving God a laundry list of wants and desires. We talk to

God about the world and what we want to see changed in it. We thank God for what is happening in our lives. But do you also spend time in quiet, calm moments, simply listening? Some might see prayer without words as a waste of time, or an inefficiency that cannot be afforded in one's busy schedule. But a relationship requires time spent listening for the answers to all the words we lift to God. Those answers may come as opportunities, an inner nudge, a growing passion, or an audible voice. But the answers will never come if we do all the talking. Instead, we must quiet our hearts, calm our minds, and steady our spirit. Only this allows us to hear what God might be saying.

~Prayer of Petition~

Evening

Better a dry crust with quiet
*   than a house full of feasting with quarrels.* (Proverbs 17:1)

Reflection

Be still my soul: your God will undertake
to guide the future, as in ages past.
Your hope, your confidence let nothing shake;
all now mysterious shall be bright at last.
Be still, my soul: the waves and winds still know
the Christ who ruled them while he dwelt below.
Be still, my soul: the hour is hastening on
when we shall be forever with the Lord,
when disappointment, grief, and fear are gone,
sorrow forgot, love's purest joys restored.
Be still, my soul: when change and tears are past,
all safe and blessed we shall meet at last.
    —Katharina von Schlegel, translated by Jane Borthwick, "Be Still, My Soul"

~Prayer of Gratitude~

Righteous

Morning Prayer of Petition

God of truth and grace, you are holy and you call us to live rightly with you and our neighbor. Center me today and bring to mind the places in my life and the world that need your Spirit:

- for people who are treated unjustly,
- for those ignored or cast aside,
- for those suffering in body or mind,
- for those in place of economic distress,
- for leaders at all levels.

May your people on earth reflect your love for all and embody your righteousness and justice. Amen.

Evening Prayer of Gratitude

Steadfast and faithful God, you show up every day and I am never without you in my life. Give me space to notice and awareness to see how you are at work:

- correcting me and setting me on a right path,
- convicting me of needed change in my life,
- forgiving me through the grace of others,
- providing for me through resources and opportunity,
- challenging me to serve you more authentically each day.

I thank you, God, for your presence today. Help me to live for you, not out of obligation, but out of gratitude. Amen.

Day 1

Morning

Please don't bring your servant to judgment,
because no living thing is righteous before you. (Psalm 143:2)

Reflection

Authentic Christianity is at once the most inclusive and exclusive faith in the world. None of us deserve God's favor or blessing. People are not ranked with some in and others out. To say that we are all sinners cuts across all of the divisions and categories that humanity devises for itself. Before God, class, race, sexual orientation, political affiliation, wealth, neighborhood, and achievement are all flattened out by the truth that we are imperfect, that we fall short. We are all sinners and, therefore, none of us is more deserving than another. What could be more exclusive than a righteousness none of us can achieve? At the same time, it is the most inclusive faith. God offers righteousness as a gift to all, regardless of what the world says about you or how culture may categorize you. None of us are any less deserving to be included in the kingdom. We all can stand with equal confidence before God because a right and whole relationship with God is something that is given as a gift, not earned as a reward.

~Prayer of Petition~

Evening

It is because of God that you are in Christ Jesus. He became wisdom from God for us. This means that he made us righteous and holy, and he delivered us. (1 Corinthians 1:30)

Reflection

It is scarcely conceivable how narrow the way is wherein God leads those who follow him and how dependent on him we must be unless we are wanting in our faithfulness to him.

It is hardly believable of what great consequence before God the smallest things are, and what great inconveniences sometimes follow those that appear to be light faults.

As a very little dust will disorder a clock and the least sand will obscure our sight, so the least grain of sin that is upon the hear will hinder its right motion toward God.

We ought to be in the church as the saints are in heaven, and in the house as the holiest people are in the church: doing our work in the house as we pray in the church, worshiping God from the ground of the heart . . .

Then shall we begin, in this fleeting life, to love God as we shall love him in eternity.

—John Wesley, "A Plain Account of Christian Perfection"

~Prayer of Gratitude~

Day 2

Morning

Christ himself suffered on account of sins, once for all, the righteous one on behalf of the unrighteous. (1 Peter 3:18a)

Harvest

Reflection

Like a lot of biblical words, the word *righteousness* has multiple, nuanced meanings. We usually think of it as being deserving or justified in our standing. More simply, we think of a righteous person as a holy one, a person who does what is right and never what is evil. But the word *righteous* can also mean steadfastly faithful. A righteous one can be depended on to always show up, always do what they promise, always be worthy of trust. In this way, righteousness is a relational word. We can depend on one who is righteous. Humanity is inherently unrighteous. Our faithfulness always has limits and conditions. Our ability to depend on another is always temporal or imperfect. But God meets our unrighteousness and inherent lack of stability in relationship with the faithfulness of Jesus. Our relationship with Christ is one that is dependable, rock-solid, and unconditional. It is truly good news to imagine that God's response to our imperfect ability to love is a promise to always be faithful to us, no matter what.

~Prayer of Petition~

Evening

God is a righteous judge,
a God who is angry at evil every single day. (Psalm 7:11)

Reflection

God is not indifferent to our actions and attitudes. God does not rest in the heavens, far removed from the concerns of earth.

Psalm 7:11 tells us that "God is a righteous judge, a God who is angry at evil every single day."

Violence enrages the heart of God. Oppression infuriates the Holy One. Arrogance exasperates the author of creation. A righteous judge cannot turn a blind eye to evil. Evil must be unmasked, disarmed, and destroyed.

Christ's light exposes the darkness of our ways. This is why the first step toward God is always repentance. So long as we are content in our sin, God's love is experienced as wrath. When we are ready to turn from our sin, the Righteous One stands ready to make us right with God.

~Prayer of Gratitude~

Day 3

Morning

The way of the righteous is like morning light
that gets brighter and brighter till it is full day. (Proverbs 4:18)

Reflection

Sometimes doing the right thing isn't immediately gratifying. The world doesn't always reward what's right. Other people often don't notice, and many don't seem to care. Any one right choice can seem insignificant in light of this reality. Why make the sacrifice when there seems to be no obvious up side? But righteousness is a way of life, not a one-time decision. Righteousness is a commitment to doing the right thing whenever, wherever. It is a way of life that may give up immediate gratification for the sake of a long-term promise. As we live into righteousness, and as we automate the practice of doing what is right, the benefits begin to show themselves over time. This way of living will be ultimately rewarding, even if in any one instance it doesn't seem that way. Living this way leads to a simplicity when it comes to decisions, a peace with who we are, an ability to sleep at night, and a reputation that can be depended on. Just as bad decisions eventually catch up with you, righteousness is a lifestyle that will show its power over time.

~Prayer of Petition~

Evening

Because the LORD is righteous!
> *He loves righteous deeds.*
> *Those whose heart is right will see God's face.* (Psalm 11:7)

Reflection

Righteousness always offends our sinful sensibilities. Comparing Jesus's life and teachings to our meager attempts at goodness is like comparing the ocean to a mud puddle. Acknowledging the people Jesus included shatters the shallow categories we construct to exclude.

The offense of the gospel leads many to reject Jesus of Nazareth, the only begotten Son of God, in favor of a Jesus of their own creation, a Jesus who confirms their prejudices and massages their bruised egos. Sadly, their Jesus will never confront, never convict, and never save.

Psalm 11:7 assures us that "those whose heart is right will see God's face."

Following Jesus the Christ requires learning to find in our offense to the gospel an invitation to draw close to the only Righteous One, to sacrifice our egos on the altar of his holiness, to fall on our knees and worship, to feel our shame cast aside and our soul saved, to lift up our eyes and behold the face of God.

~Prayer of Gratitude~

Day 4

Morning

Therefore, since we have been made righteous through his faithfulness, we have peace with God through our Lord Jesus Christ. (Romans 5:1)

Reflection

It is no fun wondering where you stand with someone. Have you ever been in a job where you had no real feedback or idea what your boss thought about you? Or have you ever had a friend with whom you had to walk on eggshells? Have you ever been in love with someone but never quite certain they felt as strongly about you? It is hard to be in a relationship if you are always questioning the stability and security of it. Against that backdrop, it is powerful to hear the news that we can be at peace in our relationship with God. Many fear that one wrong move in life could call into question their standing with God or whether God loves them. So many of us hang on to an image of God as divine hall monitor, looking for any infraction to hold over us. But we do not have to live in constant fear or wondering about where we stand with God. Because it is a relationship we don't earn, it is not one that a sin can cause us to lose. Because God's love for us comes before anything we do, we can be at peace. We don't have to constantly question this relationship. Instead, we can depend on it. When we sin, when we drift, when we openly rebel, God desires our return, our repentance, and our commitment to change. But through all of this, God's faithfulness toward us and relationship with us are never in doubt.

~Prayer of Petition~

Evening

The LORD is intimately acquainted
with the way of the righteous,
but the way of the wicked is destroyed. (Psalm 1:6)

Reflection

Putting up with people and bearing evils in meekness and silence is the sum of a Christian life. God is the first object of our love. Its next office is to bear the defects of others. And we should begin the practice of this amidst our own household. We should chiefly exercise our love toward them who most shock either our way of thinking, or our temper, or our knowledge, or the desire we have that others should be as virtuous as we wish to be ourselves.

—John Wesley, *A Plain Account of Christian Perfection*

~Prayer of Gratitude~

Day 5

Morning

If you know that he is righteous, you also know that every person who practices righteousness is born from him. (1 John 2:29)

Reflection

In school did you ever have to do logic problems, where a set of statements was presented and you had to come up with the logical conclusions? It is easy to make a mistake. That every bird has wings doesn't necessarily mean that everything with wings is a bird. Thinking about it can give you a headache. When it comes to faith, not everyone who practices righteousness is necessarily a Christ follower. We all know that people of other faiths often act in ways that are just and good. Similarly, people who claim to follow Christ do not. But one thing is clear. Those who are growing in the love of Christ also grow in righteousness, in demonstrating the fruit of the Spirit, and in loving their neighbor. This is important because there are so many people who claim to speak for God or claim to know God well. Meanwhile, their speech is divisive, their spirits are angry, and they seem more interested in condemnation than encouragement. Such is not the way with those who love Jesus. As you discern whom to listen to, whom to trust, and whose voices to allow power in your life, look for those who not only claim to follow Christ, but also show a growing righteousness, demonstrate an ever-expanding love of God and others, and live out the fruit of the Spirit.

~Prayer of Petition~

Evening

So, since we have been made righteous by his grace, we can inherit the hope for eternal life. (Titus 3:7)

Reflection

Thou hidden love of God, whose height, whose depth unfathomed no one knows,
I see from far thy beauteous light, and inly sigh for thy repose;
my heart is pained, nor can it be at rest, till it finds rest in thee.
O Love, thy sovereign aid impart to save me from low-thoughted care;
chase this self-will from all my heart, from all its hidden mazes there;
make me thy duteous child that I ceaseless may "Abba, Father" cry.
    —Gerhard Tersteegen, "Thou Hidden Love of God"

~Prayer of Gratitude~

Week 47

Humility

Morning Prayer of Petition

God of all grace, your son did not count equality with you as a thing to be grasped. Instead, he willingly emptied himself. May I learn humility in the way of Jesus so that:

- I might control my anger and frustration,
- I can seek opportunities to lift others up,
- I can listen before I speak,
- I might learn from those around me.

God, may you shape in me a humble spirit and help me to reflect that humility as I encounter others today. Amen.

Evening Prayer of Gratitude

Gracious God, daily you are working in my life. Give me a heart that can receive what you might be doing in my life, and a spirit that is willing to be shaped by you. As I see your work in me more clearly, I thank you for:

- those who have helped me to learn and grow,
- people who challenge my assumptions and expectations,
- challenging situations and obstacles that strengthen my resolve,
- opportunities and new paths opening up for me,
- relationships that surround and support me.

God, may I not take your work in my life for granted but instead be marked by gratitude for your presence in my life. Amen.

Day 1

Morning

Put on my yoke, and learn from me. I'm gentle and humble. And you will find rest for yourselves. (Matthew 11:29)

Reflection

Humility was not an obvious value in Jesus's day. Defending one's honor, fighting for one's station in life, and burnishing one's reputation were expected from people of influence. Humility made little practical sense in this understanding of power. As alien as humility must have seemed, there was something powerful about it. It was counter cultural. Humility was a protest against a culture that amassed power at all costs. Humility was a resistance movement against a zero-sum-game understanding of life. Humility was a deliberate opting out of the game of life as it was traditionally understood. And, therefore, humility was a pathway to a new way of living. It still can function this way, today. When Jesus invites us to practice humility, he isn't seeking to put us down but, rather, to invite us into a new and counter-cultural way of living. A way that sees life more clearly, not as a competition to win, but as a gift to enjoy and a meaningful project to be a part of. Humility doesn't lead to less for us but more, a freer and lighter way to be in the world. When we let go of the need to compete with everyone around us, we are able to be more comfortable in our skin, claim our own rightful places and spaces, and redirect that competitive energy into being fully ourselves in the world.

~Prayer of Petition~

Evening

When pride comes, so does shame,
but wisdom brings humility. (Proverbs 11:2)

Reflection

In ancient Greek mythology, Icarus was a boy whose father had made him a pair of wings from feathers and wax. The goal was to escape the prison that held them both by strapping on the wings and flying away. Although the boy's father warned him not to fly too close to the sun, once Icarus got a taste of what felt like divine power, he flew higher and higher. The more powerful he felt, the closer he flew to the sun.

And, just as his father had warned, the sun melted the wax from Icarus's wings, and he fell from the sky to his death. The boy's ego had become so enlarged that it led to his demise.

How many times have we flown too close to the sun? How many times have we felt God-like? How many times have we become so overwhelmed with our own egos that we ignored warnings?

Humility does not mean staying on the ground. We can fly. In fact, we are called to fly. But in the midst of our flight, may we remember our limitations. We are not God; rather, God's love provides us with wings that allow us to lift up off the ground and fly. Let us give thanks for the wings and let us use them wisely.

~Prayer of Gratitude~

Day 2

Morning

Conduct yourselves with all humility, gentleness, and patience. Accept each other with love. (Ephesians 4:2)

Harvest

Reflection

How do you conduct yourself when you are angry? How about when someone criticizes you or speaks untruthfully about you? How do you show up when you are exhausted, anxious, or overwhelmed? A true test of character and maturity is not how we act when we are at our best—well-rested, hopeful, and feeling good about life. Instead, it is instructive to consider how we show up when we are frustrated, discouraged, or under pressure. It is here that Christ calls us to a new way of living. As challenges arise in our lives, we have choices about how to see those circumstances. We can give ourselves over to frustration, impatience, selfishness, and even cynicism. Or we can choose to use challenges as opportunities to grow in patience, gentleness, and humility. As you consider the daily frustrations and challenges around you right now, how can you respond to those challenges in ways that help you to grow?

~Prayer of Petition~

Evening

Those who humble themselves like this little child will be the greatest in the kingdom of heaven. (Matthew 18:4)

Reflection

All things bright and beautiful, all creatures great and small,
All things wise and wonderful: the Lord God made them all.
Each little flower that opens, each little bird that sings,
God made their glowing colors, and made their tiny wings.
The purple-headed mountains, the river running by,
the sunset and the morning that brightens up the sky.
The cold wind in the winter, the pleasant summer sun,
the ripe fruits in the garden: God made them every one.
All things bright and beautiful, all creatures great and small,
All things wise and wonderful: the Lord God made them all.
God gave us eyes to see them, and lips that we might tell
how great is God Almighty, who has made all things well.
    —Cecil Frances Alexander, "All Things Bright and Beautiful"

~Prayer of Gratitude~

Day 3

Morning

My hand made all these things
    and brought them into being, says the LORD.

But here is where I will look:
> *to the humble and contrite in spirit,*
> *who tremble at my word.* (Isaiah 66:2)

Reflection

Humility is the starting point of growth, development, learning, and eventually wisdom. If you think more highly of yourself than you should, you usually aren't open to the perspectives of others. If you already believe you are the smartest person in the room, you rarely walk away having learned something from someone else. If you see others primarily as competition, then you will be reluctant to see in the other something that can help or teach you. On the other hand, humility is an openness to God and others. It is a recognition that we don't know everything and that, no matter how experienced we are, we always have more to learn. Humility is assuming the people around the table have something to teach you. Humility is taking the default position that others might see things you can't see. Humility allows for the possibility that God can shape and mold you at any time and through unexpected people. But all of the learning and growing, shaping and molding, that God wants to do in your life is impossible if you aren't open. Humility is the starting point of growth.

~Prayer of Petition~

Evening

In the same way, I urge you who are younger: accept the authority of the elders. And everyone, clothe yourselves with humility toward each other. God stands against the proud, but he gives favor to the humble. (1 Peter 5:5)

Reflection

While we joyfully follow and bear witness to God made known in Jesus, we also must remember that Jesus was born, lived, and died a devout Jew. This reminds us that the God we have come to know in Jesus Christ cannot be fully contained in any creedal statement, no matter how carefully constructed. God is always beyond our limited capacity to understand or experience. While we may proclaim faithfully and boldly our own experience of and trust in God, we do so with humility and gentleness as we learn to live in a community of earnest God-seekers who may have experienced and come to know God in ways different than our own.

—Reuben P. Job, *Three Simple Questions*

~Prayer of Gratitude~

Day 4

Morning

The reward of humility and the fear of the LORD
    is wealth, honor, and life. (Proverbs 22:4)

Reflection

Why lift up others around you when you could claim the credit for yourself? Why not press an advantage over another person when you have the opportunity? Why not do what you have to do to get ahead, especially since others do it freely and without qualms? The answer is because long-term humility is a better way to live. Think about people in your life whom you admire, whom you look up to. Chances are they were people who have developed a deep humility. They are people who cared about you when they didn't have to, or who gave you an opportunity when they didn't need to. Humility may sacrifice in the short-term, but it pays dividends in the long-term. Be the kind of person that you would want to look up to, and you will not regret it. Look for opportunities to lift up others; doing so will not be in vain. As you are given ever more responsibility and opportunity, develop alongside it a greater sense of humility; doing so will reward you in the end.

~Prayer of Petition~

Evening

Don't do anything for selfish purposes, but with humility think of others as better than your-
selves. (Philippians 2:3)

Reflection

Always remember, much grace does not always imply much light. These do not always go together. As there may be much light where there is but little love, so there may be much love where there is little light. The heart has more heat than the eye. Yet it cannot see. God has wisely arranged the members of the body that none may say to another, "*I have no need of you.*"

To imagine none can teach you but those who are themselves saved from sin is a very great and dangerous mistake. Give no place to it for a moment: it would lead you into a thousand other mistakes, and that irrecoverably. Obey and respect those who have charge of you in the Lord, and do not think you know better than they. Know their place and your own, always remembering that much love does not imply much light.

Not observing this has led some into many mistakes and into at least the appear-ance of pride. Oh, beware of the appearance and the thing! Let the same mind be in you that was in Christ Jesus. And clothe you all over. Let modesty and self-diffidence appear in all your words and actions. Let all you speak and do show that you are little and base and mean and vile in your own eyes.

As one instance of this, be always ready to own any fault you have done. If you have at any time thought, spoken, or acted wrongly, do not be backward to acknowledge it. Never dream that this will hurt the cause of God. No, it will further it. Be therefore open and frank when you are taxed with anything. Do not seek either to evade or disguise it, but let it appear just as it is, and you will thereby not hinder but adorn the gospel.

—John Wesley, "A Plain Account of Christian Perfection"

~Prayer of Gratitude~

Day 5

Morning

Happy are people who are humble, because they will inherit the earth. (Matthew 5:5)

Reflection

Humility and joy are not opposed to each other. Instead, one begets the other. Some people see humility as a kind of self-degradation. But humility is not holding back who we are, what we are capable of, or the voices that have been given to us. Humility is the practice of not thinking too highly of yourself, but nor is it thinking less of yourself. Humility doesn't mean giving up your voice or not claiming your space. Humility guards against the over-estimation of self, but it does not encourage the underestimation of self. This is especially important for any of us who traditionally have not had access to power, our voices valued, or a place at the table. So, claim your place, take up your space, and use the voice that has been given to you. Humility requires us to be who we are, not anything more, and not anything less.

~Prayer of Petition~

Evening

Are any of you wise and understanding? Show that your actions are good with a humble lifestyle that comes from wisdom. (James 3:13)

Reflection

There's a great *Peanuts* cartoon in which Snoopy is sitting on top of his doghouse writing a book. Charlie Brown comes by and says, "I hear you're writing a book on theology. I hope you have a good title for it," to which Snoopy responds, "I have the perfect title . . . *Has It Ever Occurred to You That You Might Be Wrong?*"

Harvest

Of all the virtues, humility seems to be least valued. This is quite possibly because it is least understood. Humility is not minimizing ourselves but, rather, being honest with ourselves and others.

It is submitting to our humanness, to our inability to know all. Humility is bowing down at the feet of the one who does know all and who greets us with love and compassion. When we are vulnerable enough to welcome humility, we are able to open ourselves to the richness of God's knowing and a freedom from not having to know everything. Embracing humility gives us peace and reminds us that we do not have to hold it all. We can trust that we love and serve a God who is holding it for us.

~Prayer of Gratitude~

Power

Morning Prayer of Petition

Great and awesome God, in your wisdom you created the earth and by your power you sustain it. I am learning to trust you and to rely on your power at work in:

- those who are suffering from illness,
- those struggling with stress and anxiety,
- people who are wrestling with addiction,
- those without access to affordable housing or healthcare,
- systems of inequality in my community and in our world.

Just as you created all that is, God, may your Spirit come and redeem all things. Amen.

Evening Prayer of Gratitude

Mighty God, as I remember the way that you have guided me in the past, I find power to live in the present. Thank you for the ways that your power was made known to me today:

- for moments that brought me life,
- for people who support me,
- for those who challenge my way of thinking,
- for moments of resilience and strength.

Thank you for blessing me with the power of your Holy Spirit. May I continue to live out of that power and not merely my own. Amen.

Day 1

Morning

LORD God, you created heaven and earth by your great power and outstretched arm; nothing is too hard for you! (Jeremiah 32:17)

Reflection

In the face of challenges in our lives, it is strange how easily we forget what God has already done for us. Forgetting is a major problem throughout the Bible. Repeatedly, when times get tough, the people of God begin to doubt God's ability and forget God's past acts. Whether it is a lack of food in the desert, doubt over the outcome of illness, or fear over a stormy sea, God's people scare easily and begin

Harvest

to wonder if God is capable of a miracle. Does God really have power in and over our lives? When we begin to waver on the question of God's power, scripture calls us to remember. We are asked to recall who God is and what God has done in the past, as a way of reminding ourselves of who is with us. God is the one who created everything, the heaven and the earth! God has great power and an outstretched arm that can reach down into any situation or circumstance we are facing. God is the one who hangs the stars in the sky and sets the planets in motion. God is not impotent in the face of life's challenges, including yours. We serve a God of great power, and remembering what God has done in the past can give us hope that God is more than capable of working in our present.

~Prayer of Petition~

Evening

You establish the mountains by your strength;
you are dressed in raw power. (Psalm 65:6)

Reflection

God of all power, and truth, and grace,
Which shall from age to age endure,
Whose word, when heaven and earth shall pass,
Remains and stands for ever sure;

That I thy mercy may proclaim,
That all mankind thy truth may see,
Hallow thy great and glorious name,
And perfect holiness in me.

Purge me from every sinful blot;
My idols all be cast aside;
Cleanse me from every sinful thought,
From all the filth of self and pride.

Give me a new, a perfect heart,
From doubt, and fear, and sorrow free;
The mind which was in Christ impart,
And let my spirit cleave to thee.

O take this heart of stone away!
Thy sway it doth not, cannot own;
In me no longer let it stay,
O take away this heart of stone!

O that I now, from sin released,
Thy word may to the utmost prove,

Enter into the promised rest,
The Canaan of thy perfect love!
> —Charles Wesley, "God of All Power, and Truth, and Grace"

~Prayer of Gratitude~

Day 2

Morning

From the dawn of time, I am the one.
> *No one can escape my power.*
> *I act, and who can undo it?* (Isaiah 43:13)

Reflection

Have you ever used the phrase, "I got this"? We use it to offer confidence to another person, usually someone who is worried about an outcome, that there is nothing to worry about. It's a way of saying that person can handle whatever is needed in the situation. Usually, this kind of confidence comes from experience that the other doesn't have. There are so many times in life when we hit speed bumps that threaten to send our lives careening off course. Perhaps your marriage is in crisis and you aren't sure that it can recover. Maybe your leadership is being questioned and criticized at work and so you are beginning to question your future. Maybe you are at your wits' end with a family member. Maybe anxiety and depression are threatening to completely overwhelm you. When we meet these situations in life, they are all-consuming. It can feel like no one understands, that we are all alone, and that nothing can really help. In the midst of this, scripture reminds us that from the beginning of time, God has dwelled in situations like this. You are not alone. The power of God has worked in situations like this in the past and is powerfully at work in your life now.

~Prayer of Petition~

Evening

God has raised the Lord and will raise us through his power. (1 Corinthians 6:14)

Reflection

The God Jesus reveals shatters all our little ideas about God and reveals a God who is author and creator of all there is. In Jesus we see a God who reverses the values of our culture and turns upside down our scheme of priorities, leaving us gasping at the sight of such bone-deep love, justice, and mercy. In Jesus we see such bold and radical truth that we tremble in awe and then cry out for help as we try to practice the faithful way of living he demonstrated so splendidly. . . .

In Jesus we see a God who is not swayed by popular opinion, loud adulation, or noisy rebellion. In Jesus we see clearly a God who is not controlled by any ideology, philosophy, concept, force, or power.

In Jesus we see a God who is never under our control but always free of any control, and who may act and create as it seems wise and is in keeping with God's will.

—Reuben P. Job, *Three Simple Questions*

~Prayer of Gratitude~

Day 3

Morning

You split the sea with your power.
You shattered the heads of the sea monsters on the water. (Psalm 74:13)

Reflection

God's power is manifested in myriad ways in scripture. Sometimes God's power is subtle and hidden. Other times God's power shows up in fantastic and obvious ways. God's power can look like a suffering servant, a word of wisdom, a healing spirit, or a still-small voice. And sometimes God's power evokes great awe and fear. God's power cannot be circumscribed, and we must be careful not to presume that we know what it looks like, and where we might find it. This means that we should always be on the lookout for God's power at work. We should never underestimate what is possible in a situation, what a person might be capable of offering, or where we may encounter greatness. Therefore, God's power gives us hope, keeps us expectant, and confronts us daily in ways that we least suspect it.

~Prayer of Petition~

Evening

Through his faithfulness, you are guarded by God's power so that you can receive the salvation he is ready to reveal in the last time. (1 Peter 1:5)

Reflection

A condition to be met in order to walk is to keep one foot on the ground and the other off. If you keep both feet down, you cannot move unless you are dragged. If you try to keep both off, you can stay up a few seconds by a jump or a hop, but the pull of the earth will inevitably bring you down. Most of us walk a good many miles during our lives without thinking of this, but no baby could ever learn to walk who did not discover it by experience.

This simple fact, transferred to the religious sphere, has very great significance. It symbolizes the need of uniting realism with idealism, nature with supernature, immanence with transcendence, time with eternity, and theology which emphasizes one of these terms to the exclusion of the other either becomes "of the earth, earthy" or moves in the clouds. The Christian religion, more than any other approach to life, makes it possible to synthesize these otherwise contradictory concepts. It keeps close to human living and human needs, but it does so through an incentive and source of power which are more than human. Without divine power there is no human achievement.

— Georgia Harkness, *Religious Living*

~Prayer of Gratitude~

Day 4

Morning

I pray that the eyes of your heart will have enough light to see what is the hope of God's call, what is the richness of God's glorious inheritance among believers, and what is the overwhelming greatness of God's power that is working among us believers. (Ephesians 1:18-19a)

Reflection

When is the last time you have seen God's power at work? What did it look like? How did it impact you? I worry that, in our quest to make faith make sense, we have downplayed God's greatness and power to show up in our world. The miracles of God do not fit nicely into any logical or scientific box that we create and, therefore, we can then stop talking about God's power, stop praying for it, or stop expecting it. What we experience in life is largely shaped by what we look for and expect. So, if we stop expecting God to act in powerful ways, we experience that power less and less. When is the last time you prayed for a miracle? When is that last time you expected God to show up and work in a powerful way in your life? If it has been a while, my prayer is that you recover a sense of expectation about what God can do in your life, in your church, and in your community.

~Prayer of Petition~

Evening

Look up at the sky and consider:
    Who created these?
The one who brings out their attendants one by one,
    summoning each of them by name.
Because of God's great strength
    and mighty power, not one is missing. (Isaiah 40:26)

Harvest

Reflection

"God said, 'Let there be light." And so light appeared'" (Genesis 1:3). Genesis makes God's creative work in forming the world appear almost effortless. Maybe it was. We think of God creating in one sweeping motion, quick, exact, and perfect. It is tempting to think of power in the same way. Power is seen in sweeping action, a firm commandment and compliant subjects. God speaks, the light obeys. God orders, the mountains move. Creative power is sweeping, but it maybe it is also slow. Our scripture today says, "Because of God's great strength and mighty power, not one is missing." Maybe at times power must be expressed slowly, so as to not forget the people for whom it works to protect. God creates with great power, and yet, God also takes the time to account for every piece, making sure that nothing is missing and that every one of us is accounted for. God gives each of us the gift of creativity and power, as well as the authority to exercise them. Today, may we ponder our power before using it, and may we use our God-given strength to slow down and notice each person around us with care.

~Prayer of Gratitude~

Day 5

Morning

He said to me, "My grace is enough for you, because power is made perfect in weakness." So I'll gladly spend my time bragging about my weaknesses so that Christ's power can rest on me. (2 Corinthians 12:9)

Reflection

We brag about what we think we are good at, what we do well, or what we want others to see. We certainly do not highlight or brag about weaknesses. We don't tell people all about our internal struggles with mental health. We don't advertise the ways we have sinned and have deeply hurt other people. We don't usually walk around telling people about the worst seasons of our marriage or relationships. Not many of us have a resumé or website highlighting our failures. Why would we? And, yet, it is often these exact moments when God's power has been most vividly on display in our lives. It is in these moments that we grow, are shaped by God, and are changed and transformed into new people. When life breaks us down, we are open to the work of God in unique ways. God does not cause these times of hardship, but God's power is at work in mighty ways during these seasons. Therefore, we do not have to lose heart or grow discouraged. Perhaps we should even grow more courageous in bragging about what God has done in our lives through our weaknesses. It can be a reminder to us and a source of hope for others.

~Prayer of Petition~

Evening

Glory to God, who is able to do far beyond all that we could ask or imagine by his power at work within us. (Ephesians 3:20)

Reflection

From the time we could speak, the word *more* was in our vocabulary. How many of us can count *more* as one of our first words? We got a bit of something sweet—a little frosting, a sweet summer peach—and before we swallowed the last bite the word *more* comes out of our mouths. *More* has become a hallmark of our indulgent society. *Enough* is an all-too-scarce-yet-holy word. *More* leaves us always grasping, never fulfilled. Saying *enough* means we now are content. And, yet, sometimes even in our contentment, there is a temptation to become complacent, even lazy. God created us to be people of power and delight and contentment, not of complacency or laziness. God's power works in and through us to create more than we could ask or imagine. Today, may we not let our contentment turn into complacency. Instead, let's ask God for more: more justice, more love, more mercy, and more unity. Today, share in God's dream that all would have enough, until earth becomes more like heaven.

~Prayer of Gratitude~

Generosity

Morning Prayer of Petition

God of all good gifts, you surround me with blessings that I can't count or repay. May your outpouring of blessing on me inspire me to be a blessing in the lives of others. May you turn my heart toward your needs in the world that I may:

- use my gifts and capabilities to impact other people,
- grow in financial generosity towards your church and other worthy missions,
- share my struggles and failures in a way that might help others,
- be present with others and offer my time where it can make a difference.

Help my life to be a mirror of your generosity towards me. Amen.

Evening Prayer of Gratitude

Good and gracious God, you have been generous to me and provided for me in ways that I did not deserve or expect. Today may I call to mind the ways you have blessed me:

- through people who nurtured and supported me when I needed it,
- with mentors and others who have invested in my growth,
- through surprising opportunities or resources that I didn't expect,
- by guiding me through challenging times with resilience and perseverance.

Thank you, God, for generously providing for me. Thank you for the ways you have gone before me, for your presence today, and for your promises in the future. Amen.

Day 1

Morning

Sell your possessions and give to those in need. Make for yourselves wallets that don't wear out—a treasure in heaven that never runs out. No thief comes near there, and no moth destroys. Where your treasure is, there your heart will be too. (Luke 12:33-34)

Reflection

Most of us naturally think that we will spend our time, energy, and money on the things we care about. If you care about family, you spend time with them. If you value your home, you will spend money on it. If you love experiences with friends, you will use your extra resources to that end. As logical as this sounds, Jesus teaches us that this is not actually the way the human heart works. It is aspirational to believe that we will spend our limited resources on what we value. The cold reality is the opposite. Our hearts follow where we spend our time, energy, and money. To know what a person cares about, don't ask them about it, look at where they spend their time. To know what is most important to a person, don't listen to their words, look at their bank statement. To know what a person truly loves, consider where they put the bulk of their emotional energy. For each of us, Jesus challenges us to audit where we spend our resources. And if we want to change what we care about, where our hearts are, then we must start with where we spend what is most precious to us—our time, our energy, our money.

~Prayer of Petition~

Evening

Generous persons will prosper;
> *those who refresh others will themselves be refreshed.* (Proverbs 11:25)

Reflection

The happiest people I know are generous people. I'm not referring to wealthy people or even generational or professional philanthropists. I'm pointing to people who give to God and others because they understand the generous nature of God. These people are filled with love, joy, expectation, and hope. They don't spend their time gate-keeping, determining worth, or counting against others. Generous people understand the economy of God in ways that people who live with a scarcity mentality do not understand. They understand that generosity begets generosity. They understand that the harvest of generosity is God's abundance. The scriptures teach us that God is abundantly generous. God is generous with love, life, forgiveness, and resources. God is not *fair* in how God spreads generosity. God is generous with sinners, tax collectors, robbers, and even murderers. God expects God's people to be generous too. In the Old and New Testaments, generosity is encouraged, praised, and rewarded. Thus, when I come across truly generous people, I am not surprised by their joy. We are made in the image of God. We are to live our lives striving to be like Jesus. If we seek joy, we should try living a generous life.

~Prayer of Gratitude~

Day 2

Morning

But he emptied himself
> *by taking the form of a slave*
> *and by becoming like human beings.*
When he found himself in the form of a human. (Philippians 2:7)

Harvest

Reflection

Generosity begins with what God did for us in Christ. The incarnation was the greatest act of generosity in human history. The word of God did count the comforts of heaven as something to hold on to or hoard. Instead, God emptied God's self. God gave these comforts and privileges away, completely. That act of generosity came with changes and sacrifices. God became human, experienced the grief of losing a friend, the disappointment and frustration of relationship, the pain of a friend's betrayal, and the visceral brutality of human violence. That act of generosity, to give up and take on something new, was all in service to a greater good. Our salvation begins with an act of generosity in the incarnation. Our salvation is won by an act of generosity on the cross. Our salvation is sealed with an act of generosity, as Christ pours out his spirit upon us. When we seek to be people of generosity, and when we teach and practice it, we do so to follow and mirror the one who emptied himself for us.

~Prayer of Petition~

Evening

Let the wicked abandon their ways
>   and the sinful their schemes.
Let them return to the LORD so that he may have mercy on them,
>   to our God, because he is generous with forgiveness. (Isaiah 55:7)

Reflection

Methodists are those who had God's love poured into their hearts through the Holy Spirit that has been given to them, who love the Lord their God with all their hearts, and with all their souls, and with all their minds, and with all their strength. God is the joy of their hearts, and the desire of their soul; which constantly cry out, *Whom have I in heaven but you? and there is nothing on earth that I desire other than you!* My God and my all! You are the strength of my heart, and my portion forever! . . . And whoever are what I preach (let them be called what they will, for names do not change the nature of things) are Christians, not in name only, but in heart and in life. By these marks, by these fruits of a living faith, do we labor to distinguish ourselves from the unbelieving world, from all those whose minds or lives are not according to the gospel of Christ. But from real Christians, of whatsoever denomination they be, we earnestly desire not to be distinguished at all, not from any who sincerely follow after what they know they have not yet attained. Whoever does the will of my Father in heaven is my brother and sister and mother. Is your heart right, as my heart is with yours? I ask no further questions. If it be, give me your hand.

—John Welsey, "The Character of a Methodist,"

~Prayer of Gratitude~

Day 3

Morning

You will be made rich in every way so that you can be generous in every way. Such generosity produces thanksgiving to God through us. (2 Corinthians 9:11)

Reflection

Generosity is as much about why we have what we have as it is about what we do with it. Why does God give us certain abilities, opportunities, and capabilities? To whatever extent you have been blessed, do you consider why God would favor you in this way? Why does God give us energy—intellectual, mental, and physical—that we can use in the world? Why do we have money, earn money, inherit money, or have access to wealth, whatever the amount? We are blessed for one simple reason: to be a blessing in the lives of others. God gives us all a unique portfolio of resources that are meant to be used for God's work in the world. So how are you blessing others with what you have? How are you using the best of your abilities, energy, and money to build the common good, benefit other people, share good news with others, or build up God's kingdom on earth? We are asked neither to feel guilty nor to find too much comfort in what we have. Instead, we are challenged to think about why we have it and how we will use it to offer thanksgiving to God.

~Prayer of Petition~

Evening

All of them are giving out of their spare change. But she from her hopeless poverty has given everything she had to live on. (Luke 21:4)

Reflection

When the Possessor of heaven and earth brought you into being and placed you in this world, he placed you here not as a proprietor, but a steward; as such he entrusted you for a season with goods of various kinds, but the sole ownership of these still rests in God, nor can ever be alienated from him. As you yourself are not your own, but God's, such is likewise all that you enjoy. Such is your soul and your body, not your own, but God's. And so is your substance in particular. God has told you in the most clear and express terms how you are to employ it for him: in such a manner that it may be all a holy sacrifice, acceptable through Christ Jesus. And this light, easy service he has promised to reward with an eternal weight of glory.

    —John Wesley, "The Use of Money"

~Prayer of Gratitude~

Day 4

Morning

Don't I have the right to do what I want with what belongs to me? Or are you resentful because I'm generous? (Matthew 20:15)

Reflection

If you grew up with siblings, you know the sensitivities we have to unfair treatment. Which of us, who grew up with siblings in our family, hasn't at some point felt like a parent favored one kid over the other, or gave more to one than to the rest? When it comes to what we have, we compare ourselves to those around us, even from the earliest age. As adults, we continue to do this—with our friends, our neighbors, our coworkers, our family. We look around and wonder why we don't have what someone else has. But this comparison distracts us from our mission and discourages us from developing hearts of generosity. If the evil one can make us believe we lack what others have, the act of generosity becomes nearly impossible. Instead of comparing ourselves to others, God invites us to see the gifts that we've been given and to focus on what we have, not what we don't. God invites us to consider the ways that we have been uniquely blessed. Only when we begin to operate out of this sense of abundance, rather than out of scarcity, will we begin to live into our purpose in the world.

~Prayer of Petition~

Evening

Tell them to do good, to be rich in the good things they do, to be generous, and to share with others. (1 Timothy 6:18)

Reflection

"Summer and winter and springtime and harvest, sun, moon, and stars in their courses above join with all nature in manifold witness to thy great faithfulness, mercy, and love." The middle verse of the great hymn "Great Is Thy Faithfulness" reminds us that everything we have is a gift of God. Every season, every day, every harvest that feeds us and sustains our lives is a fulfillment of a promise from God. It is easy to get distracted and fall prey to the belief that our work, job, or money sustains us from day-to-day. Yet, the truth remains that it is the great faithfulness of God—the generous work of God in the world and in our lives—that sustains us. What could happen if we lived as an offering of generosity to God? What would change if we lived in pursuit of opportunities to be generous? How would the world transform if we saw our way of living as an opportunity to extend God's generosity by sharing with others? What if we didn't toil over what we might not have, but instead shared with others? How would we experience the generosity of God's great faithfulness unto us?

~Prayer of Gratitude~

Day 5

Morning

Or do you have contempt for the riches of God's generosity, tolerance, and patience? Don't you realize that God's kindness is supposed to lead you to change your heart and life? (Romans 2:4)

Reflection

Think back on someone who has been surprisingly generous to you. How did their gift make you feel? Did it change you in any way? Do you find that when others are generous to you, you are more motivated to be generous to others? When we focus on what God is doing for us daily, and when we take time to remember the small ways every day that God is blessing us, it is easier and more natural to be generous ourselves. As soon as we forget, or stop paying attention to the blessings of God, we find our own hearts slowly beginning to close up. The easiest path toward a life of generosity is to develop a daily habit of recognizing God's work in your life, being grateful for it, and living out of that sense of blessing. Remember that God's daily blessings aren't supposed to flow to you, but *through* you for the sake of others.

~Prayer of Petition~

Evening

What I mean is this: the one who sows a small number of seeds will also reap a small crop, and the one who sows a generous amount of seeds will also reap a generous crop. (2 Corinthians 9:6)

Reflection

Summer and winter and springtime and harvest,
sun, moon, and stars in their courses above
join with all nature in manifold witness
to thy great faithfulness, mercy, and love.
Pardon for sin and a peace that endureth,
thine own dear presence to cheer and to guide;
strength for today and bright hope for tomorrow,
blessings all mine, with ten thousand beside!
Great is thy faithfulness! Great is thy faithfulness!

Harvest

Morning by morning new mercies I see;
all I have needed thy hand hath provided;
great is thy faithfulness, Lord, unto me!
    —Thomas O. Chisholm, "Great Is Thy Faithfulness"

~Prayer of Gratitude~

Guilt

Morning Prayer of Petition

God of truth, you know me inside and out. You see all that I am and all that I've done, and yet you love and claim me. You invite me to come to you as I am, and not as I pretend to be. Today, I pray that you would heal:

- my anger and frustration with those I care about,
- my habits and behaviors that are contrary to your will,
- my neglect of neighbors and those who are hurting in the world,
- my busyness and tendency to neglect you.

God, may my confession lead not to guilt but to the freedom that comes from your forgiveness. Amen.

Evening Prayer of Gratitude

God of grace, for freedom Christ has set me free. Help me not to submit again to the slavery of guilt. Instead, empower me as I claim your permission to:

- let go of regret and shame,
- allow myself a new start,
- experience joy and happiness again,
- no longer be entangled by the expectations and judgments of others.

Each day may I live more fully into the joy that comes from my relationship with you. Amen.

Day 1

Morning

We have sinned and done wrong. We have brought guilt on ourselves and rebelled, ignoring your commands and your laws. (Daniel 9:5)

Reflection

We think of guilt as a feeling, an inward bad conscience. In scripture, guilt is not primarily a feeling but a status, usually in a relationship. Someone is guilty when they have sinned or have broken the covenant of a relationship. This can be true between individuals (think marriage betrayal), between an individual and community (in the case of laws), or between people and God. Guilt is a consequence of sin and a recognition that sin hurts others and erodes the relationship. Therefore, guilt is not something to brush off, ignore, or reimagine as simply a feeling. If guilt is an outward reality that damages relationships, and not an inward feeling, then guilt is something we must recognize, grapple with, and address. When we emotionalize guilt, it becomes easy to dismiss. But when scripture asks us to recognize guilt, it isn't to make us feel badly, but rather to call us to take seriously the way our sins can hurt our relationship with God and others.

~Prayer of Petition~

Evening

So I admitted my sin to you;
>*I didn't conceal my guilt.*
>*"I'll confess my sins to the LORD, " is what I said.*
>*Then you removed the guilt of my sin. Selah* (Psalm 32:5)

Reflection

"Would you be free from your burden of sin?" ("Power in the Blood" by Lewis E. Jones, 1899)

Bondage of any sort—whether physical, mental, emotional, or spiritual—often utilizes the debilitating fetters of guilt and shame. Those who have experienced this in any form know all too well how easily one can come to believe that the chains themselves have more right to bind you than you have to be free. Sometimes, it's circumstances that lure us into thinking we don't matter or that whoever we are or wherever we came from somehow makes us less than others. Sometimes it's feeling so low that you become not just unsure of yourself but also convinced that everything bad in your life is somehow your own fault and you deserve to be knocked down. Sometimes, it's the voices that tell us who we should or shouldn't be and that ultimately shame us into feeling like we are incomplete. Yet, repeatedly, we are reminded that confession is good for the soul; it subverts the isolation of guilt and provides the avenue for grace to do its liberating work. Speak then, my soul, and be free!

~Prayer of Gratitude~

Day 2

Morning

I will cleanse them of all the wrongdoing they committed against me, and I will forgive them for all of their guilt and rebellion. (Jeremiah 33:8)

Reflection

Left unaddressed, our sins and wrongdoings against others will erode, and eventually undermine, our relationship with them. If we never apologize or practice forgiveness with a spouse or friend, then eventually the relationship will break under the weight of the hurt, misunderstanding, and damage that sins cause. The same is true with God. When we sin, ignoring God's wisdom, breaking God's commands, or neglecting God's direction in our lives, we undermine our relationship with God. Our sin is an active and deliberate way of telling God that we don't actually trust God, that we don't believe God's way is best for us. Just as in our relationship with others, when unaddressed, this guilt or breach of relationship does damage. But God chooses to address this broken relationship not with resentment, anger, or by cutting us off (what we often would do in our human relationships). Instead, God names our guilt, forgives the damage, and invites us to rebuild this relationship anew.

~Prayer of Petition~

Evening

Indeed, Israel and Judah have not been forsaken
*   by their God, the LORD of hosts,*
though their land is full of guilt
*   before the Holy One of Israel.* (Jeremiah 51:5 NRSVUE)

Reflection

You must dwell also on the glad remembrance of God's loving-kindness, otherwise sadness will harden the heart and lead it more deeply into despair. Let us mix honey with our absinthe, it is more easily drunk when sweetened, and what bitterness it may still retain will be wholesome. You must fix your attention on the ways of God, see how he mitigates the bitterness of the heart that is crushed, how he wins back the pusillanimous soul from the abyss of despair, how he consoles the grief-stricken and strengthens the wavering with the sweet caress of his faithful promise. . . . You will all the more easily achieve this if you let your minds dwell frequently, even continually, on the memory of God's bountifulness.

   —Bernard of Clairvaux, "Sermon 11 on Song of Songs"

~Prayer of Gratitude~

Day 3

Morning

Yes, I was born in guilt, in sin,
*   from the moment my mother conceived me.* (Psalm 51:5)

Reflection

Along with thinking of guilt as a feeling, we also consider it to be highly personal and individual. You are responsible for the things you do; I am responsible for what I do. But, in scripture, guilt can be individual or communal. The sins of some could jeopardize and undermine the community's relationship with others. The idea that we are born into guilt is troubling to most of us. We chafe at the idea that we can be guilty before we ever do anything at all. But here the psalmist is reminding us of the corporate nature of our being. Humanity is in a broken relationship with God. Humanity has a long history of ignoring, rebelling, and neglecting the God who created us. We do well to remember that we are born into a system of brokenness and into an ongoing relationship of sin and restoration. We have no choice about this, and we will eventually become part of that story. How we start, though, is not as significant as where we end. We can't control what we are born into, but we do have choices about what we do with it. We can turn back toward the God who created us, ask for forgiveness, and join God in the work of reconciliation in a broken world.

~Prayer of Petition~

Evening

Jesus said, "Father, forgive them, for they don't know what they're doing." They drew lots as a way of dividing up his clothing. (Luke 23:34)

Reflection

Our own frailty can be a real source of anxiety to us, making us want to know exactly whether we have or have not consented to a wrong desire and encouraging us to seek some kind of assurance that we are not going to consent to such desires in the future. One man wrote to ask what he should do about his unclean thoughts, of which he was afraid. The answer was, say to God: "Lord, forgive me if I have conceived of anything which is against your will, whether knowingly or not, for mercy belongs to you forever. Amen." It is not after all necessary to know whether we are guilty or not, nor to know that we shall not become guilty in the future. The mercy of God is sufficient and that is what we need to remember.

—Simon Tugwell, *The Way of Imperfection*. Includes quotation from John, "The Other Old Man," early sixth century in *Barsanuphius and John: Questions and Answers*

~Prayer of Gratitude~

Day 4

Morning

Love and faithfulness reconcile guilt;
the fear of the LORD turns away evil. (Proverbs 16:6)

Reflection

If guilt erodes and undermines relationships, love and faithfulness repair and build relationships up. We often react to guilt by feeling badly. But God doesn't desire our bad feelings. God doesn't remind us of our guilt to bring us down or make us sad. Instead, God's solution to guilt is love. It starts with God's love for us, which heals our relationships amid sin. But the same can be true for our relationship with others. Asking for forgiveness when you've hurt someone you love is a good and right starting point. But guilt is addressed over time by faithfulness and love. These are the actions of showing up for others, doing what you say you'll do, and being there in small ways daily. If there is a relationship—with a coworker, child, parent, friend, spouse—that is damaged or troubled, the pathway to restoration and reconciliation is through small, consistent, and daily acts of love and faithfulness.

~Prayer of Petition~

Evening

He touched my mouth and said, "See, this has touched your lips. Your guilt has departed, and your sin is removed." (Isaiah 6:7)

Reflection

And as soon as God's spirit opens a person's eyes, so that he recognizes and feels his misery, then he gets up with the prodigal son and says, "Father, I have sinned" (Luke 15:18). A person will not become disgusted with the world and sin until he recognizes in God's light that these things have brought him unhappiness. If a person comes this far by God's grace, that he despairs of himself and his efforts, he then sits down with Mary at Jesus' feet and cries.

In this way a person can easily know whether the Holy Spirit has his work in a person; it is when he knows and feels with agony his inner corruption of heart, and where this knowledge breaks, shames, and makes the heart humble before God. It is wherever a person becomes an enemy of sin, turns his back to the world, and hungers after Jesus. It is where all of this continues and grows (Hebrews 3:14). Whoever

Harvest

struggles here, under the discipline of the Holy Spirit, will finally be led by grace to victory. And that is the work of deliverance, Christ in us.

—Philip William Otterbein, "The Salvation-Bringing Incarnation and the Glorious Victory of Jesus Christ over the Devil and Death Delivered"

~Prayer of Gratitude~

Day 5

Morning

All the prophets testify about him that everyone who believes in him receives forgiveness of sins through his name. (Acts 10:43)

Reflection

Guilt is not something we should neglect or ignore. But guilt is also not something we should hang onto or dwell on. If guilt goes unaddressed in our life, it can fester and give bloom to shame. While we must recognize and grapple with guilt, we also need to hear God's closing word on it. God has made a decision about our guilt and given us a pathway for what to do with it. God invites us to confess it, and then God invites us back into the relationship to try again. There may be no better news than this, that guilt is not something you have to hold onto or punish yourself for. Rather, God invites us back to the table, into the house, and into the relationship to try again. Hear the good news: in the name of Jesus, you are a forgiven person. Today is a new day. God invites you to begin following anew. As much as you must recognize and grapple with guilt, you are much more invited to hear and receive this good news.

~Prayer of Petition~

Evening

My brothers and sisters, if any of you wander from the truth and someone turns back the wanderer, recognize that whoever brings a sinner back from the wrong path will save them from death and will bring about the forgiveness of many sins. (James 5:19-20)

Reflection

Repentance is essential to the community of believers. Too often we practice a "better to ask forgiveness than permission" ethic—leading to a kind of faith that rationalizes everything based on how we feel in the moment. We rationalize being cruel to each other by saying we're just "telling the truth." We rationalize abusive behavior by saying, "Toughen up." We rationalize the overuse of natural resources by saying, "It'll be fine." We rationalize greed by saying, "They're just lazy." We rationalize indifference by saying, "They deserved it." Repentance gives room to name what is right and what is wrong. Likewise, the accountability of repentance insists that God always desires mercy over sacrifice. And when mercy works in us, all self-centeredness gives way to Christ-centeredness, all legalism gives way to grace-filled accountability, and all estrangement gives way to Spirit-enabled reconciliation. If we allow it, God's mercy saves us and enlists us in saving others. Will you submit your life—your thoughts, words, actions, and relationships—to this work, so that God's mercy might be multiplied in you, by you, and through you?

~Prayer of Gratitude~

Endurance

Morning Prayer of Petition

Mighty God, you promise strength to those who hope in you. Anoint me with your Spirit so that today I may:

- have the courage to act even when I am scared,
- muster the resilience to get through the challenges facing me,
- receive the wisdom to know how to navigate decisions and situations,
- act with patience toward those who work against me,
- endure even when I do not see immediate results.

God, I hope and trust in you. Help me to run and not grow weary; to walk and not faint. Amen.

Evening Prayer of Gratitude

Even when my strength fails, you O God hold and sustain me. May gratitude well up in me as I recognize:

- your hand guiding and directing me,
- the way you've brought me through difficult seasons,
- progress in areas of struggle,
- your permission to rest even when the work is piled up.

May I depend less on my own strength, and more on your power at work in me. Amen.

Day 1

Morning

After all, you know that the testing of your faith produces endurance. Let this endurance complete its work so that you may be fully mature, complete, and lacking in nothing. (James 1:3-4)

Reflection

There is a reason that in sports most of the players who make the hall of fame not only have talent, but also longevity. No matter how good you are, there are certain aspects of the game, certain milestones, certain accomplishments, and certain kinds of influence that you can only make over time. There are, of course, bad seasons and slumps along the way. But the truly great athletes find a way to endure through and beyond them. The same is true in life—in a job, a family, a community. No matter how hard you work, how good you are, how much you try, there are certain aspects of life that are only unlocked over time. And sticking with anything over time requires endurance, the perseverance to work through difficult and dry seasons. In our culture, endurance is not in vogue. We have become a very transient people—in relationships, careers, friendships, and locations. When something is hard, the first instinct is to move on to the next thing. But remember that full maturity—that is, completeness in any aspect of life—requires enduring through and beyond temporary challenges.

~Prayer of Petition~

Evening

But not only that! We even take pride in our problems, because we know that trouble produces endurance, endurance produces character, and character produces hope. (Romans 5:3-4)

Reflection

Of all the things that Paul writes in the New Testament, Romans 5:3-4 is one of the most self-aware, and one of the most difficult. He writes, "We even take pride in our problems, because we know that trouble produces endurance, endurance produces character, and character produces hope." This is true, of course. The people who seem to have the most success trudging through adversity are people who have had to do so before. When you experience hard times, your "endurance muscle" builds up, helping you endure hard times to come.

The bad news is that hard times will come. We were never promised a pain-free life; instead, we were promised that God would walk with us through the pain and never leave us behind. When those difficult times do come, do what you can to remember this passage from Romans. Trouble does indeed produce endurance and character and hope, so that you can both use your trouble for the glory of God and be able to persevere because you have a faithful God on whom to rely.

~Prayer of Gratitude~

Day 2

Morning

Therefore, my beloved brothers and sisters, be steadfast, immovable, always excelling in the work of the Lord because you know that in the Lord your labor is not in vain. (1 Corinthians 15:58 NRSVUE)

Reflection

Have you ever vacillated between believing deeply in what you do and then wondering if it makes any difference at all? If you know, you know. For many of us, this feeling is real, especially professionally. Healthcare, teaching, social work, and ministry are all professions in which it is easy to wonder if the work is supremely meaningful or makes no difference at all. If you ever hit a season of doubt, then you can connect with what Paul is saying at the end of 1 Corinthians. It is pure encouragement for those who have begun to wonder if what they feel called to do truly matters. He answers the question convincingly, unwaveringly. It is helpful and hopeful to know that I am not the only one who has wondered if what I do matters. You aren't the only one, either. If you are in a season of doubt, repeat these words, recite them over and over as a mantra, and let their truth wash over you, seep into your spirit, and soak into your heart. Be steadfast, immovable, always excelling in the work of the Lord because you know that, in the Lord, your labor is not in vain.

~Prayer of Petition~

Evening

Look up to the heavens,
*   and gaze at the earth beneath.*
The heavens will disappear like smoke,
*   the earth will wear out like clothing,*
*   and its inhabitants will die like gnats.*
But my salvation will endure forever,
*   and my righteousness will be unbroken.* (Isaiah 51:6)

Reflection

Not so in haste my heart!
Have faith in God, and wait;
although he linger long,
he never comes too late.

He never cometh late;
he knoweth what is best;
vex not thyself in vain;
until He cometh, rest.

Until He cometh, rest,
nor grudge the hours that roll;
the feet that wait for God
are soonest at the goal.

Are soonest at the goal
that is not gained with speed;
then hold thee still, my heart,
for I shall wait His lead.
—Bradford Torrey, "Not So in Haste, My Heart"

~Prayer of Gratitude~

Day 3

Morning

You need to endure so that you can receive the promises after you do God's will. (Hebrews 10:36)

Reflection

Have you ever been to an event or large dinner where they place the dessert on the table before the meal? I have a habit of just eating the dessert right away before the salad even arrives. For some of us, it is hard to wait! In life, some of us want the rewards of a life of faith, without the discipline and time it takes to form a life of faith. We want to be able to hear from God more clearly, but we haven't been intentional in cultivating a deep prayer life. We want to know more about the Bible without establishing a rhythm of reading it regularly. We want deeper and more spirit-filled friendships, but we don't take the time to form those bonds with people. Endurance requires a willingness to put in the work so that we can begin to see the fruit of a life of faith. While God's spirit fills us when we come to faith, and forgiveness is offered when we ask for it, the full fruits of a faithful life require practice; discipline; and, during certain seasons when we aren't feeling it, endurance! But on the other side of this endurance we begin to receive the promises of a deeper and more mature faith.

~Prayer of Petition~

Evening

Youths will become tired and weary,
young men will certainly stumble;
but those who hope in the LORD
will renew their strength;
they will fly up on wings like eagles;
they will run and not be tired;
they will walk and not be weary. (Isaiah 40:30-31)

Reflection

I have heard runners talk about the distinct disciplines of sprinting and marathon running. While each distance is a race of sorts, the skills, the mindset, and even the physical attributes required are very different. The fastest mile on record was 3 minutes, 43 seconds. The fastest marathon on record was just over two hours. One cannot sprint an entire marathon; it's just too long. I have likewise heard new Christians talk about the passion they have for Christ that arrives upon becoming a Christian. This passion is undoubtedly good! And yet the skills that are required for what Eugene Peterson calls "a long obedience in the same direction" aren't exactly the same as the passion of a new Christian, for it is difficult to maintain any passion for long stretches of time. The good news is that God promises, through scripture, that we will be given endurance if we remain faithful to the gospel. This endurance is a gift, not something we achieve on our own. But, then, it is the fact of the gift that helps us to endure difficult things because God's gift of endurance is a manifestation of God's love and support for us. Truly, we are never alone.

~Prayer of Gratitude~

Day 4

Morning

You were called to this kind of endurance, because Christ suffered on your behalf. He left you an example so that you might follow in his footsteps. (1 Peter 2:21)

Reflection

There is a fine line between seeking out suffering and enduring seasons of suffering as part of faith. The former is unhealthy. God does not call us to intentionally find ways to suffer. But the latter is true; that part of faith will inevitably mean times of trial and hardship. We are called to follow Christ by remembering that living faithfully in the world will include enduring through such seasons. Part of wisdom is learning to differentiate unneeded suffering and the kind of suffering you are called to endure through. But not all hardship can be avoided, and living out the values of God's kingdom will include suffering. Christ didn't want to suffer on the cross. But the work of embodying God's love in the world led to that. He faithfully endured. At some point, doing the right thing, standing up for love, contending for the faith that Christ has given us will lead to seasons of hardship. When they do, remember that this is a path that many before you have walked, and it is worth enduring.

~Prayer of Petition~

Evening

I will strengthen the weary and renew those who are weak. (Jeremiah 31:25)

Reflection

Taking seriously the message of Jesus can be frightening and foreboding, because in my honest moments I know that on my own I cannot live the way of love that Jesus taught and lived. When I look at the immediate consequences of his life, I realize that the way of love is asking too much, and I am simply not up to living that way.

And yet, sometimes when I am newly washed in grace and nearly overcome with God's love, I do get really brave and courageous. At times like that I declare my love and loyalty to God as revealed by the life of Jesus, and I think I am ready to live the life I so easily profess. Often sooner rather than later, I bump up against the reality of my life and of our world as I become aware of my self-interest that has overcome selflessness and I realize the stain of greed on my heart and hands . . . As my courage evaporates and my faith is exposed in its weakness, I realize that I cannot live on my own the faith I profess. This is asking too much of me!

Then, like a fresh burst of wind, the realization breaks in upon me: I am not asked to do this on my own! I am asked to follow Jesus, and that means not only to do and be what Jesus calls me to do and be, but also to accept the power and presence of God to make me more than I am and enable me to live as a beloved child of God.

—Reuben P. Job, *Three Simple Questions*

~*Prayer of Gratitude*~

Day 5

Morning

Let's not get tired of doing good, because in time we'll have a harvest if we don't give up. (Galatians 6:9)

Reflection

Farming metaphors are common in scripture. Not only was farming a relatable real-world example, but also farming combines elements that are required for faithful living. Effort + Time = Harvest. Many of us throw ourselves headlong in the "Effort" part of the equation. We put in long hours, try hard, and then if that doesn't work, we try harder. If we don't immediately see the results, we assume that something we did was wrong, or that we didn't do enough of it. So, we try and try even more in order to produce the outcome we seek. We do this with our kids, in our families, in our churches, at our jobs, and in our lives. We believe that our efforts should produce results. What we often overlook is the "Time" part of the equation. Endurance is a consistent effort in one direction over time. If you are frustrated or have not yet seen the harvest that you think your effort should produce, be careful not to over-exert yourself. The solution may not be to put in more frantic effort now, but rather to continue what you are doing long enough for it to produce the desired harvest.

~Prayer of Petition~

Evening

Because you kept my command to endure, I will keep you safe through the time of testing that is about to come over the whole world, to test those who live on earth. (Revelation 3:10)

Reflection

Giving thanks for existence and life, celebrating the good things in human life, appreciating the wonders of the human body and of nature as a motive for praise, recognizing the blessings God bestows through creating and transforming human creatures—all this reaches its climax in the final picture of eternal felicity, rest, and peace in the city of God.

—Frances Young (speaking about Augustine), *God's Presence: A Contemporary Recapitulation of Early Christianity*

~Prayer of Gratitude~

Waiting

Morning Prayer of Petition

Sovereign Lord, you are over all and through all and in all. In your wisdom, you act for good in my life. Keep me expectant as I wait for you to:

- act in areas of my life where I desire change,
- heal relationships that are strained or broken,
- open up possibilities in my work or vocation,
- bring justice where we pray and work for change.

Help my trust to grow as I wait to see the fruit of your work in my life and in the world. Amen.

Evening Prayer of Gratitude

Steadfast and faithful God, your promises never fail. When I become frustrated by the gap between where I am and where I want to be, fill me with patience, I pray. And open my eyes that I may see glimpses of you at work in my life even now:

- moving obstacles and clearing a pathway,
- working in me now so that I can be prepared for what's next,
- working for peace and healing in the lives of people I love,
- providing resources and opportunities for my growth.

As I pray and as I wait, help me to see the progress I am making in you. Amen.

Day 1

Morning

Oh, I must find rest in God only,
because my hope comes from him! (Psalm 62:5)

Reflection

Some things are worth waiting for. Other things aren't. We have to do this mental calculation more than we realize. Do we wait in this lane of traffic or is the other one going to be faster? Do we wait on this person to make a commitment or is it time to find a new relationship? Do we wait until we get used to a new job, hoping that it will develop to our liking, or do we move on? Do I wait for this opportunity to finally ripen or is it time to put my hope in something else? Waiting is not necessarily a virtue. It depends what or who we are waiting *on*. In our spiritual lives, we will have to do a lot of waiting. Prayers are not always answered immediately, our work does not automatically bear fruit, people do not change instantaneously, and institutions do not redirect in weeks or even in months. If you are engaged in work that you believe God is calling you to do, then God will show up. Work, but as you work, wait. God is worth waiting for.

~Prayer of Petition~

Evening

I will wait for the LORD, *who has hidden his face from the house of Jacob, and I will hope in God.* (Isaiah 8:17)

Reflection

We are tossed and driven
on the restless sea of time;
somber skies and howling tempests
oft succeed a bright sunshine;
in that land of perfect day,
when the mists have rolled away,
we will understand it better by and by.

By and by, when the morning comes,
when the saints of God are gathered home,
we'll tell the story how we've overcome,
for we'll understand it better by and by.

Temptations, hidden snares
often take us unawares,
and our hearts are made to bleed
for a thoughtless word or deed;
and we wonder why the test
when we try to do our best,
but we'll understand it better by and by.

By and by, when the morning comes,
when the saints of God are gathered home,
we'll tell the story how we've overcome,
for we'll understand it better by and by.
  —Charles Albert Tindley, "We'll Understand It Better By and By"

~Prayer of Gratitude~

Day 2

Morning

Wait for the LORD;
> *be strong, and let your heart take courage;*
> *wait for the LORD!* (Psalm 27:14 NRSVUE)

Reflection

We too often associate strength with action and waiting with passivity. If you need something done, do it yourself. If at first you don't succeed try, try again. Waiting, on the other hand, can seem weak, like a giving up or a throwing in the towel. Some might even call it lazy. But sometimes all we can do is wait. Holy waiting is maintaining hope over time, even in the face of contrary evidence. It takes strength and courage to wait hopefully and expectantly. It takes great faith and trust to wait. Have you ever had a family member in the throes of addiction? Have you ever dealt with deep grief in your life? Have you ever badly wanted an opportunity to come your way? Sometimes the most faithful and courageous thing you can do is maintain hope over time as you wait for God's movement in your life to lead you to a new state of being.

~Prayer of Petition~

Evening

Therefore, keep alert, because you don't know the day or the hour. (Matthew 25:13)

Reflection

For the reality that everything owes its existence to an eternal love beyond time and, despite fallenness, will find fulfilment in that same love, is narrated within time in the form of a story stretching from the beginning of all things to the end.

 —Frances Young, *God's Presence: A Contemporary Recapitulation of Early Christianity*

~Prayer of Gratitude~

Day 3

Morning

Lead me in your truth and teach me,
> *for you are the God of my salvation;*
> *for you I wait all day long.* (Psalm 25:5 NRSVUE)

Reflection

Think back to some of the most important lessons you've learned in your life. What are they? What circumstances in life led to the discovery? How long did it take you to fully learn what God was teaching you through that season of life? Chances are, the most important lessons we learn come through seasons of trial and only unfold fully over time. Therefore, a key part of learning is waiting, especially in the wake of mistakes we have made or the failures we have had in our lives. But we often want to fast-forward, especially when we've made embarrassing mistakes, hurt other people, or acted in a foolish way. We want to apologize, quickly say that we have learned our lesson, and then move on. But we should be skeptical anytime we think that we have fully learned our lessons quickly, especially those stemming from our mistakes. Sometimes we must sit with those mistakes awhile, we have to excavate what is below the surface, we have to do the hard work of asking "Why?" and we have to patiently listen to the voices of those who have been impacted. Instead of moving on quickly, we have to wait for God to fully shape and teach us through these moments.

~Prayer of Petition~

Evening

Therefore, brothers and sisters, you must be patient as you wait for the coming of the Lord. Consider the farmer who waits patiently for the coming of rain in the fall and spring, looking forward to the precious fruit of the earth. (James 5:7)

Reflection

Recently, my family and I have started a garden in our backyard. It isn't anything fancy or elaborate; we simply put together a few garden boxes to hold the various vegetables we hope to harvest for the coming years. And from the moment our family started talking about the garden, it has felt like a never-ending conversation cycle, with my children asking me when the vegetables will grow, and me telling them to just wait.

But waiting hasn't meant to sit idly by, hoping something would happen. Since that first day, we bought the supplies, built the boxes, decided on the seeds, planted the seeds, watered the seeds . . . Waiting took work.

Waiting takes work. And while we trust in that day when we can experience together God's kingdom on earth as it is in heaven, we don't wait without action. We wait with care, with wonder, and we wait with the call to cultivate and nurture.

~Prayer of Gratitude~

Day 4

Morning

I hope, LORD.
My whole being hopes,
*   and I wait for God's promise.*
My whole being waits for my Lord—
*   more than the night watch waits for morning;*
*   yes, more than the night watch waits for morning!* (Psalm 130:5-6)

Reflection

If you have ever struggled with sleeping at night, you know that time seems to slow down to a crawl. Morning seems as if it is never going to come. And there is not much you can really do to make yourself sleep. In fact, sometimes the harder you try, the worse it gets. Waiting for sleep seems to take forever, as you lie there staring at the ceiling. This isn't just true of sleep. There are so many things in life and faith that don't seem like they should be so hard or take so long. It is especially frustrating when there doesn't seem like much we can do. And, sometimes, trying too hard can actually have the opposite effect of what we want. So, we are forced to simply wait. I wonder, sometimes, if in these moments, God isn't trying to teach us something. Maybe in our misguided belief that we can control everything, God is returning us to a posture of reliance and dependency on God. I wonder if, during those times of waiting, God might be trying to speak to us in a way that we could only hear when we slow down. Perhaps, if you are waiting on a desired outcome in your life, the time in between is not wasted. Maybe God is speaking. And the only way to hear is to stop trying so hard and, instead, to lie down and stare at the ceiling.

~Prayer of Petition~

Evening

Be dressed for service and keep your lamps lit. Be like people waiting for their master to come home from a wedding celebration, who can immediately open the door for him when he arrives and knocks on the door. (Luke 12:35-36)

Reflection

By gracious powers so wonderfully sheltered,
and confidently waiting, come what may,
we know that God is with us night and morning,
and never fails to greet us each new day.

Yet is this heart by its old foe tormented,
still evil days bring burdens hard to bear;

Harvest

O give our frightened souls the sure salvation
for which, O Lord, you taught us to prepare.

And when this cup you give is filled to brimming
with bitter sorrow, hard to understand,
we take it thankfully and without trembling,
out of so good and so beloved a hand.

Yet when again in this same world you give us
the joy we had, the brightness of your sun,
we shall remember all the days we lived through,
and our whole life shall then be yours alone.

    —Dietrich Bonhoeffer, translated by Fred Pratt Green, "By Gracious Powers"

~Prayer of Gratitude~

Day 5

Morning

Be still before the LORD,
    and wait for him.
Don't get upset when someone gets ahead—
    someone who invents evil schemes. (Psalm 37:7)

Reflection

How many times do you compare your life to those around you? We probably do it hundreds of times a day without always realizing it. We, especially, are tempted to look at the timeline of someone's life and wonder why ours isn't following suit. Why aren't we at the same place in our careers as they are? How do they already get to take these kinds of vacations (we see where they are on social media)? How could they afford that house? Or why are they able to start a family when we have been trying longer? The list goes on. When we are waiting on something, one of the greatest temptations is to look around and notice that others have what we want, what we are waiting for. If we aren't careful, this kind of comparison can leave us feeling like we are uniquely being left out or left behind by God. In reality, no one's life is as perfect as it looks. And what may look like success of one kind could be hiding catastrophe of another. We never truly know what another person is going through, and it is wise to remember this fact. Our lives are our own and God's. God's intentions for you are tailor-made for your journey. As you wait for your life to unfold, resist the temptation to look around and compare your journey to those around you.

~Prayer of Petition~

Evening

There is still a vision for the appointed time;
> *it testifies to the end;*
> *it does not deceive.*
If it delays, wait for it;
> *for it is surely coming; it will not be late.* (Habakkuk 2:3)

Reflection

Life is full of waiting. We wait in lines to checkout at stores, and we wait to be seated when we go out. Some wait for school to begin, others wait for school to end. We wait for meetings, we wait on hold, we wait for food to finish cooking, we wait for coffee to brew....

And, sometimes, we wait for things that really matter, like the results of a medical test or a phone call to update us on the status of a loved one. Or we wait for a child or grandchild to be born, or for someone to take their last breath in hospice.

Often, we wait for things to happen so intensely that we lose sight of the present. There is a holiness to waiting, itself; there is a holiness in the moments of waiting. Perhaps we are being invited to let go of all that will come and to be content in the waiting...

~Prayer of Gratitude~

Index of Themes

Contributors

Matt Miofsky, General Editor and Contributing Writer; serves in the Missouri Conference of The United Methodist Church.
Authored all prayer texts, prayer prompts, and morning reflections. Selected scripture passages, determined weekly themes, and contributed to the structural design of this book.

Laceye Warner, Contributing Editor; Duke Divinity School, Duke University, Durham, North Carolina.
Contributed content sources for evening reflections and provided guidance throughout the development, writing, and production of this book.

Contributing Writers

These authors wrote original material for the evening prayer practices in this volume. Each writer's contributions are listed below by the week and day.

Tori Butler serves in the Baltimore-Washington Conference of The United Methodist Church. *Week 2, Day 2; Week 2, Day 4; Week 3, Day 1; Week 3, Day 3; Week 4, Day 1; Week 28, Day 2; Week 28, Day 5*

Wil Cantrell serves in the Holston Conference of The United Methodist Church. *Week 9, Day 2; Week 9, Day 3; Week 21, Day 1; Week 21, Day 2; Week 37, Day 1; Week 37, Day 5; Week 46, Day 2; Week 46, Day 3*

Rachel Cornwell serves in the Baltimore-Washington Conference of The United Methodist Church. *Week 16, Day 3; Week 16, Day 5; Week 17, Day 3; Week 17, Day 5; Week 18, Day 1; Week 18, Day 2; Week 19, Day 2; Week 19, Day 5; Week 36, Day 4; Week 36, Day 5*

Elizabeth Duffin serves in the Texas Conference of The United Methodist Church. *Week 5, Day 1; Week 5, Day 3; Week 6, Day3; Week 6, Day 4; Week 41, Day 1; Week 41, Day 5; Week 44, Day 2; Week 44, Day 4*

R. DeAndre Johnson serves in the Texas Conference of The United Methodist Church. *Week 12, Day 3; Week 12, Day 4; Week 26, Day 2; Week 26, Day 4; Week 39, Day 4; Week 39, Day 5; Week 50, Day 1; Week 50, Day 5*

Joseph Kim serves in the Pacific Northwest Conference of The United Methodist Church. *Week 8, Day 1; Week 8, Day 3; Week 45, Day 1; Week 45, Day 3; Week 52, Day 3; Week 52, Day 5*

Amy Lippoldt serves in the Great Plains Conference of The United Methodist Church. *Week 15, Day 1; Week 15, Day 3; Week 23, Day 1; Week 23, Day 3; Week 31, Day 3; Week 31, Day 4*

Dalton Rushing serves in the North Georgia Conference of The United Methodist Church. *Week 20, Day 2; Week 20, Day 5; Week 32, Day 1; Week 32, Day 5; Week 42, Day 1; Week 42, Day 4; Week 51, Day 1; Week 51, Day 3*

Chelsea Simon serves in the California-Pacific Conference of The United Methodist Church. *Week 11, Day 1; Week 11, Day 2; Week 22, Day 3; Week 22, Day 5; Week 29, Day 1; Week 29, Day 4; Week 47, Day 1; Week 47, Day 5*

Katie McKay Simpson serves in the Louisiana Conference of The United Methodist Church. *Week 10, Day 3; Week 34, Day 3; Week 35, Day 2*

Jasmine Smothers serves in the North Georgia Conference of The United Methodist Church. *Week 27, Day 2; Week 27, Day 3; Week 40, Day 2; Week 40, Day 4; Week 49, Day 1; Week 49, Day 4*

Donna Claycomb Sokol serves in the Baltimore-Washington Conference of The United Methodist Church. *Week 7, Day 3; Week 7, Day 4; Week 25, Day 1; Week 25, Day 4; Week 33, Day 1; Week 33, Day 3; Week 38, Day 2; Week 38, Day 5*

Audrey Warren serves in the Florida Conference of The United Methodist Church. *Week 13, Day 1; Week 13, Day 5; Week 24, Day 3; Week 24, Day 4; Week 30, Day 1; Week 30, Day 2; Week 43, Day 3; Week 43, Day 5; Week 48, Day 4; Week 48, Day 5*

Contributing Scholars

These Methodist scholars recommended specific historical and contemporary spiritual writing for inclusion as evening reflections.

Wendy Deichmann, President Emerita and Professor of History and Theology, United Theological Seminary, Dayton, Ohio

Edgardo Cólon-Emeric, Dean of Duke Divinity School, Irene and William McCutchen Professor of Reconciliation and Theology, Director of the Center for Reconciliation, Durham, North Carolina

Sarah Lancaster, Professor of Theology, Werner Chair, Methodist Theological School in Ohio, Delaware, Ohio

Hyemin Na, Assistant Professor of Worship, Media, and Culture; Chapel Elder, Oxnam Chapel, Wesley Theological Seminary, Washington, D.C.

Amy Oden, Visiting Professor of Early Church History and Spirituality, Saint Paul School of Theology, Leawood, Kansas

Laceye Warner, Royce and Jane Reynolds Associate Professor of the Practice of Evangelism and Methodist Studies; Associate Dean for Wesleyan Engagement and Hybrid Programs, Duke University, Durham, North Carolina

Karen Westerfield-Tucker, Professor of Worship, Boston University School of Theology, Boston, Massachusetts

Sources

Advent

John Wesley, *The Scripture Way of Salvation* (1765), III. 18

Howard Thurman, *Meditations of the Heart* (Beacon, 2014), 211

Charles Wesley, "Come, Thou Long-Expected Jesus," *UMH* (*The United Methodist Hymnal* [United Methodist Publishing, 1989]), 196

Amanda Berry Smith autobiography, from *In Her Words*, edited by Amy Oden (Abingdon, 1994), 310

Julia A. J. Foote, "A Brand Plucked from the Fire" in *Sisters of the Spirit: Three Black Women's Autobiographies of the Nineteenth Century*, edited by William L. Andrews (Indiana University Press, 1986), 209

Francis of Assisi, "Lord, Make Me an Instrument of Thy Peace," *UMH* 481

Charles Wesley "Love Divine, All Loves Excelling," *UMH* 384

Excerpt from The Martyrdom of Perpetua—visions, by Perpetua (203), from *In Her Words*, edited by Amy Oden, 32–33

Pope Francis, *Evangelii Gaudium: Apostolic Exhortation on the Proclamation of the Gospel in Today's World*. In *The Holy See*: www.vatican.va/content/francesco/en/apost_exhortations/documents/papa-francesco_esortazione-ap_20131124_evangelii-gaudium.html, paragraph 6.

Martin Janus, "Jesus, Joy of Our Desiring," *UMH* 644

Christmas

Joseph Mohr, "Silent Night," *UMH* 239

Mary McLeod Bethune, "Address to a World Assembly for Moral Re-Armament" (Caux, Switzerland on July 27, 1954) in *Mary McLeod Bethune: Building a Better World*, edited by McCluskey and Smith (Indiana University Press, 1999), 56

Charles Wesley, "And Can It Be That I Should Gain," *UMH* 363

Afro-American Spiritual, adapted by John W. Work, Jr., "Go, Tell It on the Mountain," *UMH* 251

Charles Wesley, "Hark! the Herald Angels Sing" *UMH* 240

Epiphany

Charles Wesley, "Let Heaven and Earth Combine," *Hymns for the Nativity of Our Lord*, 2nd ed. (Strahan, 1745), 5

Bonganjalo Goba, "What Is Faith? A Black South African Perspective," in *Lift Every Voice*, eds. Susan Brooks Thistlethwaite and Mary Potter Engel (Orbis, 1998), 27

Jacque B. Jones, "You Formed Creation By Your Word," GIA Publications

Jarena Lee, *The Religious Experience and Journal of Jarena Lee* (Harvard College, 1849), 60-61, 101, 123, 152

Jan Richardson, "The Magdalene's Blessing" from *Circle of Grace: A Book of Blessings for the Seasons*; janrichardson.com

John Wesley, "The Witness of the Spirit," I.7, I.12

Ida B. Wells-Barnett, "The Requisites of True Leadership," in Marcia Y. Riggs, ed., *Can I Get a Witness?* (Orbis, 1997), 66

Daniel Charles Damon, "Broken, Bitter, Bruised We Come," Hope Publishing Co.

Charles Wesley, "Lord, I Hear of Showers of Blessing"

George MacDonald, *A Guide to Prayer for All God's People* (Upper Room, 1990)

Gordon MacDonald, *Restoring Your Spiritual Passion* (Oliver-Nelson Books, 1986)

The Wesley Study Bible (Abingdon, 2009), 1536

Fyodor Dostoevsky, *The Brothers Karamazov*

C. S. Lewis, *The Problem of Pain*

Mary Louise Bringle, "Can You Feel the Seasons Turning," GIA Publications, Inc.

Adam M L Tice, "What Comfort Can Our Worship Bring," GIA Publications, Inc.

Mary Bosanquet Fletcher, "Merciful" sections 3-7, in "Watchwords: The Names of Christ," as reprinted in *The Asbury Journal* 61 no. 2 (2006):13-94, 66

African American Spiritual, "There Is a Balm in Gilead," *UMH* 375

Thomas H. Troeger, "God Weeps with Us Who Weep and Mourn," GIA Publications, Inc.

The Wesley Study Bible, 1192

Will L. Thompson, "Softly and Tenderly," *UMH* 248

Lent

Mary McLeod Bethune, "The Lesson of Tolerance" (1952)

Parker Palmer, *Let Your Life Speak* (Jossey-Bass, 2000), 4

Julian of Norwich, *Revelations of Divine Love* (1670)

Fyodor Dostoevsky, *The Brothers Karamazov* (1880)

Claudia F. Hernaman, "Lord, Who Throughout These Forty Days," *UMH* 269

Amy Oden, *Right Here, Right Now: The Practice*

Sources

of *Christian Mindfulness* (Abingdon, 2017), 3

Roberta Bondi, *To Love as God Loves: Conversations with the Early Church* (Fortress, 1987)

Angelina E. Grimké, "Appeal to Christian Women of the South" (1836)

Ancient Irish; translated by Mary E. Byrne, "Be Thou My Vision," *UMH* 451

Julia A. J. Foote, "A Brand Plucked from the Fire" (1879)

Fanny J. Crosby, "Blessed Assurance, Jesus Is Mine!" *UMH* 369

Rubem Alves, *I Believe in the Resurrection of the Body* (Wipf & Stock, 2003), 8

John of Damascus, "Come, Ye Faithful, Raise the Strain," *UMH* 315

Matthew Bridges, "Crown Him with Many Crowns," *UMH* 327

Charles Wesley, "Christ the Lord Is Risen Today," *UMH* 302

Robert Robinson, "Come, Thou Fount of Every Blessing," *UMH* 400

The Wesley Study Bible, 1573

2016 Book of Resolutions, #3066

Charles Wesley, "O That I Could Repent!"

Mother Theresa, *A Simple Path* (1995)

Charles Wesley, "To Whom Should Thy Disciples Go," *Short Hymns on Select Passages of the Holy Scriptures*, vol. 2 (Farley, 1762), 114

John Wesley, from *John and Charles Wesley* (Paulist, 1981), 129

Ruth Duck, "We Humans Build to Frame a Life," GIA Publications, Inc.

Julian of Norwich, *Julian of Norwich: Showings*, translated by Edmund Colledge and James Walsh (Paulist, 1978), 256

Natalie Sleeth, "Hymn of Promise," *UMH* 707

Phoebe Palmer, from *In Her Words*, edited by Amy Oden, 290-91

Elizabeth of the Trinity, *Complete Works*, vol. 1, translated by Sister Aletheia Kane OCD (Institute of Carmelite Studies, 1984), 183-84

Reginald Heber, "Holy, Holy, Holy," *UMH* 64

Pentecost

Georgia Harkness, *Understanding the Christian Faith* (1947), from *In Her Words*, edited by Amy Oden, 331

Shannon Craigo-Snell, from *The CEB Women's Bible* (Common English Bible, 2016), 693

Mary Nelson Keithahn, "How Can We Sing Our Love for God," in *Hymns in Times of Crisis* (2017), #19

Mary McLeod Bethune, "Spiritual Autobiography" (1946)

Isaac Watts, "O God, Our Help in Ages Past," *UMH* 117

John Keble, "Blest Are the Pure in Heart," *Ancient and Modern: Hymns and songs for refreshing worship* (1819), #602

Anselm, An Address (Proslogion) in *A Scholastic Miscellany: Anselm to Ockham*, edited and translated by Eugene R. Fairweather (Westminster, 1961), 92

Martin Luther, *Luther's Works* (Fortress, 1958), 32:24

Henry Francis Lyte, "Abide with Me," *UMH* 700

Karen Baker-Fletcher, *Dancing with God: The Trinity from a Womanist Perspective* (Chalice, 2006), p. x

Mary Bosanquet-Fletcher, *The Life of Mrs. Mary Fletcher* (1818), 132

"The Ten Hallmarks of Benedictine Education," *Journal of Catholic Higher Education* 21:9 (2010), 46-47

Shirley Erena Murray, "Let My Spirit Always Sing," Hope Publishing Co.

Susanna Wesley, Letter, June 8, 1725

Andrew Sung Park, *The Wounded Heart of God* (Abingdon, 1993), 10

Isaac the Syrian (8th century)

Monica Moss, *The CEB Women's Bible*, 89

Charles Wesley, "Love Divine, All Loves Excelling," *UMH* 384

Isabel Crawford, "A Native American Interpretation of the 23rd Psalm"

Marth Luther, "A Mighty Fortress Is Our God," *UMH* 110

Walter Wangerin, *The Book of God: The Bible As a Novel* (Zondervan, 2003), 255

Sow

Marilynne Robinson, *Gilead* (Farrar, Straus and Giroux, 2004)

Rabbi Abraham Heschel, *The Sabbath* (1951)

Wendell Berry, "Sabbaths 1999, VII," *Given* (Counterpoint, 2006)

Óscar Romero, "The Final Homily of Archbishop Romero," Anniversary Mass for Sara Meardide Pinto, Chapel of the Divina Providencia Hospital, El Salvador, March 24, 1980. http://www.romerotrust .org.uk/homilies-and-writings/homilies /final-homily-archbishop-romero

Thomas Merton, *The Seven Storey Mountain* (Harcourt Brace, 1948)

Esther de Waal, *Living with Contradiction* (Morehouse, 1997)

Mary Louise Bringle, "Abba, Deliver Us from Evil," GIA Publications, Inc.

Howard Thurman, *The Inward Journey* (Friends United, 2007)

Thomas O Chisholm, "Great Is Thy Faithfulness," *UMH* 140

Jarena Lee, *The Religious Experience and Journal of Jarena Lee*, 123

Jan Richardson, "The Magdalene's Blessing" from *Circle of Grace: A Book of Blessings for the Seasons*; janrichardson.com

Washington Gladden, "O Master Let Me Walk With Thee," *UMH* 430

Evelyn Underhill: The Spiritual Life (Hodder & Stoughton, 1937), 222

St. Therese de Lisieux, The Story of the Soul, translated by Thomas N. Taylor (Cosimo, 2007), 175, 194

Thomas Merton, *Thoughts in Solitude* (Ferrar, Straus and Giroux, 1999), 79

Cynthia Weems, *The CEB Women's Bible*, 1421

John Wesley, *John and Charles Wesley*

Mireya Martinez, *The CEB Women's Bible*, 1473

Harvest

Richard Allen, Absalom Jones, Richard Allen, "A Narrative of the Proceedings of the Black People During the Late Awful Calamity in Philadelphia in the Year 1793" (Eastern Acorn, 1993)

Katherina von Schlegel, translated by Jane Borthwick, "Be Still, My Soul" *UMH* 534

Charles Wesley, "Love Divine, All Loves Excelling," *UMH* 384

John Wesley, from "A Plain Account of Christian Perfection," *A Longing for Holiness: Selected Writings of John Wesley* (Upper Room, 1998), 50-51

Gerhard Tersteegen, "Thou Hidden Love of God," translated by John Wesley, *UMH* 414

Cecil Frances Alexander, "All Things Bright and Beautiful," *UMH* 147

Reuben Job, *Three Simple Questions* (Abingdon, 2011), 64-65

Charles Wesley, "God of All Power, and Truth, and Grace" (1742)

Georgia Harkness, *Religious Living* (Association Press, 1958), 57-58

John Welsey, "The Character of a Methodist," *A Longing for Holiness: Selected Writings of John Wesley* (Upper Room, 1998)

John Wesley, "The Use of Money," *A Longing for Holiness: Selected Writings of John Wesley*

Bernard of Clairvaux, "Sermon 11 on Song of Songs," 11.2

Simon Tugwell, *The Way of Imperfection: An Exploration of Christian Spirituality*, Templegate (1985), 468; includes quotation from John, "The Other Old Man," early 6th century, in *Barsanuphius and John: Questions and Answers*, ed. Derwas Chitty, Patrologia Orientalis, XXXI, 3 (Paris 1966)

Philip William Otterbein, "The Salvation-Bringing Incarnation and the Glorious Victory of Jesus Christ over the Devil and Death Delivered," in *Early German-American Evangelicalism: Pietist Sources on Discipleship and Sanctification*, edited by John Steven O'Malley (Scarecrow, 1995), 27

Bradford Torrey, "Not So in Haste, My Heart," *UMH* 455

Frances Young (speaking about Augustine), *God's Presence: A Contemporary Recapitulation of Early Christianity* (Cambridge University Press, 2013), 135

Charles Albert Tindley, "We'll Understand It Better By and By," *UMH* 525

Frances Young, *God's Presence: A Contemporary Recapitulation of Early Christianity*, 225

Dietrich Bonhoeffer, translated by Fred Pratt Green, "By Gracious Powers," *UMH* 517